D1867001

DIY, Subkulturen und Feminismen

Alma Marta

Herausgegeben von
Sarah Czerney, Lena Eckert und Silke Martin

DIY, Subkulturen und Feminismen

Reihe Aspekte

Alma Marta

Die Deutsche Bibliothek verzeichnet diese Publikation
in der Deutschen Nationalbibliografie.
Detaillierte bibliografische Daten sind im Internet abrufbar unter
http://dnb.d-nb.de

Besuchen Sie unsere Verlage im Internet:
www.alma-marta.de
www.marta-press.de

1. Auflage Januar 2021

Printed in Germany.
ISBN 978-3-948731-01-4

Inhalt

Do it yourself!
Subversive Praktiken und informelles Wissen

von Sarah Czerney, Lena Eckert und Silke Martin

Gebastelt wurde zu allen Zeiten und überall: Untergrundorganisationen drucken heimlich Flugblätter auf umgebauten Waschmaschinen, Hobbybastler*innen verbringen Stunden in dunklen Kellern, Tüftler*innen hoffen auf den Durchbruch ihrer Erfindungen, Techniker*innen ergänzen ihre Labormaschinen mit Alltagsgegenständen, Punkbands rebellieren gegen normative Autoritäten, Wissenschaftler*innen suchen auf Barcamps nach alternativen Formen des Wissensaustauschs.

Selbermachen ist eine gesellschaftlich und zeitlich übergreifende Kulturpraxis. In Zeiten der Knappheit erlaubt Basteln eine Alternative zu den offiziellen Ressourcen. In den letzten Jahren wird die Selbermach-Idee zunehmend der Kapitalismuskritik verpflichtet, etwa in Form von Recyclingbasteln. So oder so positioniert sich Selbermachen als Gegenpol zum offiziellen, geregelten und kontrollierten Umgang mit Ressourcen. Selbermachen kann aber auch politisch vereinnahmt oder Teil der Mainstreamkultur werden wie in der Zrób-to-Sam und in den Do-it-yourself-Bewegungen der 1970er Jahre in Ost- und Westeuropa.

Diese kurze Aufzählung verdeutlicht, was sich auch in diesem Band spiegelt: die große Diversität und Interdisziplinarität des Themas DIY. Der Versuch, einen lückenlosen Überblick über das

Feld zu geben müsste insofern notgedrungen scheitern. Stattdessen werden wir in dieser Einleitung die theoretischen Grundannahmen umreißen, auf denen die Publikation beruht, und einige grundlegende Fragen stellen. Dafür lesen wir den Titel wörtlich bzw. Wort für Wort.

Do

Die Konferenz, auf die dieses Buch zurückgeht, versammelte Vorträge zu sehr heterogenen Themen und stellte eine Plattform dar, um mit unterschiedlichen Formaten zu experimentieren:[1] neben klassischen akademischen Panels gab es persönliche Berichte von DIY-Erfahrungen (Sirtl) sowie einen Workshop zum Thema Schreiben als Empowermenttechnik (Eckert/Martin).

Die Artikel in diesem Sammelband stammen von Autor*innen mit unterschiedlichen Hintergründen, sowohl geografisch als auch hinsichtlich akademischer Disziplinen. So finden sich in diesem Buch Beiträge von Kunsthistoriker*innen und Künstler*innen, Medien- und Genderwissenschaftler*innen, aber auch Soziolog*innen – was sie jedoch alle gemeinsam haben ist ein sehr interdisziplinärer Umgang mit ihren jeweiligen Gegenständen. Nicht

---

[1] Es handelt sich um folgende Konferenz: Do-it-Yourself! Subversive practices and informal knowledge, Annual Conference of the Leibniz Graduate School ‚History, Knowledge, Media in East Central Europe', 18. bis 20. November 2015, Herder-Institut, Marburg, organisiert von Sarah Czerney, Jan Surman und Eszter Gantner, weitere Informationen elektronisch veröffentlicht unter: https://www.herder-institut.de/en/events-exhibitions/conferences/2015/do-it-yourself-informal-knowledge-and-subversive-practices.html [Stand: 26.08.2020] sowie unter: https://www.hsozkult.de/conferencereport/id/tagungsberichte-6381 [Stand: 26.08.2020].

nur in der Wissenschaft profitieren die Gegenstände oft von einem multiperspektivischen Zugang, sondern auch das „Tun“ erfordert häufig eine überfachliche Annäherung.

Was die Beiträge zudem in ihrer Heterogenität eint, ist ihr Fokus auf DIY als Praktik(en). Selbermachen als Praktiken zu denken, bedeutet dabei nicht nur, nach den Ergebnissen des DIY zu fragen, sondern auch auf den Prozess des Machens zu fokussieren. Es bedeutet, die Frage nach dem Selbermachen mit folgenden Fragen zu kombinieren: Was bedeutet ‚etwas selber machen‘ in der jeweils spezifischen Situation (sei es beim Denken, Schreiben, Hacken, Basteln etc.)? Wer und was sind am Prozess des Selbermachens beteiligt? Wie und unter welchen Bedingungen wird etwas selber gemacht? Was sind die materiellen Gegebenheiten, welche die soziopolitischen, historischen und ökonomischen Bedingungen des Selbermachen? Welche Medien und Technologien werden eingesetzt und welche Netzwerke spielen eine Rolle? Auf Praktiken zu blicken bedeutet, vereinfacht gesagt, nach Verben anstatt nach Substantiven zu fragen; es bedeutet, die Frage nach dem Was mit der Frage nach dem Wie zu vereinen.

It

Das „it“ in DIY steht für das, was selber gemacht oder selber produziert, gebastelt, gehackt, erforscht etc. wird. Es kann nicht vom Prozess des Machens getrennt werden und demnach auch nicht von dessen materiellen Bedingungen und seinem soziopolitischen und historischen Kontext. Zum Beispiel bedeutete DIY in kommunistischen Ländern vor 1989 etwas ganz anderes als heutzutage im kapitalistischen Neoliberalismus, wo Praktiken des DIY oftmals Teil des kapitalistischen Mainstreams geworden sind, anstatt wegen Mangelwirtschaft pure ökonomische Notwendigkeit zu sein.

Die Verwobenheit der Bedingungen des Selbermachens mit „it“ (dem, was selbst gemacht wird) kann darüber hinaus auch in kleineren Maßstäben beobachtet werden. Beispielsweise macht es einen Unterschied, ob ich mit einem Stift auf Papier schreibe oder die Buchstaben über eine Tastatur in ein Textverarbeitungsprogramm im Computer eintippe. Auch die Räume, in denen akademische Konferenzen wie die, auf die dieses Buch zurückgeht, stattfinden, die Art und Weise, wie Tische und Stühle aufgestellt sind, beeinflussen, was in diesen Räumen getan, gesagt und gedacht werden kann, und was nicht. Unser Denken verändert sich mit den Bedingungen, unter denen es stattfindet. Die hier versammelten Beiträge vereint, dass sie die verschiedenen materiellen, menschlichen und nicht-menschlichen Akteur*innen mitdenken, die den Prozess des Selbermachens beeinflussen.

Damit verbunden ist ein weiterer Gedanke, der für den hier präsentierten Blick auf DIY wichtig ist: was selber gemacht werden kann, wird nicht nur von Netzwerken menschlicher und nichtmenschlicher Akteur*innen, nicht nur von politischen und historischen Bedigungen beeinflusst, sondern auch durch den Standpunkt, von dem aus etwas selbst gemacht, gesagt, gefragt, gebastelt, geschrieben oder erforscht wird.

Yourself

Der letzte Buchstabe des DIY bezieht sich auf ein ‚Selbst', auf ein Ich – und damit auf die Positionierung, von der aus etwas selber gemacht wird. Um zu verstehen, wie dieses ‚Ich' den Prozess des Selbermachens beeinflusst, kann es hilfreich sein, seinen*ihren Standpunkt offenzulegen und zu reflektieren. Die feministische Standpunkttheorie bietet hierfür das methodische Werkzeug.[2] Der Begriff des Standpunkts geht auf die Philosophin Nancy Hartsock zurück. Aufbauend auf marxistischer Theorie zu einem proletarischen Standpunkt fordert Hartsock die Entwicklung eines feministischen Standpunkts, der die geschlechtsspezifische Sozialisierung des Selbst und die damit zusammenhängende ökonomische Situation berücksichtigt. Ob wir als Frau oder als Mann erzogen werden, beeinflusst Hartsock (1986) zufolge fundamental, wie wir die Welt wahrnehmen, welche Fragen wir stellen und welches Wissen wir generieren. Die Wissenschaftshistorikerin Donna Haraway (1988) greift diesen Ansatz in ihrem berühmten Text „situated knowledges" auf und betont die Situiertheit jeder Wissensproduktion. Wir alle sprechen und handeln von spezifischen sozio-historischen Standpunkten aus, die von Kategorien wie Geschlecht, Race, Klasse, Alter etc. strukturiert werden. Das Anliegen der Standpunkttheorie ist es, diese Positionierungen sichtbar zu machen und offenzulegen, um so Universalisierungen und den „god trick" des „seeing everything from nowhere" zu vermeiden (Haraway 1988: 581). So ist es uns ein Anliegen, im Nachdenken über

[2] Auch wenn der Begriff eine geschlossene Theorierichtung suggeriert, meint er eine Vielzahl an Ansätzen. Für einen Überblick siehe Singer 2008.

DIY das Selbst und seine soziale, historische und ökonomische Positionierung und deren materiellen Verflechtungen – zumindest in Ansätzen – sichtbar zu machen.

Dabei verstehen wir das ‚Self' in ‚Do it yourself' nicht als einzelne Person, als isoliertes Individuum, sondern als Selbst, das verbunden ist mit anderen Menschen, Texten, Ideen und Techniken. Wir denken 'Do it yourself' als kollaborative Praxis. In Bezug auf akademische Forschung formuliert Rosi Braidotti das wie folgt: „Thinking and writing, like breathing, are not held into the mould of linearity, or the confines of the printed page, but move outwards, out of bonds, in webs of encounters with ideas, others, texts" (Braidotti 2013: 166). Das Selbst in DIY bedeutet nicht ein kohärentes, stabiles Selbst, sondern ein Selbst, das in einem Netz aus Verbindungen mit anderen Akteur*innen lokalisiert ist, sowohl menschlichen als auch nicht-menschlichen Ursprungs. Dieses Konzept eines eingebundenen und verbundenen Selbsts, das die Verantwortung für seinen*ihren Standpunkt übernimmt, widerspricht dem Mythos des männlich geprägten Genies, das allein im Studierzimmer oder im Hobbykeller sitzt und durch Konzentration brillante Ideen entwickelt.

‚Do it yourself' so verstanden meint nicht ‚Mach es allein', sondern, ganz im Gegenteil, eine kollaborative Praxis. In diesem Sinn hoffen wir, dass wir mit diesem Band und der Konferenz, auf die er zurückgeht, einen Raum schaffen, in dem Menschen, Ideen und Texte aufeinander treffen, sich verbinden und etwas Neues selber machen.

Die Beiträge in diesem Band

Die britische Autorin Ellen Foster benutzt in ihrem Beitrag zu „Critical Engagement within Hacker and Maker Communities" die Methode der feministische Epistemologie um Gruppen zu beschreiben, die sich soziale Gerechtigkeit innerhalb des „Maker Movement" zum Ziel gesetzt haben. Sie untersucht hierbei die besondere Herangehensweise dieser Gruppen, die das DIT, das Do-It-Together praktizieren. Es geht Foster in erster Linie darum, diese Praktiken des Teilens von Fähigkeiten in Hinblick auf feministische Pädagogiken zu untersuchen. Im Zentrum stehen hier feministische Hackerspaces, die versuchen, dekolonial zu arbeiten und Umweltverschmutzung zu thematisieren und zu bekämpfen. Der technologische Aspekt dieser zunehmend aktivistisch arbeitenden Kollektive wird von Foster ebenso diskutiert wie ihr Potential Wissenschaftskritik zu üben.

Am Beispiel zweier polnischer Künstlerinnen zeigt Constance Krüger in ihrem Betrag zu „Rosa Zimmer und Kressekleid oder 'Do-it-yourself' zwischen Rezeption und Produktion. Die künstlerischen Praktiken bei Maria Pinińska-Bereś und Teresa Murak", wie DIY als Ermächtigungsstrategie fungiert, die Erkenntnisprozesse initiieren und zu einem kritischen, feministischen Künstlerinnenverständnis führen kann. Während die erste Künstlerin mit rosafarbenen, weichen Stoffskulpturen arbeitet, verwandelt die zweite Künstlerin Kressesamen zu grünen Kleidern. Hierbei bilden Erfahrungen der Künstlerin als Frau sowohl in ihrer körperlichen als auch in ihrer biografischen Verfasstheit den zentralen Wissenshorizont. Die Arbeitsweise beider Frauen kann als experimentell beschrieben werden, in materieller Hinsicht ebenso wie in

Hinblick auf den offenen Ausgang ihrer Ergebnisse. Dabei ist die künstlerische Praxis von Pinińska-Bereś und Murak nicht nur mit Aspekten von Weiblichkeit, sondern auch mit Aspekten von (Kunst-)Politik verwoben. Weiblichkeit wird jeweils in einen sozio-politischen Kontext gestellt. Der DIY-Aspekt beider Künstlerinnen zielt dabei nicht nur darauf ab, die Betrachterinnen an der künstlerischen Arbeit zu beteiligen, sondern er bezeichnet auch eine Methode der gezielten Erkenntnisgewinnung als Künstlerin.

Sarah Helds Beitrag zu „'Not Just Boys Fun' - Perspektiven auf Gender in der DIY-Hardcore/Punk-Szene" beschäftigt sich mit dem Verhältnis von Feminismus und Hardcore Kultur in der Riot-Grrrl-Bewegung. Durch eine Analyse verschiedener Artefakte wie Liedtexte, Zines und Interviews aber auch Praktiken und Events wie das ladyfest innerhalb der Szene deckt Held den männerdominierten Gestus dieser Subkultur auf. Sie endet mit einem wie sie sagt, nicht-akademischem Schlusswort: *Up the female-punx!*

Christin Sirtls Erfahrungsbericht „Selbermachen als feministische Ermächtigung – eine Jungimkerin erzählt" über das Imkern als feministische Do-it-yourself-Strategie zeigt nicht nur die Möglichkeiten von Empowerment und Emanzipation, sondern deckt auch patriarchale Strukturen in der Hobbyimkerei auf. Die fast hundertjährige Tradition des Imkerns in Sirtls Familie hat dabei mehrere politische Systeme überlebt und immer wieder einen anderen Zweck erfüllt. So wird das Imkern von Christin Sirtl bis heute gemeinsam mit ihren Eltern und Großeltern praktiziert. Imkern beschreibt für die Autorin in erster Linie – anders als für ihre Familienmitglieder – eine feministische Selbermach-Tätigkeit. Mit ihrem Erfahrungsbericht führt sie nicht nur durch ihre Familiengeschichte seit 1925, sondern macht auch einen Streifzug durch die verschiedenen politischen Systeme Deutschlands – von der Weimarer Republik hin zum Nazi-Regime, DDR-Sozialismus und heutigen Kapitalismus. Sirtl bezeichnet sich selbst als Traditionsimkerin. Ihre Erfahrung als Mitglied in einem ortsansässigen Imkerverein vergleicht sie mit dem Internet-Imkern, das, wie sie herausfindet, anders als die herkömmliche Imker-Vereinsstruktur Potential zur Selbstermächtigung in feministischer Perspektive bietet.

Wie sich Praktiken des Selbermachens und institutionalisierte Strukturen / Praktiken zueinander verhalten, untersucht Christiane Lewe in ihrem Text „Wie man Harvard ein Gesicht gibt“ am Beispiel von Scrapbooks und Jahrbüchern der Elite-Universität Harvard. Anhand dieser medialen Praxis, die auch an heutige social media Praktiken denken lässt, fragt Lewe, wie „kinds of people“ entstehen. Wie werden Harvard-Studierende auf institutioneller und individueller Ebene zurechtgemacht und wie entwerfen sie sich selbst? Dabei zeigt sie auf, dass Praktiken des Selbermachens nicht außerhalb von gesellschaftlichen Machtverhältnissen passieren, sondern diese allenfalls dynamisieren können.

Lena Eckert und Silke Martin untersuchen in ihrem Beitrag „Schreiben als Empowerment“ die alltägliche Kulturtechnik des (wissenschaftlichen) Schreibens als Praktik des Selbermachens. Der Artikel dokumentiert ein Schreibgespräch von fünf Nachwuchswissenschaftler*innen, das in einem von Eckert und Martin angeleiteten Schreibworkshop entstanden ist. Was es bedeutet, als weiblich gelesene Person in der Wissenschaft zu schreiben, wie Schreiben im Kollektiv funktionieren und wie Schreiben eine Praktik des Empowerments sein kann, sind die zentralen Fragen des Textes.

Lisa Conrad und Matthias Maier beschreiben in ihrem Beitrag zu „Das Maker Movement: Perspektiven der Mikroökonomie, der Feldtheorie und der Praxistheorie" die Maker*innen Bewegung aus ökonomischer und sozialwissenschaftlicher Perspektive. Das verstärkte Wiederaufkommen von Maker*innen und DIY Bewegung in den letzten zehn Jahren veranlasst die beiden Autor*innen dazu, verschiedene Fragen nach dem Ursprung, der Ausformung und den Innovationen des Maker*innen Movement zu stellen. Dabei dienen ihnen drei (sozial-)theoretische Rahmungen – die erweiterte Mikroökonomie, die Bourdieu'sche Feldtheorie und die Praxistheorie – um diesen Fragen nachzuspüren. Geht es zunächst um die Entstehung der Maker*innen Bewegung im Kontext von Hacker*innenkultur und Arts-and-Crafts Bewegung sowie um deren Ästhetiken und Praktiken so werden anschließend aus den Perspektiven von Mikroökonomie, Bourdieu'scher Feldtheorie und Praxistheorie Einordnungen des Maker*innen Movement getroffen. Interessanterweise verändert sich die Beschreibung der Maker*innen Bewegung, je nachdem, welche der drei konzeptionellen Herangehensweisen Conrad und Maier wählen. Dies zeigt, dass der Artikel selbst eine experimentelle Anordnung darstellt.

Literaturverzeichnis

Braidotti, Rosi (2013): The Posthuman. Cambridge.

Haraway, Donna (1988): “Situated Knowledges: The Science Question in Feminism and the Privilege of Partial Perspective”, *Feminist Studies* 14 (3): 575-599.

Hartsock, Nancy C. M. (1986): The feminist standpoint: developing the ground for a specifically feminist historical materialism. In: Harding, Sandra/Hintikka, Merrill B. (Hrsg.): Discovering Reality. Feminist Perspectives on Epistemology, Metaphysics, Methodology, and Philosophy of Science. Dordrecht, Boston, London, 283-310.

Singer, Mona (2008): Feministische Wissenschaftskritik und Epistemologie: Voraussetzungen, Positionen, Perspektiven. In: Becker, Ruth/Kortendiek, Beate (Hrsg.): Handbuch Frauen- und Geschlechterforschung: Theorie, Methoden, Empirie. Wiesbaden, 285-294.

Critical Engagement within Hacker and Maker Communities

von Ellen K. Foster

This paper is an analysis using feminist epistemologies to examine alternative pathways set forth by social justice oriented groups associated with the 'Maker Movement.' It takes skill-sharing practices and the infrastructures built up around them as points at which to analyze and instantiate change within Do-It-Yourself (DIY) or Do-It-Together (DIT) cultures and communities – arguing for a more engaged and feminist pedagogical approach. But what *does* it mean to share skills and instantiate technology development and change from within feminist hackerspaces or through a decolonial mindset with relation to waste and pollution? While this paper does not fully answer this question, it helps to lay the groundwork to do so.

Introduction

My research contributes to an emerging scholarly field that looks at community design and making practices (Disalvo/Lukens 2009; Ratto 2011), while specifically querying how feminist (Toupin 2014), marginalized (Nascimento 2014), and radical groups make and appropriate technology (Eglash et al. 2004) for their own purposes. Instead of glossing over practices as identifying with one mindset or ethic in hacker and maker cultures, I tease out the multiplicity of ideologies at play in these collectivities and spaces.

While my object of study is geared more towards skill-sharing practices, my research has also focused on the physical instantiation of makerspaces associated with maker cultures and the 'Maker Movement.' The makerspace is touted as an exciting and often liberatory venue in which interested individuals can tinker, explore, appropriate, manipulate, and innovate technology. While associated with hackerspaces and hacklabs, some claim that makerspaces are a divergence from these groups which have historically focused on creating space for skill-sharing around free and open source software (F/OSS) and the political implications therein (Maxigas 2014). Scholars and participants relate that there is a focus on subversive acts and political intervention more prevalent within hackerspaces and hacklabs, while makerspaces and maker culture are geared toward social entrepreneurship, capitalistic tendencies, and consumerist material production. Yet the delineation of such spaces is complex and messy, with many so-called maker groups focusing on community-building activities and social justice practices alongside entrepreneurial endeavors. Meanwhile makerspaces and cultures have further entrenched technological manipulation into the material world via 3D printing and the advent of the Arduino micro-controller. Self-identifying as hackers and makers, different sets of individuals gather for collective collaboration in both makerspaces and hackerspaces.

In this paper, I parse out some examples in this field of study, what might constitute more critically-minded practices, share a few specific stories in terms of tactical measures taken by some of these groups, and then illustrate possible steps for my own methodology and explorations moving forward – what I hope to instantiate in my research into particular informal skill-sharing and hands-on praxis. I also examine diverse aspects of maker and hacker cultures in terms of what is increasingly being called the Maker Movement. While I focus in the above text on my own working definition of hackerspaces and makerspaces, my actual research for this paper highlights groups that are often mobile – something I would call hacker or maker collectivities.

Background: Maker cultures and Critical Design

Maker and hacker groups push for material empowerment through the acquisition of skills, technical literacy, and tool accessibility. More so than hackerspaces, makerspaces and maker cultures have put forth rhetoric arguing for ultimate inclusivity, claiming everyone as a maker on at least some level in their everyday lives – but who really populates these spaces and cultures? And who has the time or desire to take part in personal production practices? A certain amount of boundary work (Gieryn 1983) on the part of the Maker Movement gatekeepers is often taking part in order to validate what is counted as a 'making' practice. Making and hacking are already happening at the margins of society, but it may not be recognized in the maker cultural realm, or deemed appropriate by the dominant maker milieu. While makerspaces and maker programming is touted as open and accessible to all, there are often dominant norms or narratives that rise to the surface, and implicit barriers of cost, elitism, or location may keep certain people out of a space or out of a particular practice of skill-sharing. As the proponents of maker practices begin to influence innovation and development frameworks at the level of national governments (Kraft 2014), public education (Libow/Stager/Stager 2013), and the industrial economy (Charter/Keiller 2014), this is an important moment to document and assess their approaches geared toward the democratization of technoscience. An avenue through which to do this critique is in the field of design studies.

Critical design studies scholarship explores the possibility for practices that address the need for user-generated and user-centric technologies in various forms, including participatory design (Le Danetc/Disalvo 2013), reflexive design (Sengers 2005), 'critical-making' (Ratto 2011) and 'critical technical practices' (Agre 1997; Disalvo/Lukens 2009). Participatory design is rooted in changing the practices of design, while working to design a system, in an iterative format and in relation to users, researchers, materials, and the designers therein involved (Boehner et al. 2005). Engaging the concept of 'DIY Citizenship' (Ratto/Boler 2014), design studies scholars have also extrapolated what kinds of citizenship and publics are established and reworked through these different and possibly participatory design narratives.

Reflexive design focuses on Human Computer Interaction (HCI) development. HCI is the study of interactive computer systems in which efficacious human interaction is designed into the system. This work has theoretical implications for how other types of technology development can evolve by enacting participation through use (Boehner et al. 2005), and might be productively applied to the Maker Movement to further explore sociocultural dimensions of design. Paul Dourish (2010) calls upon HCI, and other fields that create participatory technological systems, to engage and more deeply understand the political implications of design, querying the 'design of politics.' He problematizes the design narrative of the individual user of technology, highlighting the need to recognize that users function in a community and develop use via sociocultural context, a theme appropriate to makers working in collectivities. Reflexive design and critical technical practice are in conversation with participatory design and inclusive design (Reed/Monk 2011) scholarship, but further develop the definitions of expertise, knowledge, community, and empowerment. This study joins in on these conversations highlighting the implicit politics designed into interactive systems, since it explores implicit narratives designed into maker and hacker communities and technologies.

By critically engaging maker rhetoric, I eventually hope to give a nuanced description – unpacking terms such as 'accessibility', 'inclusion', and 'empowerment' – of how maker subject formation is influenced by overarching cultural contexts while producing new relations to design, technological production, and material fabrication. These environments and discourses influence which knowledges are considered important for enacting and taking part in technological (re)production. It is these interests and critical inquiries, especially those grounded in the work of critical making and critical technical practice, which have led to setting the stage for critical inquiry of skill-sharing workshops and knowledge dissemination within maker cultures.

Theoretical Influences and Underpinnings

By focusing on mobile collectivities rather than concrete spaces as my object of study, I have identified groups that hope to create an alternative pathway for the production and use of technology in a DIY capacity – although I see each group as situated and heterogeneous in terms of participant interests, ethics, and ideologies. I am grounding my interest in particular groups with J. K. Gibson-Graham's elucidation of the existence and possible cultivation of alternative economies (Gibson-Graham 2005) that exist regardless of monolithic capitalist tendencies so prevalent in Western societies. While myself critical of the effects that a subset of hacker and maker practices might have on large-scale technology development and use, I am hopeful for these small yet transformative and empowering disruptions. This hope is further influenced and cultivated by Michel de Certeau's theorization of subversive tactics (1984) in relation to practices of everyday life. Although they may start at a base-level and through micro-interactions, subversive interventions into technological use, interpretation, and appropriation can have impact on local communities and the individuals that take part – toward something that many individuals in these groups identify as empowerment.

The cultivation of technological imaginaries outside of dominant structures points toward an opening up of methodologies and practices that follow from José Muñoz's (2009) queer utopian futures – which move beyond the pragmatism of the here and now. By envisioning an alternate future with different modes of production and consumption that play with, yet take seriously, issues of gender, race, and socio-economic class, these collectivities are engaging with a different relationality to technological production and use. Yet there are still boundary-making aspects to the haves and have nots of maker and hacker communities, including time-commitment, capacities, skill, and comfort-levels – which often create an implicit or systemic preference of one population over another to take part in these practices. The problems therein are something serious to address and unpack in hacker and maker cultures, especially when they tend to use a rhetoric of inclusion and accessibility. It is also important to consider questions of for whom, by whom, and for what purpose when taking into account the labor around and within technological production. Due to my interest in critical engagement, I have sought out spaces that are already open to reflexive and critical mindsets as possible testing beds for these approaches, or as places to observe new and mindful ways in which to share skills when taking into consideration marginalized publics or knowledges. This interest has led me to explore the practices of feminist hacker collectives, Fixers Collectives or Repair Cafes, and library makerspaces.

My explorations of interventions into the structure of skill-sharing in DIY projects, are rooted in the engaged, feminist pedagogy of bell hooks and critical pedagogy as explored by Donna Riley (2003). Breaking from the norms of engineering education, Riley challenges her students to question sociocultural framings and definitions of science, technology, and engineering as they go through a higher education program. As she explains in her article "Employing Liberative Pedagogies in Engineering Education", Riley is directly influenced by the work of Paolo Freire, hooks, and others. In particular, hooks defines engaged pedagogy as creating a classroom environment where people can speak and relate freely. Even though this may result in discomfort, her method is to talk through issues of difference towards mutual understanding. "Rather than focusing on safety, I think that a feeling of community creates a sense that there is shared commitment and a common good that binds us" (hooks 1994: 40). The shared commitment results in a more democratic and participatory environment. This method of pedagogy builds community by "recogniz[ing] the value of each individual voice" (hooks 1994: 40). According to hooks, unless the harsh realities and tensions regarding issues of marginalization along lines of gender, race, and socio-economic class are talked about directly, resolutions and transgression beyond current systemic beliefs may not transpire. This pedagogical shift also relates to breaking down the preference of one type of voice, or knowledge, over another. Hacker and maker groups usually focus on sharing soldering, 3D printing, coding, and electronic tech skills – shutting many different people from feeling useful and able to contribute relevant or useful skills. Beyond the technical, skills such as active listening, organization, sustaining practices, promotion, design, care, maintenance, and management are just as important, in their own right, for running such a group -- something that the feminist hacker groups recognize.

While many makers and hackers are explicit about the politics of opening up the black-box of technology, some are adamant that their practices are just about having fun and tinkering in their free time. Critical reflection does not always factor into these practices, and the hackerspace or makerspace sometimes embody less a community of practice than a clubhouse for friends to tinker and play around with shared tools. In reaction to this, some hackerspaces or groups acknowledge issues connected to the 'politics of no politics' and are explicit about the politics they want to impart within their practices and skill cultivations. With the concept 'politics of no politics' I am invoking Donna Haraway's (1997) work to think about Chris Kelty (2008) and Gabriella Coleman's (2013) research into issues of openness among hacker groups. Both scholars have explored how, in the stead of such openness, certain dominant voices and structures often tend to assert themselves. This phrasing is also based upon Traweek's (1992) explanation of a 'culture of no culture' within her book *Lifetimes and Beamtimes*, a laboratory study of the culture in a Japanese high energy physics lab. In her work, Traweek argues that the high demand to be objective results in an erasure or glossing over of the politics and culture embedded in daily scientific practices.

Case Study 1: Feminist hacker collectives

Acknowledging the systemic power dynamics and dominant structures of innovation that are often reproduced via claims of 'no politics,' feminist hackerspaces often take a socially political stance in their groups. As with other spaces, their focus is on experiential learning of tacit knowledge. However, alongside this interest in technical and fabrication knowledges, they question norms of technical skill-sharing and cultivate a particular politics as important for moving forward into a constructively critical realm. The possibility in this framework is to recognize these acts as exploratory and subversive. Nevertheless, the delineation needs to be made as to which acts are reproducing cultural norms or breaking their bounds by producing new practices, discourses, and actions.

Precedence of tactics employed by feminist hacker collectives traces back to the Consciousness-raising groups of the 1960s, stitch n' bitch sharing circles, and the riot grrrl movement of the 1990s. These groups used the concept of 'safe space' to create an exclusive setting that allowed for open exploration of ideas, failures, skills, and knowledges. In-line with hooks, they were seeking to build community and trust via identity and among subject-formations in order to create their own cultures and alternative routes for subverting what dominant cultural practices and beliefs were telling them: that they did not have the capacity to do certain things and that their particular standpoints and knowledges were irrelevant in the greater context of culture. Instead of taking these judgments to heart, these previous movements and groups created their own cultures of belonging – something that feminist hacker groups also seek to do in the face of a tech culture that is predominantly white, male, and upper-class dominated – typically in an overtly misogynistic, or what is often termed 'machismo,' manner.

Feminist hacker collectives are operationalizing politics and inclusionary or exclusionary tactics in order to open up complex discussions regarding the tech industry, empowerment, knowledges, pedagogy, accessibility, and inclusion. They are trying to escape the capture of dominant consumerist tendencies of maker culture by creating a community of care towards different types of people with different types of knowledge. Not all are enacting the same critique, though, and some are more tech, white, and upper-class oriented (Rosner/Fox 2016) with empowerment helping certain marginalized communities and possibly excluding others.

Even as their intention is to question notions of accessibility and inclusion, and they take this seriously in terms of gender and sexuality, they can still struggle with issues of intersectionality (Crenshaw 1991) regarding race, socio-economic class, and mobility (Rosner/Fox 2016).

One feminist group working to shift narratives in the hacker activist scene of Montreal is Femhack. Some members of Femhack were originally part of a different hacker collective in Montreal, but a move away from an originally politicized agenda and gender imbalance in the hackerspace presented difficulties that sometimes resulted in micro-aggressions and unchecked discomfort. As a result, interested individuals created a feminist meet-up group within the hackerspace to establish solidarity and a safe space mentality. They partly created this exclusionary safe space in which to hack and rethink technological use and knowledge, and eventually they broke from the main group to meet elsewhere. Sophie Toupin (2014) as well as and Daniela K. Rosner and Sarah E. Fox (2016) have also observed these tactical exclusionary practices in other feminist hacker collectivities such as Double Union, Liberating Ourselves Locally (LOL), and Mothership Hacker Moms.

Members of the Femhack collective have described various events at which discomforts arose as a reason to cultivate safe space. In one such example, they were hosting a workshop when an outsider to Femhack took what participants and Femhack members saw as a machismo attitude to teaching and skill-sharing. At the end of the information session, the outsider instructed participants to come to him with their problems as opposed to helping them establish sustainable and autonomous practices. His reasoning was that it was too complicated for them to understand. In reflection and talking with Femhack members afterward, the outsider recognized the issue within himself and apologized – but things were not addressed and changed in the moment. In part, Femhack saw this as an issue within their own abilities to deal with such interactions in their programming, and as an organizational failure brought on by the uncertainty of collaborating with an outsider to run an event.

Femhack members wanted to set up a different way of reacting to these tensions in the moment and worked to conceptualize this later in the winter of 2015. Not wanting to react in an aggressive or escalating way, the tactic they landed upon was that of *jouissance* – to take the belittlement or attempts of control as farcical, and to bring levity and humor into the situation; to undercut acts of bravado or belittlement with laughter instead of rage or silence. Femhack had also decided that they wanted to establish alternative space and framing through the formation of their group – they were not setting out to topple the machismo attitudes they felt was prevalent in male-dominated hacker cultures by going to spaces and asserting their own values. Instead, they wanted to create their own collectivity, an alternative route similar to the alternative economies that Gibson-Graham (2005) highlight as a way to create an economic account that destabilizes capitalism. It is the possibility to foster these multiplicities within the greater maker and hacker milieu that seem to cultivate feelings of possibility, utopia, transgression, transformation, and change for feminist hacker collectives through pursuit of their practices. Beyond *jouissance* and safe space, there are a few other ways in which Femhack hopes to accomplish the task of creating an alternative frame.

Rather than having self-proclaimed experts teaching courses and skills, participants in Femhack are interested in creating an atmosphere where it is permissible to learn together and have diverse styles to approaching a problem. In this sense, there is more than one way to solder a circuit. Everyone has some knowledge, whether it be technical, organizational, emotional, or otherwise to bring into the craft-work – and the feminist hacker and maker groups to whom I have talked want to foster an acknowledgement of such contributions. This was also revealed by Rosner and Fox as a practice of Mothership Hacker Moms, when members were encouraged to bring ideas and projects to the table that they felt they would never be able to accomplish on their own. The hope being that members can garner advice and support from the others in the group who have different expertise, knowledges, and experiences, and thus accomplish a project through the collectivity (Rosner/Fox 2016).

Femhack members are part of a larger network of similarly-minded groups, collectives, and individuals which run some aggregate initiatives such as autonomous feminist servers, including the AnarchaServer project. Launched in 2014 by residents of the "post-capitalist colony" Calafou and participants of a feminist hacker event being hosted there, the AnarchaServer is a self-proclaimed feminist server. In part, it "aims to develop autonomous infrastructure on the Internet for feminist projects" (o.J.: o.S.). AnarchaServer also functions as a working experiment to establish and train female-identifying peoples as System Administrators (sys admins) – a classically male-dominated field in the realm of Information Technology and hacker cultures. Members of their network live throughout the world, including in Austria, Catalunya, Quebec, and Switzerland. Much of the original physical infrastructure for the AnarchaServer is based in Calafou which is housed in an abandoned textile factory outside of Valbona, Catalunya. Creating an autonomous and alternative data server infrastructure is putting the imaginary of alternative pathways into practice in a very tangible way, but it also poses issues regarding the resource-intensive realities of running and maintaining a reliable data server, especially in Calafou, an off-the-grid colony that has power outages from time to time.

Calafou hosted the TransHackFeminist! Convergence of 2014, and is also home to the feminist healthcare hacker group Gynepunk. Gynepunk hopes to reclaim female health care practices for women, much in the way that the feminist consciousness-raising groups of the 1960s hoped to do. Beyond the creation of online manuals and texts, Gynepunk's main mode of intervention is through the production of serious at home testing kits via a DIY Bio lab, and 3D printed speculums that they plan to make freely available to sex workers and the resource poor. There is a slight flip-side to this narrative as strains of neoliberalization increasingly take hold of healthcare, often making the individual fully accountable and responsible for their own needs and cares. The possibility to take such health concerns into one's own hands assumes a lot in terms of labor, time, and affordance in many ways. However, in creating a collective (as opposed to individual) experience around these DIY methods and sharing practices, experimentations, stories, tools, and failures, Gynepunk hope to sidestep neoliberal tendencies, establishing an alternative narrative through collective becoming and accountability.

Case Study 2: Collaborative Civic Science Platforms

In the vein of critical practice, groups such as the Public Laboratory for Open Technology and Science (Public Lab), as well as the Agbogbloshie Makerspace Platform (AMP) initiative in Accra, Ghana are compelling case studies for the effects of alternative knowledges in conversation with DIY practices. Particularly in how their cultivation might affect Big Science policy as well as everyday understandings of how scientific knowledge intertwines with local knowledges and the productive possibilities for both to co-produce one another.

Both initiatives have an interest in using DIY and DIT narratives for social justice works by developing tools of informal scientific practices within the public or informal sphere, while engaging and developing different forms of expertise. Public Lab enacts these goals by sharing open-source blueprints for overhead mapping technology – which are helpful for documentation during pollution and oil spill events – water-temperature sensing flotation devices, and other toxin detection devices. As a research group, Public Lab works to make these instruments easy to acquire, fabricate, and tweak for local situations. They have also created infrastructure for online and offline communities of tinkerers, data collectors, and community advocates who are invested in their local environmental story, helping to instigate events that bring awareness to locally-contingent pollution issues. Participants in a network of working groups share their experiences, victories, and documentations on the Public Lab website. There is no one exact or right way to deploy the openly developed technologies, and success is deeply grounded on locally "situated knowledges" (Haraway 1991) and available materials with which devices can be changed for a particular need. Conceptually, situated knowledges make visible the positionality of those who produce knowledge, as well as the effect that certain tools and methods might have on the data produced. It complicates the outcome of scientific practices and gives room for alternative knowledges to take part.

While the Public Lab group may not directly affect scientific policy practices, in the "stories" section of their website they list several instances in which the use of their DIY technologies and the communities connected to the research group have made indirect impacts on policy, legislation, or further investigation into instances of unregulated industrial pollution. Further investigation was the result of one such case involving a mismanaged coal pile at a United Bulk facility, of which Public Lab members were able to gather informational photography. "The images they secured of the coal pile over time changed the Gulf Restoration Network's (GRN) understanding of the extent of Oiltanking/United Bulk's alleged environmental crimes and led to funding for further documentation and water quality analysis of this facility, culminating in a notice of intent to sue under the Clean Water Act" (Public Labs o.J.: o.S.). (Data gathered using Public Lab shown in Image 1 by eustatic and Gulf Restoration Network)

Image 1: Data gathered showing a coal pile changing over time using Public Lab DIY tools. Source: Stories. United Bulk Coal Terminal Monitoring, in: Public Labs, URL: https://publiclabs.org/wiki/stories (Accessed on 18.10.2016). Image by eustatic and the Gulf Restoration Network (GRN).

The two community-members who acted as part of Public Lab in this instance used the Public Lab training, tools, and support in conjunction with their own local knowledge of the area, connections to GRN, and their understandings of local weather conditions in order to use the data gathering tools productively. While the data would most likely have not made an impact when reported in isolation, by connecting to previous studies, data, and existing infrastructure, actions and impacts were made.

In his book *Street Science* (2005) Jason Corburn speaks about the promises and downfalls of citizen mapping and citizen sensing. Here, citizen mapping is defined as the creation of maps that incorporate publicly and/or collectively gathered data, aggregating the situated knowledges of citizens including personal stories, experiences, and information from citizen sensing. Citizen sensing uses low-cost or DIY technologies to measure and monitor local pollutants or contaminants. Corburn argues that while community mapping may not be fully convincing for policy-makers or in legislation hearings, it works to embellish and collate many different reports and information to create an evocative re-telling and re-problematizing from situated standpoints. As he reveals, such methods were able to create a more nuanced and readable story of micro-level pollution events in Brooklyn neighborhoods in the early 2000s.

In the cases that Corburn studies, and often in the case of Public Lab, the work that the citizen-mapping does was to help form community coalitions and set the groundwork for further investigations or legislative support towards action and change. It also gave communities the feeling that they had a voice, an issue around which to organize, and a material practice to support what they had already been experiencing – it gave further weight to their own expertise. "As street scientists generate maps that reframe and reorient definitions of "problems," and as these same scientists develop the sophisticated skills of computer-aided mapping, they will continue to blur the line between professional and local knowledge and whose evidence counts as credible in environmental health decision making" (Corburn 2005: 199). These DIY tools and practices do not work in isolation. Their power comes more from community development and support toward instantiating change and reframing the problems at hand, as well as blurring the lines and making clear that situated, local knowledge can impact greater infrastructures.

Similarly, the Agbogbloshie Makerspace Platform (AMP) project is invested in working with and cultivating the knowledge of the scrapping community in an electronic-waste (e-waste) and informal scrapyard site located in Accra, Ghana. Started by Yasmine Abbas and D.K. Osseo-Asare, the initiative hopes to facilitate in remediation practices and to rethink what scrapping practices can do on-site. This has involved ethnographic interviews and surveys of scrappers, their working environment, and the practices they have developed to deal with large amounts of e-waste in the area. The AMP research team are positioning themselves to neither romanticize nor patronize the scrapping community. While acknowledging that the scrappers are dealing with very harsh working conditions, AMP also recognizes that they have expertise and local knowledge that can contribute to remediation efforts and improvement of working standards and best practices. This work is also done in the context of a global interest in maker cultures and in conversation with the Maker Movement discourse. "We're trying to make the argument [that] look, there *is* already a Makerspace in Ghana. And it's not the only one. [...] But let's see them as Makerspaces and bring them into the discourse and not just focus on the negative sides, but try to use the positive sides to change the negative sides" (Osseo-Asare 2014: o.S.) AMP hopes to enroll the scrapping community in transformation and change, and is creating a locally-sourced semi-permanent infrastructure on-site for sharing knowledge, talking about practices, and initiating conversation.

Traditionally, workers in Agbogbloshie focus on the scraping of the materials that make their way to the dumping ground. AMP is interested in helping to establish more small-scale fabrication on site for the scrappers so that they might move beyond selling materials to outside processing centers toward doing their own processing on site, thus building local entrepreneurial practices. This includes the melting down of plastics to make bricks or buckets (tools for processing shown in Image 2 and experimental examples shown in Image 3). On site production facilities are also inspired by a blacksmith and metal-working group already on site.

Image 2: Local instruments used in creating plastic tiles.

Image 3: Tiles made from 1. PET 2. PP 3. HDPE 4. PP 5. Inpregnated fabric 6. LDPE 7. PP 8. PP. Source: "Experimenting with plastics" URL: https://qamp.net/2014/07/15/experimenting-with-plastics/ (Accessed on 18.10.2016).

The interactions and informal practices of knowledge sharing and production are not bound by the physical site at Agbogbloshie and include an extended constellation of collaborators which AMP is building in an intentional manner. By engaging local college students and recent graduates in the fields of chemistry, architecture, biology, anthropology, and material sciences, AMP is starting something that Osseo-Asare calls "inter-class innovation." They hope to create a coalition of scrappers and the students who have an interest in social justice and the informal or DIY fabrication practices within Ghana.

[Y]ou have latent potential in both of those two communities and you can create linkages and create a hybridized social network. The theory is that you can create opportunities for new forms of entrepreneurship. So that's one of the leading points of departure for AMP as an idea to try to forge those links. (Osseo-Asare 2014: o.S.)

An important aspect of AMP, is to work within existing infrastructure and subvert dominant discourse in order to innovate and change practices. This entails working from the ground-up in contrast to a top-down perspective. “I think the other idea of the change-making is that if you take the existing system and you tweak it or you hack it, you can create new outputs” (Osseo-Asare 2014: o.S.). Abbas is particularly interested in thinking about place and the changes that happen with changing environments and structures. For her, the transformation of a hostile e-waste dumping site starts from changing the physicality of the place, but in collaboration with those already present.

I really believe that you can change this place. If you seed something relevant, you can probably change the ecosystem and hence the way people see or perceive the place or environmentally behave. I'm interested in that aspect of design. Learning from the practices there and proposing a design that somehow seeds changes in that place – in that community, but also in the larger Ghanaian community in terms of: how do you appreciate waste generated and how do you engage with that Agbogbloshie community. (Abbas 2014: o.S.)

Through DIY practices, and a focus on building a "generative context" (Lyles et al. 2016) with collective resources and community engagement, inter-class collaborations and grass-roots knowledge production is advanced. In this way, AMP proposes a culturally-contingent fabrication culture that uses maker narratives, yet is positioned outside of the dominant discourse, and as a possible alternative to the Silicon-Valley maker cultures that contribute so heavily to the e-waste problem with which Agbogbloshie is now burdened.

Both Public Lab and AMP propose alternative frameworks to create worlds and narratives beyond the dominant discourse of what counts as legitimate knowledge and who can take part. Yet there are pitfalls. Researchers within Public Lab describe an inquiry from police to use their open-source and accessible technology to monitor crowds at different public events.

While we declined to participate or collaborate with this particular inquiry, it emphasized the need to clearly situate our technology as an *alternative* to government and corporate information production, and to draw explicit attention to our work as a grass-roots community of practice who are offering a critique of traditional map making. The responsibility for developing strong ethical norms and exploring potential risks must be addressed both before, during, and after the development of accessible technologies. (Dosemagen/Warren /Wylie 2012)

This continual process of engaging and addressing embedded politics, ethics, and social implications within technology development and use is crucial for following through on the promises of DIY and critical engagements within the Maker Movement and maker/hacker cultures.

Conclusion

The communities explored (feminist hacker collectives, Public Lab, and AMP) highlight differentiated local knowledges and bring them into conversation with dominant discourse with the intention to open up technology in subversive ways. They create room to be critical and reflexive of practices that are inherently political and often give preference to certain types of knowledges or prerogatives over others. Working through artistic practice and Science and Technology Studies (STS), my work engages performativity and critical work-shopping (Foster 2015) as a site of critique, research, and new methodologies. I am interested in exploring how the spectacular and creative can instigate new spheres of public discourse, critique, knowledge sharing, and bottom-up production practices.

The projects I have explored here are clear examples of interventions into design and DIY practices that critically engage the various cultural dynamics and assumptions that dominant discourse and various subject formations bring forth – particularly by enabling the cultivation of local, situated, and alternative knowledges. What might scholars studying cultural dynamics of technology and science do to further engage these communities and incite interventions or to highlight such communities that do subvert by remaking culture, however slightly, and thus decenter the norm?

Critical reflexivity, or strong objectivity, does not dodge the world-making practices of forging knowledges with different chances of life and death built into them. All that critical reflexivity, diffraction, situated knowledges, modest interventions, or strong objectivity "dodge" is the double-faced, self-identical god of transcendent cultures of no culture, on the one hand, and of subjects and objects exempt from the permanent finitude of engaged interpretation on the other. (Haraway 1997: 37)

Haraway describes that by engaging ways in which to identify the cultures and politics inherent in different knowledge systems, we gain a better understanding of what is at stake and the power involved in the "world-making practices of forging knowledges." As she argues, however, the recognition alone is but a step toward any kind of transformation divergent from a preference or focus on dominant practices. It is possible that through critical pedagogical practices, and by questioning the very ways in which we learn and transfer knowledge, some shifts may occur. It remains to be seen if it is possible to follow and help the alternative narratives herein described, possibly through cultivation via critical pedagogy, without them being co-opted by the capitalist, commercialistic powers deeply embedded within the Maker Movement and its subsequent cultures.

Acknowledgements

The author would like to acknowledge NSF grant DGE-0947980 in support of this work as part of an NSF grant on community situated STEM (Eglash/Foster 2017) which facilitated travel to conduct research in Ghana and subsequent analysis of collected interviews and observations.

Literaturverzeichnis

Abbas, Yasmine [Interview: 03.08.2014].

Agre, Philip E. (1997): Toward a Critical Technical Practice. Lessons Learned in Trying to Reform AI. In: Bowker, Geoffrey C./Star, Susan Leigh/Turner, William/Gasser, Les (Hrsg.): Bridging the Great Divide. Social Science, Technical Systems, and Cooperative Work. New York, 131-157.

Boehner, Kirsten/David, Shay/Kaye Joseph 'Jofish'/Sengers, Phoebe (2005). "Critical Technical Practice as Methodology for Values in Design", *Chi Workshop*: o.S.

Charter, Martin/Keiller, Scott (2014): Grassroots innovation and the Circular Economy. A Global Survey of Repair Cafes and Hackerspaces. In: (o.A.): The Center for Sustainable Design. o.O., o.S.

Coleman, Gabriella (2013): Coding Freedom. The Ethics and Aesthetics of Hacking. Princeton, Oxford.

Corburn, Jason (2005): Street Science. Community Knowledge an Environmental Health Justice. Cambridge.

Crenshaw, Kimberle (1991). "Mapping the Margins: Intersectionality, Identity Politics, and Violence Against Women of Color", *Stanford Law Review* 43: 1241-1299.

De Certeau, Michel (1984): The Practice of Everyday Life. London.

Disalvo, Carl/Lukens, Jonathan (2009). "Towards a Critical Technological Fluency. The Confluence of Speculative Design and Community Technology Programs", *Proceedings of the Digital Arts and Culture Conference:* 1-6.

Dosemagen, Shannon/Warren, Jeffrey/Wylie, Sara (2012). "Grassroots Mapping. Creating a Participatory Map Making Process Centered on Discourse", *Journal of Aesthetics & Protest* 8: o.S.

Dourish, Paul (2010). "HCI and Environmental Sustainability: The Politics of Design and the Design of Politics", *ACM, Proceedings from DIS Conference, Aarhus Denmark* (8): 16-20.

Eglash, Ron/Croissant, Jennifer L./Di Chiro, Giovanna/Fouché, Rayvon (2004): Appropriating Technology. Vernacular Science and Social Power. Minneapolis.

Eglash, Ron/Foster, Ellen (2017): On the Politics of Generative Justice: African Traditions and Maker Communities. In: Eglash, Ron/Foster, Ellen: What Do Science, Technology, and Innovation Mean from Africa, Clapperton Chakanets Mavhunga. Cambridge, o.S.

Foster, Ellen (2015). "Critical Work shopping. The Contact Microphone", *Hyperrhiz* 13: o.S.

Gibson-Graham, J. K. [Graham, Julie/Gibson, Katherine] (2005): The End of Capitalism As We Knew It. Minneapolis.

Gieryn, Thomas (1983). “Boundary-Work and the Demarcation of Science From Non-Science. Strains and Interests in Professional Ideologies of Scientists”, *American Sociological Review* 6 (6): 781-795.

Haraway, Donna (1991): Situated Knowledges. In: (o.A.): Simians, Cyborgs, and Women. The Reinvention of Nature. New York, 183-203.

Haraway, Donna (1997): Modest_Witness@Second_Millennium. FemaleMan–Meets–OncoMouse. Feminism and Technoscience. New York.

hooks, bell (1994): Teaching to Transgress. New York.

Kelty, Christopher M. (2008): Two Bits. The Cultural Significance of Free Software. Durham, NC.

Kraft, Caleb (2014). White House Maekr Faire Attendee List Released. [Link: http://makezine.com/2014/06/18/white-house-maker-faire-attendee-list-released; 18.06.2014].

Le Dantec, Christopher A./Disalvo, Carl (2013). “Infrastructuring and the Formation of Publics in Participatory Design”, *Social Studies of Science* 43 (2): 241–64.

Libow, Sylvia/Stager, Martinez/Stager, Gary S. (2013). How the Maker Movement is Transforming Technology. [Link: http://www.weareteachers.com/hot-topics/special-reports/how-the-maker-movement-is-transforming-education; 18.10.2016].

Lyles, Daniel/Lachney, Michael/Foster, Ellen K./Zatz, Zoe (2016). "Generative Contexts. Generating Value between Community and Educational Settings", *Revista Teknokultura* 13 (2): 613-637.

Maxigas, Peter (2014). "Hacklabs and Hackerspaces – Tracing Two Geneaologies", *The Journal for Peer Production* 2: o.S.

Muñoz, Josè Esteban (2009): Cruising Utopia. The Then and There of Queer Futurity. New York, London.

Nascimento, Susana (2014). "Critical Notions of Technology and Promises of Empowerment in Shared Machine Shops", *Journal of Peer Production* 5: o.S.

o.A. (o.J.). Anarcha Section. [Link: http://anarchaserver.org/mediawiki/index.php/Main_Page#Anarchaserver; 27.11.2017].

o.A. (o.J.). Stories. United Bulk Coal Terminal Monitoring. [Link: https://publiclabs.org/wiki/stories; 18.10.2016].

Osseo-Asare, D. K. [Interview: 03.08.2014].

Ratto, Matt (2011). "Critical Making: Conceptual and Material Studies in Technology and Social Life", *The Information Society* 27 (4): 252-260.

Ratto, Matt/Boler, Megan (2014): DIY Citizenship: Critical Making and Social Media. Cambridge, Boston.

Reed, Darren/Monk, Andrew (2011). “Inclusive Design. Beyond Capabilities Towards Context of Use”, *Universal Access in the Information Society* 10 (3): 295-305.

Riley, Donna (2003). “Employing Liberative Pedagogies in Engineering Education”, *Journal of Women and Minorities in Science and Engineering* 2 (9): 137-158.

Rosner, Daniela K./Fox, Sarah E. (2016). “Legacies of Craft and the Centrality of Failure in a Mother-Operated Hackerspace”, *New Media & Society* 18 (4): 558–580.

Sengers, Phoebe/Boehner, Kirsten/David, Shay/Kaye Joseph ‘Jofish’ (2005): Reflective Design. In: (o.A.): Proceedings of the 4th decennial conference on Critical Computing: between sense and sensibility, ACM Press. o.O., 49-58.

Toupin, Sophie (2014). “Feminist Hackerspaces as Safer Spaces?”, *Feminist Journal of Arts and Digital Culture* 27: o.S.

Traweek, Sharon (1992): Beamtimes and Lifetimes. The World of high Energy Physicists. Cambridge.

Rosa Zimmer und Kressekleid oder „Do-it-yourself" als Selbstbehauptung – Künstlerische Strategien bei Maria Pinińska-Bereś und Teresa Murak

von Constance Krüger

In der kunstgeschichtlichen Auseinandersetzung wird mit Do-it-yourself (DIY) vornehmlich eine Kunst verbunden, die eine „Mitmach"-Aufforderung an das Publikum richtet.[1] Im Zentrum stehen also Kunstwerke, die erst durch das Agieren der Rezipientinnen[2], durch eine vorher von den Künstlerinnen bestimmte und festgelegte Handlung zu solchen werden. So definiert Anna Dezeuze das DIY-Kunstwerk folgendermaßen: "I will be defining as 'do-it-yourself' artworks a range of artistic practices that require an active physical and/ or conceptional participation on the part of the spectator" (Dezeuze 2010: 1). Der Fokus verschiebt sich demnach von den Kunstwerken als statische Objekte hin zu künstlerischen Praxen, welche die Aktivierung des Publikums miteinschließen – die-

[1] Diese Mitmach-Aufforderung bezeichnet der Kunsthistoriker Oskar Bätschmann als Erfahrungsgestaltung. Darunter versteht er Kunstwerke, „die das Publikum von Ausstellungen mit einer unerwarteten Situation überraschen oder in einen Vorgang einbeziehen und danach einen Prozess der Erfahrung auslösen sollen. [...] Erfahrungsgestaltung ... richtet sich auf Partizipation und Einbezug durch Einladung, Verlockung, Überwältigung, Schock und Gefährdung" (Bätschmann 1996: 254-255).

[2] Zur besseren Lesbarkeit des Textes verwende ich ausschließlich die weibliche Form, die männliche Form ist hierbei stets mitgedacht.

ses stellenweise gar in Form einer Ko-Autorschaft konzeptualisieren (Blunck 2005). Dadurch werden gleichzeitig die Begriffe von Produktion und Rezeption obsolet – verwirklicht sich das Kunstwerk doch erst durch den aktiven Beitrag der Rezipientinnen. Bei den handlungsorientierten Aufforderungen an das Publikum geht es jedoch weniger darum, künstlerisch Gemälde oder Skulpturen zu gestalten. Vielmehr wird es aufgefordert, Tätigkeiten des Alltags auszuführen und diese somit in das Feld der Kunst zu übertragen. Es ist nicht verwunderlich, dass unter dem Begriff der DIY-Kunst schwerpunktmäßig die 1960er Jahre (Pop-Art, Fluxus, Konzeptkunst) im Mittelpunkt stehen, also Kunstformen fokussiert werden, die sowohl die Auflösung tradierter Definitionen von (Hoch-)Kunst als auch eine Neuausrichtung der Rolle der Künstlerin propagierten (Cichocki 2012: 8). Gerade die Ausrichtung auf nicht-künstlerische Materialien und damit verbunden auch auf Techniken wie Kleben und Arrangieren, die nicht einer akademisch-künstlerischen Ausbildung bedürfen, machen diese Kunstformen anschlussfähig an Überlegungen, bei denen das Bild der Künstlerin als Bricoleuse, als Bastlerin und Amateurin, aufgerufen wird.[3]

Zwei polnische Künstlerinnen – Maria Pinińska-Bereś (1931-1999) und Teresa Murak (*1949) – können als solche Bastlerinnen verstanden werden. Während sich die erste auf rosafarbene, weiche Stoffskulpturen fokussiert, arbeitet die zweite mit Kressesamen, die sie zu grünen Kressekleidern verarbeitet. Kann „Do-it-

[3] Der Begriff des *Bricoleur* wird unter Bezugnahme auf das bei Lévi-Strauss entwickelte Konzept in Auseinandersetzung mit der Pop-Art immer wieder genannt. Vgl. Lévi-Strauss 1977, Wiedemeyer 2015.

yourself“, also „Mach-es-selbst“, hier als eine Ermächtigungsstrategie der Künstlerin verstanden werden, durch welche die künstlerische Arbeit buchstäblich (wieder) in die eigenen Hände genommen wird? Oder anders formuliert: Werden durch die angewandten Techniken und Materialien bestimmte Erkenntnisprozesse in Gang gesetzt, die zu einem kritischen, feministischen Künstlerinnenverständnis führen?

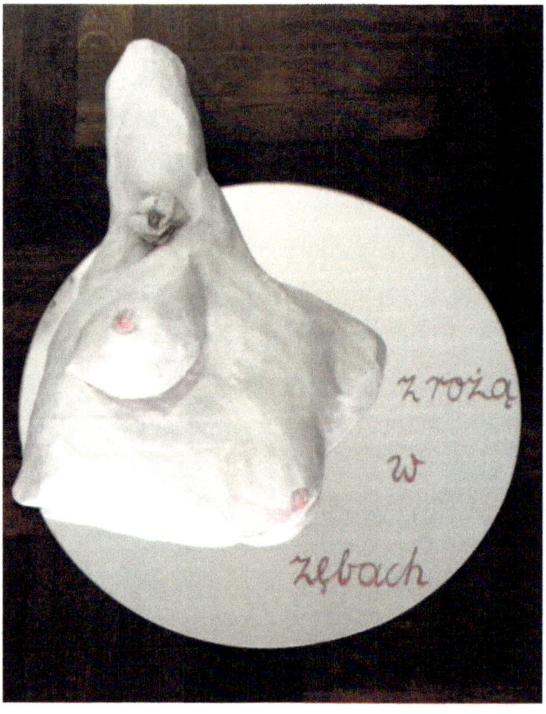

Abb. 1: Maria Pinińska-Bereś: Z różą w zębach / With a rose in teeth, 1970, Spiegel, Sperrholz, Papiermaché, Tempera, 75x58x15 cm, Privatbesitz.

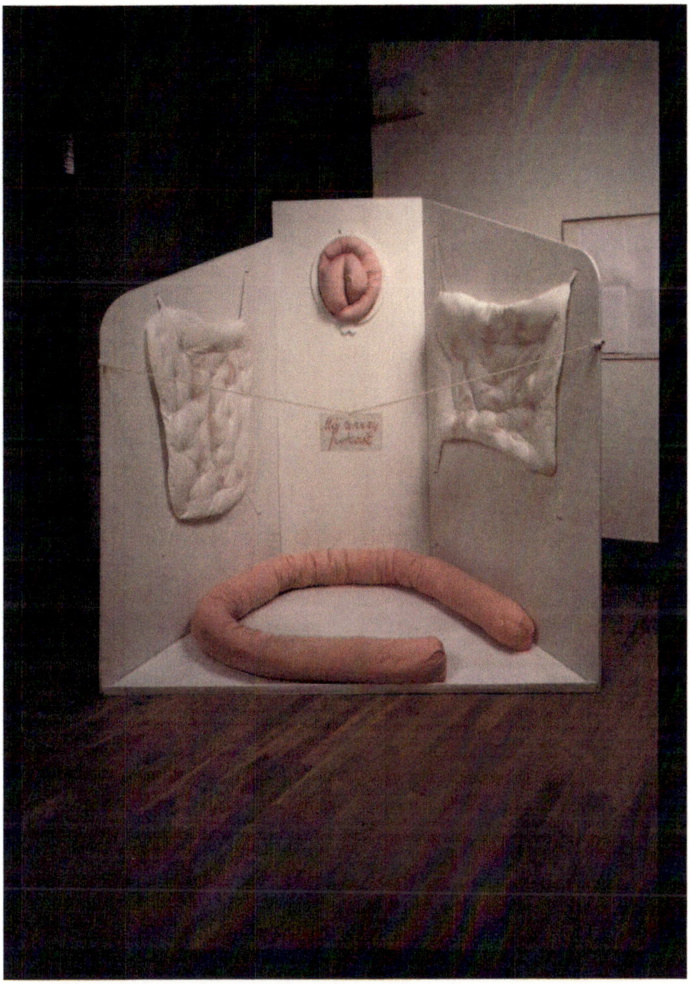

Abb. 2: Maria Pinińska-Bereś: Mój uroczy pokoik / My enchanting little room, 1975, Baumwolle, Acryl, Baumwollfäden, Holz, Sperrholz, mit Watte und Schwämmen beklebte Leinwand, Steppelemente, 102x163x172 cm, Sammlung des Nationalmuseums Krakau, Inv. Nr. MNK II-rz-913.

Abb. 3: Teresa Murak: Dywan Wielkanocny / Easter Carpet, 1974, Aktion in Kielczewice, Fotografie von Marek Banach, Archiv Teresa Murak.

Abb. 4: Teresa Murak: Rzeżucha. Lady's Smock, 1975, Performance, Galeria Sztuki MDK Labirynt, Lublin, Fotografie von Andrzej Polakowski, Archiv Teresa Murak.

Maria Pinińska-Bereś – Vom Handeln zum Schauen

Wenn der Fußhebel eines handelsüblichen Mülleimers betätigt werden muss, um das grinsende Frauengesicht der Arbeit „Keep Smiling“ (1972) sichtbar zu machen, oder wenn bei „Maszynka Miłości“ / „Love Machine“[4] (1969) erst durch die Betätigung einer Kurbel die Beine der dargestellten Frau in Bewegung versetzt werden, dann sind dies Elemente, die von Maria Pinińska-Bereś als Aufforderung an die Betrachterin zu einer aktiven Rezeption, nämlich zu einer körperlichen Betätigung, eingesetzt werden. Diese Kunstwerke kommen ganz im Sinne der oben skizzierten DIY-Lesart durch die Aktivierung des Publikums zu ihrer vollständigen Wirkung. Der Großteil der Arbeiten von Pinińska-Bereś zeichnet sich jedoch durch eine weniger stark aktiv-rezeptive Aufforderung aus und thematisiert eher eine ambivalente Form des Mit-Machens. In diesen Arbeiten steht vor allem das Spiel mit dem Blick der Betrachtenden im Mittelpunkt.

Für die Arbeit „Z różą w zębach“ / „With a rose in teeth“ (1970, Abb. 1) benutzte Pinińska-Bereś einen handelsüblichen Spiegel, auf den sie einen aus Papiermaché und Sperrholz geformten und anschließend mit Acrylfarbe bemalten weiblichen Torso aufklebte. Der Torso zeigt den Ansatz des rechten Armes, der gleichzeitig als Phallus lesbar ist. In die Achselhöhle der Figur ist eine Rose gemalt. Der Titel des Werkes erscheint als rosafarbenes Schriftbild auf der Spiegelfläche. Beim Betrachten der Arbeit

---

[4] Die englischen Übersetzungen der polnischen Originaltitel entnehme ich Maria Pinińska-Bereś 1999.

wird die jeweilige Person gleichzeitig mit ihrem eigenen Spiegelbild konfrontiert. Die Kunstbetrachtung führt Pinińska-Bereś hier als eine aktive Handlung vor – den voyeuristischen Blick auf den nackten Körper einer Frau stellt sie entlarvend zur Schau. Die Betrachtenden als Handelnde, nämlich Blickende, haben keine Wahl zwischen aktivem Mit-Machen oder passivem Anschauen. Wollen sie die Arbeit betrachten, resp. konsumieren, werden sie sichtbar.

Für die Arbeit „Mój uroczy pokoik“ / „My enchanting little room“ (1975, Abb. 2) erarbeitet sich Pinińska-Bereś auf einer trapezförmigen Bodenplatte einen Innenraum, dessen Wände aus Holz bzw. Sperrholz gearbeitet und mit rosa Acrylfarbe bemalt sind. An den Seitenwänden befinden sich mit Schnüren befestigte gesteppte Leinen-Kissen, die mit Watte und Schwämmen ausgestopft und ebenfalls mit weißer und rosa Acrylfarbe bemalt sind. An der Rückwand wurde ein ovaler Durchbruch – eine Art Guckloch – mit einem dunkelrosafarbenen Gebilde zugestopft. Aus dem gleichen Material ist die auf dem Boden liegende Stoffschlange gearbeitet. Eine Schnur, die zwischen die beiden Seitenwände gespannt ist und ein Täfelchen mit der Aufschrift „Mój uroczy pokoik“ trägt, hält die Betrachtenden davon ab, diesen Raum zu betreten. Bei dieser Arbeit ist der DIY-Aspekt als Mitmach-Aufforderung nur noch vage angelegt. Er bezieht sich als Negation auf die von der Künstlerin hervorgerufene Aktion des Betretens, Berührens, sich Niederlassens. Materialwahl und Herstellungsprozess machen deutlich, dass Pinińska-Bereś auf weiblich konnotierte Handarbeiten wie Nähen oder Patchwork zurückgreift und den häuslichen Kontext fokussiert. Das Zimmerchen wird als das der Künstlerin beschrieben. Die Künstlerin selbst spricht an anderer Stelle von ihrer „eigenen, kleinen intimen Welt, einer Welt der

Weiblichkeit mit all ihren Attributen."[5] Diese intime Welt ist auch in der hier diskutierten Arbeit entworfen, die dadurch einen persönlichen Charakter erhält. Der angebliche Einblick in eine private Sphäre ist jedoch ein vorgetäuschter, da es sich tatsächlich um eine künstlerische Arbeit handelt. Die Künstlerin erhebt einen eigenen, privaten Raum in den Bereich der Kunst, den sie museumsgerecht durch das Absperrband präsentiert.

Im Verlauf der 1970er Jahre erhalten die Arbeiten der Künstlerin einen immer stärker persönlich wirkenden Charakter. Damit einhergehend werden die Betrachterinnen immer mehr in den Möglichkeiten des Mitmachens, des Sich-Körperlich-Aneignens, eingeschränkt. Wurden sie zunächst zu körperlicher Aktion aufgerufen, verschiebt sich der Fokus der Arbeiten zunehmend auf die Auseinandersetzung mit Blickregimen, um letztlich im Ausschluss der Betrachtenden ihren Höhepunkt zu finden.

Teresa Murak – Vom Schauen zum Handeln

Bereits als Studentin der Malerei an der Warschauer Kunsthochschule zu Beginn der 1970er Jahre entwickelte Teresa Murak eine künstlerische Praxis, in der Objekte und Performances mit Kresse im Zentrum standen, wie es beispielsweise die Aktion „Dywan

---

[5] Der Ausspruch „Ja mam swój intymny mały świat" [Ich habe meine eigene, kleine intime Welt] findet sich an den Zaunlatten der Arbeit „Ogródek" / „Garden" (1974) und wird in den Artikeln von Andrzej Sawicki aus demselben Jahr immer wieder aufgegriffen, ohne jedoch die Quelle zu benennen. Auch in seiner Ausstellungsbesprechung im Dziennik Polski weist der Autor darauf hin, dass sich Pinińska-Bereś mit „Geschlecht und all seinen Attributen" beschäftigen würde. Vgl. Sawicki 1975.

Wielkanocny" / „Easter Carpet" (1974, Abb. 3) vorführt. Diese Aktion wurde anlässlich der Osterfeierlichkeiten in Kiełczewice, dem Geburtsort der Künstlerin nahe Lublins, entwickelt. Hierfür bestreute Murak ein 70 Meter langes Leinentuch mit Kressesamen, das sich unter der Pflege ortsansässiger Nonnen innerhalb einer Woche in einen grünen Kresseteppich verwandelte.[6] Dieser Teppich wurde am Karsamstag in einer Prozession, an der sich neben der Künstlerin auch Freunde sowie Kinder des örtlichen Kinderheimes beteiligten, vom Kloster zur Kirche getragen und dort vom Altar, durch den Kirchenraum, über das Eingangsportal und die Stufen der kleinen Anhöhe hinunter ausgelegt, in die liturgische Feier der Osternacht eingebunden und schließlich dem nahe liegenden Fluss übergeben. Muraks Arbeit kann im Sinne einer kollektiven Kunst verstanden werden, wobei die Künstlerin mit Laien zusammengearbeitet hatte. Erst diese Kollaboration der unterschiedlichen Akteure ermöglichte die Umsetzung der Idee von Murak in eine Kunstaktion. Mach-es-Selbst bezieht sich hier auf ein gruppendynamisches „Machen-wir-es-selbst!"

Neben dieser Form der Gemeinschaftsarbeit machte Murak verstärkt ab Mitte der 1970er Jahre den Entstehungsprozess ihrer Arbeiten im Ausstellungskontext sichtbar: Während der mehrtägig angelegten Performance „Przyjście Zieleni" / „Die Ankunft des Grün" in der Warschauer Galeria Repassage (21. Februar bis 3. März 1975) konnte das Keimen und Wachsen der Kressesamen direkt beobachtet und verfolgt werden. Murak schlüpfte dazu in

---

[6] Vgl. die Beschreibung der Künstlerin in Murak, Kubica-Bielska, Smalcerz, Marcinek: Teresa Murak. Album., Galeria Bielska BWA, Bielsko-Biała 1983: 42. Hier zitiert nach Rymarz 2011: 138.

ein Kressesamen-Kleid.[7] Ihre Körpertemperatur war mitverantwortlich für die Keimung und Entwicklung der Samen zu Pflanzen. Auch im Rahmen der Performance „Rzeżucha“ / „Lady's Smock“, die sie kurze Zeit später in der Galeria Sztuki MDK Labirynt in Lublin (3. bis 8. Juni 1975, Abb. 4) durchführte, brachte Murak die Samen an ihrem eigenen Körper zur Keimung. Anschließend präsentierte sie sich den Lubliner Passantinnen, die nicht zur Performance in die Galerie gekommen waren.[8] Eine ähnliche Performance im Innenstadtraum ohne ausgewiesenes Galerie-Publikum hatte sie bereits ein Jahr zuvor mit „Procesja“ / „Lady's Smock“ [Prozession. Lady’s Smock, 1974) durchgeführt. Hier spazierte die Künstlerin in einem langen grünen Pflanzenmantel durch die Warschauer Innenstadt. Murak setzte also auch bei den Orten – und damit verbunden bei den Menschen, die diese Orte besuchen – verstärkt auf nicht-künstlerische Momente.

Durch die Verwendung von Kressesamen und handelsüblichen Leinenstoffen sowie der Sichtbarmachung des Entstehungsprozesses der Arbeiten können die Performances von Murak als Gebrauchsanweisung für ein Nachahmen verstanden werden. Es handelt sich hier nicht um eine Anleitung im Sinne eines ausformulierten Textes oder einer Zeichnungsserie, sondern um eine lebendige Anleitung am bzw. durch den eigenen Körper. Einige Arbeiten – etwa Dywan Wielkanocny – sind darüber hinaus in Zusammenarbeit unterschiedlicher Personen entstanden und stehen

---

[7] Eine fotografische Dokumentation der Performance findet sich in Dokumentacja Plastyki Współczesnej IS PAN [Dokumentation der Zeitgenössischen Bildenden Kunst, Kunsthistorisches Institut der Polnischen Akademie der Wissenschaften], Akte Teresa Murak, Warschau.
[8] Die Galerie befand sich zu dieser Zeit am Marktplatz 8 im Keller eines Hauses aus dem späten Mittelalter.

im Kontext einer partizipativen Kunst, bei der das Kunstwerk seinen Status als visuelles Anschauungsobjekt verliert und als liturgisches Objekt in ein außerkünstlerisches Handeln eingebunden wird. Die Vorbildhaftigkeit dieser Kunstaktion zeigt sich in ihrer Übernahme in die religiöse Praxis des Ortes: Über viele Jahre hindurch wurde ein solcher Teppich für die Osterfeierlichkeiten geschaffen und in die Liturgie eingebunden, ohne dass die Künstlerin davon Kenntnis hatte.[9]

DIY im Produktionsprozess

Wie in der DIY-Kunst üblich, arbeiteten Pinińska-Bereś und Murak mit außer-künstlerischen Materialien, mit denen sie während ihrer Ausbildung nicht konfrontiert wurden.[10] Der künstlerische Schaffensprozess unterscheidet sich demnach von traditionellen Techniken der Bildhauerei und Malerei und lässt die Künstlerinnen als Bastlerinnen erscheinen:

---

[9] „Next year, the woman who looked after the carpet for me, did the sowing all by herself, and carried it to the church. She did so for a few years, as I learnt only in 1981", Murak 1983: 69. Die christliche Symbolik der Kresse im Rahmen der Osterfeierlichkeiten wird im vorliegenden Artikel nicht besprochen. Zur Verwendung von Kresse als Symbol der Erneuerung vgl. Cichocki 2012: 10.

[10] Pinińska-Bereś studierte in den Jahren 1950-56 Bildhauerei an der Krakauer Kunstakademie bei Xawery Dunikowski. Ab den 1960er Jahren erweiterte die Künstlerin ihre Materialien um weiche Stoffe. Ab Ende der 1970er Jahre arbeitete sie verstärkt performativ, vgl. Maria Pinińska-Bereś 1999. Teresa Murak schloss ihr Studium zwar im Bereich der Malerei ab, arbeitete aber bereits als Studentin vor allem performativ, vgl. Teresa Murak 1998.

> Der Bastler oder Amateur, auf den im Allgemeinen lange hinabgeblickt wurde, arbeitet in erster Linie anders als der Profi. Er macht etwas (selbst), wozu er nicht ausgebildet ist. Aber gerade, weil die Tätigkeit nicht seiner Profession entspricht, verlangt es Leidenschaft, sie auszuüben. Die emotionale Bindung und Hingabe schlagen sich sowohl in der Tätigkeit als auch im Produkt nieder. (Hornung/Nowak/Kuni 2012: 9)

Auch die künstlerische Praxis von Murak und Pinińska-Bereś kann als „emotionale Bindung und Hingabe" beschrieben werden. Während Pinińska-Bereś sich im Laufe ihrer künstlerischen Entwicklung immer mehr der Bricolage näherte und sich immer stärker auf das Nähen verlegte, ist Muraks Vorgehen an gärtnerische Techniken angelehnt, bei der sie den Pflanzensamen zu ihrer Keimung verhalf. Beide künstlerischen Techniken sind, so werde ich zeigen, eng an die Person der Künstlerinnen gebunden – sei es die körperliche Erfahrung bei Murak oder die biografische bei Pinińska-Bereś.[11] „Emotionale Bindung und Hingabe" scheint hier eine persönliche Kunst hervorzubringen, die gleichsam ein gesellschaftskritisches Potenzial birgt.

---

[11] Pinińska-Bereś verweist selbst auf diesen Zusammenhang in einem Statement aus den frühen 1990er Jahren. Jüngst hat Agata Jakubowska die Verknüpfung von künstlerischer Entwicklung mit biografischen Elementen als künstlerische Strategie herausgearbeitet, vgl. Jakubowska 2014.

Erfahrungswissen

Rückblickend beschreibt Pinińska-Bereś ihre künstlerische Entwicklung von traditionellen Bildhauermaterialien wie Stein und Gips, mit denen sie während ihrer Ausbildung und bis in die Mitte der 1960er Jahre gearbeitet hat, hin zu den weichen Stoffen als eine Suche nach einer authentischen, und in ihrem Verständnis weiblichen Sprache:

> I felt however … a need to create art wholly authentic, that grew from the authors personality. […] The author here was a woman, with the baggage of experience that today would be classified as feminist. […] Yet when I once decided to speak with my own voice, when I had unblocked that female reservoir there flowed a river. (Pinińska-Bereś 1999: 162)

Die Künstlerin spricht davon, eine authentische Kunst schaffen zu wollen, die aus ihrer Persönlichkeit als Frau schöpft. Diese Frau trüge ein „baggage of experience" – einen Erfahrungsbalast – mit sich, der durch eine eigene Sprache freigelassen werden konnte. Diese Sprache ist eine künstlerische, die sich in Form- und Farbgebung manifestiert: pinkfarbene, weiche, teilweise bestickte und bemalte Stoffobjekte, welche die Künstlerin zu Arrangements und Installationen zusammenfügt.

Pinińska-Bereś knüpft die Suche nach dieser, ihrer eigenen künstlerischen Sprache, an persönliche Erfahrungen und Erinnerungen, die sie als „female reservoir" bezeichnet. Einmal geöffnet ist dieses Reservoir Quelle künstlerischer Schöpfung und Auseinandersetzung. Die Suche nach dem „richtigen" Material für ihre

Arbeiten kann daher als künstlerische Forschung verstanden werden, bei der u.a. biografische und psychische Elemente ins Bewusstsein gehoben und anschließend verarbeitet werden. Diese Erforschungs-Arbeit ist gleichzeitig als künstlerischer Bewusstwerdungsprozess zu verstehen.

Inwiefern das weibliche Erfahrungswissen für die künstlerische Praxis der 1970er Jahre an Bedeutung gewinnt, zeigt ein Blick auf zwei Plakate, die in einem Abstand von 10 Jahren entstanden sind. Das erste Plakat von 1970 wurde anlässlich ihrer ersten Einzelausstellung im Krakauer Club „Pod Baranami“ gestaltet. Hier beschreibt die Künstlerin ihre Entwicklung in selbstbewussten und kämpferischen Worten, die sich – ganz im Sinne der Avantgarde – gegen die traditionellen Schranken und Beschränkungen innerhalb der Bildhauerei richtet, ist jedoch noch ohne den frauenspezifischen Bezug formuliert:

> Mein Weg von der Skulptur aus Stein, Zement über das Abenteuer mit Stoff, zur Papierskulptur ist keine aufgezwungene Laune, sondern eine Form des Protests gegen die Fachwelt und die kommerziellen Skulpturen-Denkmäler. Ich setze mich ein für die ungehinderte Überschreitung der fachlichen Normen, was mir erlaubt, eine uneigennützige Kommunikativität zu erreichen. (Pinińska-Bereś 1970, Übersetzung C. K.)[12]

1980 entsteht im Rahmen des Kunstfestivals „Sztuka Kobiet“ / „Kunst von Frauen“ in Poznań ein Plakat, bei dem der Bezug zu Weiblichkeit stärker in den Vordergrund tritt:

---

[12] Die Aussage ist auch abgedruckt in Tatar 2010: 98.

> Charakteristisch ist die Wahl der von mir eingesetzten Farben: neutrales Weiß und signalhaftes Rosa. Die rosa Farbe kam früh zu mir und wurde mit der Zeit zu meinem Markenzeichen. Der Einsatz war inhaltlich begründet und bezog sich auf mein Interesse an der Frauenthematik bzw. Geschlechterproblematiken in den Jahren 1965 bis 1977. (Pinińska-Bereś 1980, Übersetzung C. K.)

Hebt Pinińska-Bereś in der Aussage von 1970 auf ihre stilistische und inhaltlich motivierte Abgrenzung zu zeitgenössischer Bildhauerei ab, so formuliert sie zehn Jahre später ihre künstlerische Handschrift selbstbewusst und eindeutig weiblich. Der eingangs proklamierte Protest zur Überwindung der bildhauerischen Tradition scheint zu einer weiblichen Formensprache zu führen; die Denkmäler werden durch Objekte aus der Frauenthematik ersetzt. „Ich denke, dass die Künstlerin vor allem aus der Perspektive ihrer eigenen Erfahrung sprach, in der die Kategorie Gender und oft sogar das Geschlecht der Künstlerin selbst eine wichtige Determinante für die von ihr und ihr gegenüber getroffenen Entscheidungen war." – hält die polnische Kunsthistorikerin Ewa Tatar fest (Tatar 2010: 96). Zu dieser eigenen Erfahrung zählen u.a. die Sphäre des Haushalts, die sich künstlerisch verarbeitet in einer Reihe von Objekten wiederfindet – und im vorliegenden Text anhand der eingangs besprochenen Arbeiten visualisiert wurde. Es ist die Sphäre der Frau (My enchanting little room) und das Alltagsleben, welche in den Blick rücken. Neben der thematischen Eingrenzung wird jedoch stärker auf der ästhetischen Ebene auf diese „Welt der Weiblichkeit" Bezug genommen, wenn Pinińska-Bereś mit Haushaltswaren wie Decken experimentiert und ihre Objekte verstärkt in den Farben Weiß und Rosa erstellt.

Experimental Practices

In ihrer Einleitung in den Sammelband *The Do-it-yourself Artwork* verweist die Kunstwissenschaftlerin Anna Dezeuze auf die Nähe der Praktiken von DIY-Kunst zu naturwissenschaftlichen Methoden. Sie bezeichnet sie als

> experimental practices, which share with scientific experimental protocols a concern in maintaining a belance between limited variables and an openess to a range of results, including unexpected ones. (Dezeuze 2010: 9)

Diese hier vorgeschlagene Fokussierung auf den experimentellen Ansatz künstlerischen Handelns mit begrenzten Variablen und einem offenen Ende halte ich für produktiv, um die geschlechtsspezifische Konnotation der Arbeiten von Teresa Murak sichtbar zu machen. So fand die Aktion „Przyjście Zieleni“ (1975) nicht nur im öffentlichen Galerieraum statt, wobei das Publikum die Entwicklung des Pflanzenmantels über mehrere Tage verfolgen konnte. Vielmehr dokumentierte die Künstlerin den Entstehungsprozess des Objektes minutiös in einem Tagebuch. Ihre Aufzeichnungen wurden 1983 publiziert. Sie geben einen lebhaften Einblick in das mehr als einwöchige künstlerische Experiment:[13]

> The seeds of cress sown on my shirt and sprinkled with water have swollen and burst in the dark. I water them every hour. I do not sleep. I keep watching them with the light on. Saturday, Feb.22. The sprouts begin to penetrate

[13] In leicht abgewandelter Form erscheint der Text in Hegyi 2011: 61.

> the fabric. They cannot pierce it. I help them with light. I water them more frequently. [...] Sunday, Feb.23. The roots are strong, germinant, white. [...] Monday, Feb.24. (Balance upset). I try to help putting wet gauze underneath. It does not help. I have watered them seventy-five times so far. Night, I change the arrangement of the shirt. I take it down from the hanger. I cut it and spread it on foil, the roots down. All the leaves develop within two hours. The roots lift the fabric. The cress has grown fully and healthy. [...] Monday, March 3. After eleven days I put the cress shirt on and my body gets into contact with it. The contact will go on long, untill I get tired in a half-sitting position. I want to hold out as long as possible. (Murak 1983: 69)[14]

Einige zentrale Merkmale naturwissenschaftlichen Experimentierens werden hier sichtbar: Einerseits beschreibt Murak ihre einzelnen Schritte sowie die Entwicklung der Pflanzen sehr detailliert, teilweise mit Zeitangaben.[15] Sie legt ihren eigenen Einsatz offen – die Pflanzen sind unter ständiger Beobachtung der Künstlerin, so dass diese jederzeit eingreifen kann, sogar unter Schlafverzicht. Interessant ist vor allem die von Murak vorgenommene Änderung im „Versuchsaufbau“, durch die das Ergebnis – ein fertiges Pflan-

---

[14] In leicht abgewandelter Form erscheint der Text in Hegyi 2011: 61.

[15] Ich setze mich hierbei klar von der allgemeinen Forschung ab, die Muraks Arbeiten in einem spirituellen, archaisch-religiösen Kontext setzen. Die Religiosität Muraks und ihre Widerspiegelung in der Kunst möchte ich nicht infrage stellen, an dieser Stelle interessiert mich aber eine andere Seite der künstlerischen Praxis, die bislang nicht beleuchtet wurde. Bislang wurde auch übersehen, dass Murak Kleidungsstücke anfertigt, also den Bereich der Kultur und der weiblich konnotierten Handarbeiten betritt.

zenkleid – erst erzielt werden kann. Dem Experiment des Entstehens des Pflanzenkleides wird in einem zweiten Schritt ein Experiment zur Seite gestellt, in dem das Produkt des ersten als Mittel für das folgende benutzt wird. In diesem tritt das Kleid in Kontakt und Austausch mit Muraks Körper. Der Körper der Künstlerin rückt nun ins Zentrum der Untersuchung – und wird daraufhin geprüft, inwieweit er dem Pflanzenkleid standhalten kann. In der Arbeit „Rzeżucha“ / „Lady's Smock“ (1975) verband Murak beide Elemente miteinander und ließ ihren Körper direkten Anteil haben an der Entwicklung der Samen. Auch dies hielt sie schriftlich fest: „I cover my whole body with the sticky seeds of lady's smock. The plants germinate and grow directly on my skin, kept warm by the heat of my body.“ (Murak 1975, o. S.) Sowohl die Kresse als auch der Körper sind Materialien des Kunstwerks, deren Eigenschaften zu seinem Gelingen beitragen. Inwieweit der Prozess des Sähens auch mit unvorhersehbaren Ereignissen verbunden ist, zeigt diese Aktion. In einem Kommentar in der Lubliner Tageszeitung „Sztandar Ludu“ / „Volksflagge“ konstatiert der Autor das Missglücken des Experiments: „Die Kresse ist nicht aufgegangen“, und gibt dafür zwei Gründe an: Neben einer eher naturwissenschaftlichen Erklärung, die Samen hätten nicht die richtige Qualität gehabt oder seien überlagert gewesen, fügt er einen sexistischen Gedanken hinzu, wonach die Künstlerin zwar gut gebaut, aber nicht heiß genug gewesen sei. (Bartek 1975) Ähnlich wie gescheiterte naturwissenschaftliche Experimente führte auch Murak ihre Performance noch einmal durch und hatte im zweiten Versuch Erfolg. Die Entwicklung des Pflanzenkleides wurde fotografisch begleitet und in einem Ausstellungskatalog dokumentiert (Murak 1975).

Die hier dargelegten künstlerischen Praxen von Pinińska-Bereś und Murak können als Selbstexperimente bezeichnet werden, bei denen die eigenen Erfahrungen genuiner Teil des Kunstwerkes werden. Diese Erfahrungen werden durch die Materialwahl visualisiert und in Kunst übersetzt. Sie beziehen sich einerseits auf situative körperliche Eindrücke (bei Murak) und andererseits auf biografische Erlebnisse (bei Pinińska-Bereś). Damit thematisieren beide Künstlerinnen praktische Erfahrungen. Hier zeigt sich ein Ansatz der DIY-Kunst und -Kultur, bei dem der Praxis ein wissensgenerierender Wert zugeschrieben wird:

> Wer meint, mit einem enzyklopädischen Wissen automatisch auch schon für die Praxis gerüstet zu sein, der irrt. Tatsächlich sind auch von anderen bereits erprobte, detailgenaue Anleitungen kein Garant für den eigenen Erfolg. Vielmehr verlangt die zukünftige Anwendbarkeit von Wissen, dass zuvor Lernen in und an der Praxis stattgefunden hat. (Hornung/Nowak/Kuni 2012: 14)

Lernen in und an der Praxis ist also eine mögliche Form von Wissensgenerierung. Die Art und Weise der künstlerischen Praxis bei Pinińska-Bereś und Murak kann als ein Lernen – oder als Wissensgenerierung – verstanden werden, bei der die Erfahrungen der Künstlerin als Frau sowohl in ihrer körperlichen als auch ihrer biografischen Verfasstheit den zentralen Wissenshorizont bilden. Dabei arbeiten beide experimentell – sowohl in Hinblick auf die eingesetzten Materialien als auch in Hinblick auf den offenen Ausgang der Ergebnisse. Anders ausgedrückt: Körperliche und biografische Erfahrungen der Frau führen zu einem speziellen weiblichen Wissen, das durch bestimmte Materialien und Techniken in

Kunst übersetzt wird, die wiederum das Subjektive und Private als Quellen der Werke nicht nur nicht verdeckt, sondern offenkundig zur Schau stellt und damit die Verortung der Kunst in einen weiblichen Erfahrungshorizont bewusst vornimmt.

DIY als Selbstermächtigung

Mit der bewussten Entscheidung für bestimmte Materialien und Techniken rekurrieren beide Künstlerinnen auf außer- bzw. nichtkünstlerische Tätigkeiten, wie sie für die Kunst der 1960er und 1970er Jahre auch für die Volksrepublik Polen bekannt sind. Inwiefern sind die hier beschriebenen Praxen des DIY als kritischer Kommentar auf die als autoritäre Vormundschaft empfundene Kunstpolitik der VR Polen, aber auch auf das modernistische Verständnis von Kunst, zu verstehen? Sowohl Pinińska-Bereś als auch Murak sprechen durchaus kunstpolitische sowie geschlechtsspezifische und damit genderpolitische Aspekte an. Durch die dargelegte subjektive und private Sprache des künstlerischen Handelns ist ihre Kunst als ein Aushandeln, als ein Sich-Positionieren zu verstehen, und zwar sowohl hinsichtlich der kulturpolitischen Relationen als auch hinsichtlich der geschlechtsspezifischen Situation als Frau und Künstlerin in einem männlich dominierten Kunstfeld.[16] Selbstverwirklichung und Selbstbehauptung durch künstlerisches Handeln ist einerseits eine emanzipatorische Strategie, die für die Kunst der Avantgarde(n) in Anspruch genommen

[16] Zur Einschätzung der polnischen Neoavantgarde und polnischen Nachkriegskunst als männlich dominiertes Feld siehe Pejić 2009; Toniak 2010; Jakubowska 2011.

wird, andererseits bezieht sie sich im feministischen Sinne auf die Subjektwerdung als Künstlerin.

Kunstpolitischer Kontext

Muraks Bezugnahme auf die Kresse ist gleichzeitig eine radikale Abkehr zur Museumskunst – die Kresse existiert nur einige Tage, danach verwelkt sie und damit verschwindet das Kunstwerk. Der ephemere Charakter ist aber auch in den Arbeiten von Pinińska-Bereś wiederzufinden, vergleicht man ihre Stoff- und Klebeobjekte mit Bronzen oder Steinskulpturen. Die verwendeten Materialien und Techniken sind zugleich auf einer kunstpolitischen Ebene als mindestens kritische Kommentare lesbar: So konnte das notwendige künstlerische Material nur auf Zuteilung durch den Berufsverband „Związek Polskich Artystów Plastyków" (ZPAP) [Verband der Polnischen Bildenden Künstler] bezogen werden; und diese Zuteilung war wiederum an eine Auftragsvergabe gebunden.[17] Durch den Gebrauch von Industrietextilien und -waren, Acrylfarben und anderen Bastelmaterialien entzogen sich beide Künstlerinnen dieser Zuteilungspolitik und konnten Plastiken, Ob-

---

[17] Eine systematische Aufarbeitung der Kunstpolitik der Volksrepublik Polen steht weiterhin aus. Hinweise zu Ausschreibungs- und Wettbewerbsverfahren finden sich in den zeitgenössischen Tageszeitungen und Fachzeitschriften und in den Äußerungen der Künstlerinnen. So verweist Teresa Gierzyńska auf das Verhältnis von Auftragsarbeit und „eigenständiger, unabhängiger" künstlerischer Tätigkeit in ihrem Tagebuch, vgl. Gierzyńska-Dwurnik 2014: 141-158. Vgl. auch Cieślińska 1998: 1. Zu den wenigen Publikationen, die sich speziell mit der Kunst in der VR Polen auch unter einem weitgefassten soziologischen Ansatz befassen, zählt Gryglewicz / Szczerski 1999.

jekte und Performances auch unabhängig vom Auftragsvergabesystem schaffen. Eine ähnliche Positionierung kann bei beiden Künstlerinnen auch hinsichtlich der Produktionsstätte der Arbeiten festgestellt werden. Da beide über einen längeren Zeitraum kein eigenes Atelier hatten, mussten andere Räume für die Kunstproduktion gefunden werden. So nähte Pinińska-Bereś den überwiegenden Teil ihrer Stoffobjekte am heimischen Küchentisch. Bei Murak waren die verschiedenen Orte, an denen sie die mit Kressesamen bedeckten Leinentücher bzw. Leinenkleider auslegte, oft bereits Teil der Aktion oder Performance.

Weder die angedeutete Absage an die Auftragspolitik noch die Wahl der künstlerischen Produktionsstätte ist jedoch dahingehend zu verstehen, dass es sich hier um Formen einer Untergrund-Kunst handeln würde oder dass die Künstlerinnen einer inoffiziellen Szene angehörten. Es handelt sich vielmehr um eine graduelle Distanzierung, deren politische Implikation aber deswegen nicht weniger brisant ist. Pinińska-Bereś stellte ihre Arbeiten in den vom polnischen Künstlerverband geführten Ausstellungsräumen[18] aus und vertrat 1983 die VR Polen auf der Biennale São Paulo. Ihre künstlerischen Wandlungen können auch als Antwort auf eine Kulturpolitik verstanden werden, die – dies vor allem auch für Bildhauerinnen – stark von der Auftrags- und damit Materialvergabe des zentralen Künstlerverbandes abhing. Pinińska-Bereś war Mitglied im ZPAP und über viele Jahre Mitorganisatorin der Ausstellungen zur polnischen Skulptur, den sogenannten Rzeźba-

[18] Es handelt sich hierbei um Galerieräume für zeitgenössische Kunst, die im ganzen Land eingerichtet wurden und unter der Kurzbezeichnung BWA (Biuro Wystaw Artystycznych, Büro für Kunstausstellungen) stellenweise auch heute noch fungieren.

Roku-Ausstellungen. Diese gaben einen Überblick über die Entwicklungen der zeitgenössischen Skulptur in der Volksrepublik Polen. Pinińska-Bereś stellte ihre Arbeiten immer wieder in diesem Kontext aus und wurde mehrfach ausgezeichnet.

Pinińska-Bereś war, wie viele ihrer Kolleginnen, mit der mehrfachen Rolle als Künstlerin, Hausfrau, Mutter (Geburt der Tochter Bettina 1958) und Ehefrau konfrontiert. Die Verankerung in Krakau, die Nähe zur dortigen Avantgardeszene rund um die „Grupa Krakowska" [„Krakauer Gruppe"] und der stete Vergleich mit ihrem Künstlerehemann Jerzy Bereś haben ihre künstlerische Entwicklung genauso geprägt wie ihre Kindheit. Markowska verweist auf den elitären Männerbund, bei dem Frauen als Künstlerinnen eigentlich nicht vorgesehen und nur grummelnd gedudelt wurden (Markowska 2010). Während ihr Ehemann Jerzy Bereś, mit dem sie gemeinsam 1955 das Bildhauerstudium abschloss, bereits 1966 Mitglied der Krakauer Gruppe wurde, gelang dies Maria Pinińska-Bereś erst 1979.[19] Ihre erste Einzelausstellung in den Räumlichkeiten der Gruppe, Galeria Krzysztofory, fand erst 1980 statt. Hier soll nicht die Frage erörtert werden, inwiefern Pinińska-Bereś in ästhetischer und inhaltlicher Sicht zum Programm der Gruppe gehörte. Es bleibt festzuhalten, dass sie seit Beginn der 1960er Jahre in engem Kontakt zur Gruppe stand und dass ihre eigene Karriere nach der Aufnahme in die Gruppe einen Sprung machte – u.a. mit Ausstellungen im Ausland. Es ist also durchaus die These zu formulieren, dass die institutionelle Anbindung eine

[19] Nach der Aufnahme in die Gruppe häufen sich dann auch die Einzelausstellungen und die Katalogpublikationen. Ihre Mitarbeit und Initiierung der erfolgreichen Rzeźba Polska-Ausstellungen, bei denen Pinińska-Bereś mehrmals ausgezeichnet wurde, werden kaum in der Forschung besprochen.

ganz zentrale Rolle für die Sichtbarkeit und Anerkennung der Künstlerin gespielt hat.

Die progressiven, im Kontext der Kunstpolitik der VR Polen nicht verständlichen Performances brachten Teresa Murak in Schwierigkeiten. So wurde ihre als Stadtspaziergang geplante Performance „Procesja" / „Lady's Smock" (1974) zunächst von einem Milizionär gestoppt.[20] Die Kunsthaftigkeit der Aktion war dem Mann ebenso unersichtlich wie die „Frechheit" der Künstlerin, eine solche unangemeldet im öffentlichen Raum durchzuführen. Denn trotz einer gewissen Freiheit, die der künstlerischen Entwicklung in der VR Polen zugewiesen wurde, fand Kunst weiterhin vor allem in den traditionell dafür vorgesehenen Räumen wie Galerie, Atelier, Museum oder Hochschule statt. Nur wenige Künstlerinnen erschlossen sich den öffentlichen Raum. Ist der Weg nach draußen bereits als eine Form von Institutionskritik zu verstehen, so ist die von der Künstlerin eingeschlagene Route hochgradig symbolisch aufgeladen: Der historische Königsweg, die Kunsthochschule und der Aufmarschplatz[21] sind Orte, die traditionell mit Macht verbunden (Herrschaft, Akademie, Militär)

---

[20] Teresa Murak: „Es war im vierten Studienjahr, als ich schon nicht mehr im Studentenwohnheim Dziekanka wohnte, sondern in Żoliborz. Und stell dir vor, als ich nur mit meinem Pflanzenmantel bekleidet die Straße ul. Słowackiego entlangging, stoppte mich auf der Höhe des Kino Wisła ein Milizionär. Er sagte mir, dass ich so nicht weitergehen könne. Glücklicherweise hatte ich den Fotografen Antoni Zdybiak mitgenommen, der einen Freund anrief, und dieser holte uns dann mit dem Auto an. Wir warteten wohl 1½ Stunden, bis er endlich kam. Wir fuhren direkt zur Straße Krakowskie Przedmieście, wo eigenartigerweise keine Miliz war, die mich hätte anhalten können... und wo wie üblich viele Spaziergängerinnen unterwegs waren." Murak 2016, Übersetzung C. K.

[21] Es handelt sich hierbei um den heutigen Plac Piłsudkiego im Zentrum von Warschau. 1974 fungierte er unter dem Titel Plac Zwycięnstwa (Siegesplatz)

und männlich konnotiert sind. Murak schreibt sich als Frau in diesen Machtraum ein und ist durch ihre auffallende Kleidung besonders sichtbar. Der künstlerische Ausdruck verlässt hier den rein ästhetischen Bereich und wird in einem politischen Rahmen verhandelt. Murak rüttelt hier, zumal als Studentin, an dem Pakt, der zwischen Künstlern und dem Staat geschlossen wurde und auf den der polnische Kunsthistoriker Piotr Piotrowski immer wieder hingewiesen hat[22]: „Der Künstler war frei in seinen Entscheidungen der künstlerischen Ausdrucksmittel und er freute sich über seine Freiheit, solange er keinen politischen Weg einschlug“ (Piotrowski 1999: 177).

Geschlechtsspezifische Konnotation

Es ist deutlich geworden, wie sehr in der künstlerischen Praxis von Pinińska-Bereś und Murak die Auseinandersetzung mit Aspekten der Kunstpolitik verwoben ist mit Aspekten von Weiblichkeit. Sowohl auf der Ebene der Material- und Technikwahl als auch auf

und diente u.a. als Aufmarschort von Militär und Staatsapparat zu den großen (nationalen) Festlichkeiten. In nächster Umgebung zum Platz befindet sich die Zachęta – eines der zentralen und damals als CBWA (Zentrales Büro für Kunstausstellungen) eines der wichtigsten Ausstellungshäuser zu zeitgenössischer Kunst. Inwiefern das Stolzieren der Künstlerin VOR dieser Galerie auch als ein Zeigen ihrer Ausgrenzung aus dem institutionellen Kunstsystem der VR Polen verstanden werden könnte, ist hier lediglich als Frage zu formulieren.

[22] Vgl. Piotrowski 1991, 1999, siehe auch die Einschätzung bei Cieślińska „... die Künstler [... bestimmten, CK] selbst die Grenzen, die Kunst nicht überschreiten sollte“ (Cieślinska 1998: 15, Kowalcyzk 1999: 57-64).

der Ebene der verschiedenen Räume, in denen die Künstlerinnen wirkten, kann von einer kritischen Stellungnahme gesprochen werden. Weiblichkeit wird jeweils in einen sozio-politischen Kontext gestellt.

Bei Murak wird Weiblichkeit zunächst durch den Einsatz des eigenen Körpers thematisiert. Der weibliche Körper wird besonders über die Einbindung in das künstlerische Handeln sichtbar. Do-it-yourself wird hier verstanden als eine Aufforderung an den Körper der Künstlerin, durch seine physische Präsenz etwas Neues hervorzubringen. Der weibliche Körper bringt im Zusammenspiel mit den Pflanzen das Kunstwerk hervor. Er ist produktiver Teil im Entstehungsprozess. Damit lässt sich auch in Muraks Arbeit die Verbindung zwischen Frau und Natur herstellen, die gleichzeitig durch die naturwissenschaftlich anmutende experimentelle Methode einer rein essentialistischen Zuschreibung enthoben wird. Nicht nur ihr Körper, sondern auch die anderen Materialien verweisen auf die geschlechtsspezifische Positionierung der Künstlerin. In den Pflanzensamen sind darüber hinaus weibliche Metaphern wie Fruchtbarkeit, Zeitlichkeit bzw. der Kreislauf des Lebens angelegt.

Stärker als Murak rekurriert Pinińska-Bereś neben den benutzten Materialien auch in ihren künstlerischen Techniken auf die Sphäre, die traditionell der Frau zugewiesen wird. So werden die Industriewaren wie Stoffe, Bettdecken oder Spiegel, die dem Häuslichen, der Sphäre der Frau, zugeordnet werden, durch Nähen, Patchwork und Arrangieren in die Kunst überführt. Pinińska-Bereś scheint hier all die Materialien zu benutzen, die sie in ihrer Umgebung vorfindet, um sie gleichfalls zweckentfremdend für ihre Objekte und Installationen zu verarbeiten. Die Nähe zur

Bricolage wird hier besonders augenscheinlich. Zugleich kann diese Überführung als eine „Praxis von Frauen [verstanden werden, bei der] die Tätigkeit der Produktion neue und andere 'Handlungsmuster' sowie Möglichkeiten der Intervention“ eröffnen würden (Hornung 2012: 52). Der Akt der Überführung der Handarbeit in künstlerische Praxen könne demnach verstanden werden als eine „Dekonstruktion geschlechtlicher Zuschreibung durch feministische Handarbeiterinnen“, wodurch sich „neue Handlungsspielräume“ eröffnet hätten (ebd.). Handarbeit ist demnach ein Mittel, um „widerspenstige Praktiken“ (ebd.) zu entwickeln – und gleichzeitig dient sie als Mittel eines künstlerischen Ausdrucks und damit eines Erkenntnisprozesses.

Schluss

Die künstlerischen Praxen von Maria Pinińska-Bereś und Teresa Murak wurden im vorliegenden Beitrag um Rahmen der DIY-Kunst diskutiert und hinsichtlich ihrer kunstpolitischen und geschlechtsspezifischen Konnotationen untersucht. Wie herausgearbeitet werden konnte, bezieht sich der DIY-Aspekt beider Künstlerinnen nicht nur darauf, die Betrachterinnen an der künstlerischen Arbeit zu beteiligen, sondern bezeichnet eine Methode der gezielten Erkenntnisgewinnung als Künstlerin. Zwar werden die Betrachterinnen auch als Rezipientinnen angesprochen, der Fokus liegt jedoch auf dem Produktionsprozess der Arbeiten, der unter Rückgriff auf nicht-künstlerische Materialien auf Techniken rekurriert, die einerseits als Alltagstätigkeiten und andererseits als weiblich konnotierte Handlungen zu beschreiben sind. Der Produktionsprozess löst zugleich einen Erkenntnisprozess aus, der im Sinne des „Consciousness-Raising“ – also der Bewusstseinswerdung – als Selbstermächtigungsstrategie verstanden werden kann. Die vorgestellten künstlerischen Praktiken sind durchaus im Kontext einer künstlerischen Forschung zu verstehen, bei der ästhetische und wissenschaftliche Elemente zusammenfließen. Pinińska-Bereś und Murak entwickeln dabei jeweils eigenständige Formsprachen, die ihrer Kunst einen eindeutigen Wiedererkennungs- und Zuschreibungswert geben. Beide Künstlerinnen rekurrieren dabei gleichzeitig auf das Persönliche, Intime, Weibliche. Entgegen einer essentialistischen Zuschreibung wird hier Weiblichkeit jedoch als Strategie entwickelt, der Fokus liegt bei beiden Künstlerinnen auf dem Prozesshaften.

Der bewusste Bezug auf das Handwerkliche, auf außerkünstlerische Materialien und Techniken, auf die bewusste Ansprache des (nicht nur kunstinteressierten) Publikums zeigen die Möglichkeiten einer DIY-Kunst auf, die über den einfachen Mitmach-Gedanken hinausreichen und sich hin zu einer kritischen Reflexion zu geschlechtlichen und politischen Machtstrukturen entwickeln. DIY ist hier gerade nicht eine reine Bastelanleitung, sondern eine Strategie der künstlerischen Selbstbehauptung. Insofern lösen die beiden polnischen Künstlerinnen das ein, was Blume fordert:

> Do It Yourself aus der stupiden Bastelanleitung auf die Rezeptionsebene nicht nur von Kunstwerken, sondern auf die Wahrnehmung, auf die Erkenntnisfähigkeit von Welt hin ausgedehnt, heißt nichts anderes als Emanzipation von allen Anleitungen, heißt sich selbst herzustellen,

> sich selbst zu finden in einem Labyrinth von Vorschriften, Interpretationen und Auslegungen all dessen, was den Einzelnen umgibt. [...] Es ist die populäre Beschreibung der Ideenkunst eines künstlerischen Selbst. (Blume 2005: 2)

Bei beiden Künstlerinnen ist diese kritische Reflexion untrennbar an die eigene Person, den eigenen Körper und die eigenen Erfahrungen gekoppelt. Sie bezieht sich dementsprechend auch auf eine kritische Reflexion zu Fragen des Künstlerinnen-Seins: Das künstlerische Selbst ist in den hier beschriebenen Beispielen ein dezidiert weibliches Selbst – ein Künstlerinnen-Selbst.

Literaturverzeichnis

Bartek (Pseudonym) (1975): „Zrobieni w minotaura“ [Zu einem Minotaurus gemacht], Sztandar Ludu [Volksflagge], 10.06.1975: o.A.

Blume, Eugen (2005): Editorial. In: Hamburger Bahnhof-Museum für Gegenwart (Hrsg.): Do it yourself. Positionen von den 1960er Jahren bis heute. Ausst. Kat. Hamburger Bahnhof-Museum für Gegenwart. Berlin, 2-3.

Blunck, Lars (2005): Do it yourself. Die Geburt der Ko-Autorschaft aus dem Geiste Duchamps. In: Hamburger Bahnhof-Museum für Gegenwart (Hrsg.): Do it yourself. Positionen von den 1960er Jahren bis heute. Ausst. Kat. Hamburger Bahnhof-Museum für Gegenwart. Berlin, 10-13.

Cichocki, Sebastian (2012): Earthworks. Teresa Murak and the Spiritualisation of Slime. In: Tersa Murak 2012, 8-12.

Cieślińska, Nawojka (1998): “Die Kunst der Volksrepublik Polen im Spiel mit der politischen Wirklichkeit“, Zeitschrift für Politik 45(1): 1-19.

Dezeuze, Anna (Hrsg.) (2010): The 'do-it-yourself' artwork. Participation from Fluxus to New Media. Manchester-New York.

Gierzyńska-Dwurnik, Teresa (2014): The „One Month of my Live“ Contest. In: Nad rzeką, ktorej nie ma / By the River, That Isn't.

Ausst. Kat. Galeria Sztuki Współczesnej BWA Sokół. Nowy Sącz, 141-158.

Gryglewicz, Tomasz/Szczerski, Andrzej (Hrsg.) (1999): Sztuka w okresie PRL'u. Metody i przedmiot badań [Kunst während der Volksrepublik Polen. Methoden und Forschungsgegenstände]. Kraków.

Hegyi, Dóra (Hrsg.) (2011): Art has always its consequences. Artists Texts from Croatia, Hungary, Poland, Serbia 1947-2009. Berlin.

Hornung, Annabelle (2012): Fingerhut und Feminismus. Die beschäftigte weibliche Hand. In: Hornung/Novak/Kuni 2012, 52-59.

Hornung, Annabelle / Novak, Tine / Kuni, Verena (Hrsg.) (2012): Do-it-yourself. Die Mitmach-Revolution, Ausst. Kat. Museum für Kommunikation Frankfurt am Main. Mainz.

Jakubowska, Agata (Hrsg.) (2011): Artystki Polskie [Polnische Künstlerinnen]. Bielsko-Biała.

Jakubowska, Agata (2014). "Ambigous Liberation: The Early Works of Maria Pinińska-Bereś", Konsthistorisk tidskrift / Journal of Art History 83 (2): 168-182.

Kowalcyzk, Izabela (1999): Polityczna apolityczność i bezcieleesne ciała a przypadek Alina Czapocznikow [Das politische Unpolitische und der körperlose Körper am Beispiel von Alina Szapocznikow]. In: Gryglewicz/ Szczerski 1999, 57-64.

Lévi-Strauss, Claude (1977): Das wilde Denken. Frankfurt am Main.

Markowska, Anna (2010): Artystki Grupy Krakowskiej [Künstlerinnen der Grupa Krakowska (Krakauer Gruppe)]. In: Toniak 2010, 105-122. Wiederabdruck in: Markowska, Anna (2012): Dwa przełomy. Sztuka Polska po 1955 i 1989 roku [Zwei Wendepunkte. Polnische Kunst nach 1955 und 1989]. Toruń, 209-229.

Maria Pinińska-Bereś. 1939-1999 (1999). Ausst. Kat. Galeria Sztuki Współczesnej Bunkier Sztuki. Kraków.

Murak, Teresa (1983): "Ziarno. The Seed", Projekt 1: 69.

Murak, Teresa (2016): Zasiew. Rozmowa z Teresą Murak [Saatgut. Gespräch mit Teresa Murak] [Link: http://www.dwutygodnik.com/artykul/6582-zasiew.html (14.07.2016); 17.08.2020].

Pejić, Bojana/Museum Moderne Kunst Stiftung Ludwig (Hrsg.) (2009): Gender Check. Feminity and Masculinity in the Art of Eastern Europe. Ausst. Kat. Museum Moderne Kunst Stiftung Ludwig Wien. Köln.

Pinińska-Bereś, Maria (1999): On Feminism in Art? In: Pinińska-Bereś 1999, 162.

Piotrowski, Piotr (1999): Znaczenie Modernizmu, W stronę historii sztuki polskiej po 1945 roku [Die Bedeutungen des Modernismus in der polnischen Kunstgeschichte nach 1945]. Poznań.

Rymarz, Ferdinand (2011): Dzieje Parafii w Kiełczewicach [Die Geschichte der Pfarrei Kiełczewice]. Lublin.

Sawicki, Andrzej (1975): „o.T.“, Dziennik Polski [Täglich Polnisch], 21.5.1975: o.A.

Tatar, Ewa (2010): W poszukiwanie ciała – w poszukiwaniu siebie [Auf der Suche nach dem Körper – auf der Suche nach sich selbst]. In: Toniak 2010, 93-103 [Erstveröffentlichung in Rzeźba Polska 2008].

Teresa Murak (1998). Ausst. Kat. Galeria Bielska BWA, Bielsko Biała.

Teresa Murak. Do kogo idziesz? [Zu wem gehst du?] (21012). Ausst. Kat. Galeria Labyrint Lublin.

Toniak, Ewa (Hrsg.) (2010): Jestem artystką, we wszystkim, co niepotrzebne. Kobiety i sztuka około 1960 roku [Ich bin Künstlerin, in allem, das nicht notwendig ist. Frauen und Kunst um 1960]. Warszawa.

Wiedemeyer, Nina (2015): „Ästhetik des Provisorischen. Über Bricoleur und Provisoriker/in“, wissenderkuenste (4), Das Provisorische, [Link: wissenderkuenste.de/#/text/aesthetik-des-provisorischen-ueber-bricoleur-und-provisorikerin/; 16. 01. 2016].

Quellen

Maria Pinińska-Bereś, Ausstellungsplakat, Galeria Pod Baranami, Kraków 1970, Dokumentacja Plastyki Współczesnej IS PAN [Dokumentation der Zeitgenössischen Bildenden Kunst, Kunsthistorisches Institut der Polnischen Akademie der Wissenschaften], Akte Maria Pinińska-Bereś, Warschau.

Sztuka Kobiet. Maria Pinińska-Bereś, Ausstellungsplakat, Galeria O.N., Poznań 1980, Dokumentacja Plastyki Współczesnej IS PAN [Dokumentation der Zeitgenössischen Bildenden Kunst, Kunsthistorisches Institut der Polnischen Akademie der Wissenschaften], Akte Maria Pinińska-Bereś, Warschau.

Teresa Murak. Rzeżucha. Lady`s Smock (1975), Ausst.Kat., Galeria Sztuki MDK Labirynt, Lublin, Dokumentacja Plastyki Współczesnej IS PAN [Dokumentation der Zeitgenössischen Bildenden Kunst, Kunsthistorisches Institut der Polnischen Akademie der Wissenschaften], Akte Teresa Murak, Warschau.

"Not Just Boys Fun" – Perspektiven auf Gender in der DIY-Hardcore/Punk-Szene[1]

von Sarah Held

I just want to play punk rock, [...]and get rad ...
you can fucking quote me on that.
Jenny Angelillo, Neighborhood Brats

Über ein Feld zu schreiben, das so heterogen strukturiert und von vielfältigen Lesarten, Erfahrungen und Attitüden durchzogen ist wie die DIY-Punk/Hardcore-Szene evoziert Dissonanzen wie Assoziationen gleichermaßen. Das führt zum Wiedererkennen und Einschreiben individueller Subjekte in den hier thematisierten Sachverhalt. Gleichzeitig sind Exklusionen durch andere Lesarten und Erfahrungen als meine eigenen vorprogrammiert. Ebenso wenig wie die zwar oft einheitlich und uniformiert wirkende Szene ausschließlich von homogener Natur ist, möchte mein Artikel keine universale und allgemeingültige Aussage über die DIY-Punk/Hardcore-Szene treffen.[2] Er stellt vielmehr eine subjektive

---

[1] Der vorliegende Artikel ist im Zuge des Symposiums „Selbermachen! Informelles Wissen und subversive Praktiken" im November 2015 entstanden. Der Artikel ist daher als Momentaufnahme aus 2015/2016 zu betrachten, da nur marginale Überarbeitungen vor der Veröffentlichung durchgeführt wurden.

[2] Die Unterscheidungsmerkmale der im Untergrund angesiedelten DIY-Punk-Hardcore-Kultur zum Mainstream wird an späterer Stelle erklärt.

Position dar. Diese Auseinandersetzung versucht wie eine Vielzahl (semi)wissenschaftlicher Publikationen, das Feld aus der jeweiligen Position zu analysieren. Oft publizieren szeneimmanente Akteur_innen diese Schriften (Büsser 2000). Häufig produzieren Szeneoutsider ebenfalls wissenschaftlich dazu. Diese haben nicht selten einen hölzernen Anstrich und wirken meist unglaubwürdig. Daher provozieren sie, oft verdient, nur ein müdes Lächeln bis großes Unverständnis bei Insidern.[3]

Wenn sich im Folgenden auf die zeitgenössische DIY-Punk/Hardcore-Szene bezogen wird, liegt der besondere Fokus auf dem deutschsprachigen Raum. Für die szenefremden Leser_innen folgt eine kurze Merkmalskizzierung der oben genannten Szene. Diese umfasst ein Milieu, das der Mainstream in der Regel als Untergrund assoziiert. Dort wurde der Ethos von DIY einerseits stark internalisiert und andererseits sehr stark geprägt. Amy Spencer, die früher eigene Zines herausgegeben, ein eigenes DIY-Plattenlabel betrieb und mittlerweile an der Goldsmith Universität, London promoviert, beschreibt den Ethos der DIY-Bewegung folgendermaßen: „[t]he DIY movement is about using anything you can get your hands on to shape your own cultural identity; your own version of whatever you think is missing in mainstream culture“ (Spencer 2008: 11). Sie meint damit Strategien, welche die Punk- und Hardcore-Bewegung verfolgt, um nach eigenen Bedürfnissen ausgerichtete, nicht-kommerzielle Veranstaltungen jenseits großer Arenen zu realisieren. Es findet eine selbstverwaltete Kulturproduktion statt, die versucht u.a. anti-

[3] Exemplarisch hier das Teilforschungsprojekt von Prof. Dr. Ronald Hitzler https://jubri.jugendkulturen.de/teilvorhaben-i.html.

sexistische, anti-rassistische und LBTGQIA-freundliche Räume zu generieren.[4] Gemeint sind subkulturelle Veranstaltungsorte wie autonome Zentren, besetzte Häuser, selbstverwaltete Kulturräume und seltener auch kommunal unterstützte Räume. Innerhalb dieser Untergrundkulturproduktion werden nicht nur Konzerte selbstgemacht, sondern auch Plattenlabels, Zines, Merchandise-Produkte und vor allem die Musik und die dazugehörigen Tonträger. Dezidiertes Ziel ist es, gesellschaftliche, geschlechterbedingte und kapitalistische Machtverhältnisse mittels verschiedener Veranstaltungsstrategien und Interventionen zu reflektieren, zu hinterfragen und zu unterminieren. Dabei handelt es sich zwar um eine David-gegen-Goliath-Aufgabe, die kein völlig autarkes System generiert, allerdings hat sich seit den 1970er Jahren eine annährend global vernetzte Gegenkultur entwickelt.

Diese Einleitung dient somit als eine Art How-To zur persönlichen Verortung sowie des Artikels selbst im (wissenschaftlichen) Diskurs zu verstehen. Dieser erhebt keinesfalls den Anspruch aus einer soziologischen Perspektive subkulturtheoretisch korrekt zu sein, noch soll er das erzielen. Er ist vielmehr eine subkulturelle Berichterstattung aus der Perspektive einer Gender- und Kulturwissenschaftlerin. Beiden Welten angehörend, einerseits als Nachwuchswissenschaftlerin, die in ihrer Dissertation Weiterentwicklungsaspekte der Do-It-Yourself-Kultur an der Schnittstelle zu künstlerischem Aktivismus gegen sexualisierte Gewalt und Femicides erforscht hat; andererseits als aktive Akteurin im subkultu-

---

[4] Die Abkürzung LBTGQIA steht für die englischen Begriffe lesbian, gay, transgender, queer, inter- und asexual.

rellen DIY-Punk/Hardcore-Milieu, möchte ich durch meine subjektive Erfahrung und jahrelange Zugehörigkeit, Einblicke in die aktuelle DIY-Hardcore-Punk-Szene im deutschsprachigen Raum geben.

Mein Beitrag ist in drei Teile gegliedert. Zu Beginn eröffne ich mit einem knappen historischen Überblick das Thema. Im Anschluss werden Interventionen und Aktivitäten von Frauen* innerhalb der genannten Szene beschrieben.[5] Auch wenn sich diese größtenteils als emanzipatorisch versteht, entstehen doch immer wieder knisternde Spannungsfelder und damit einhergehende Paradoxien. Es werden unterschiedliche Praxen und verschiedene subkulturelle Haltungen kritisch reflektiert. Diese werden in den abschließenden Betrachtungen und einer knappen Analyse des ausgewählten Feldmaterials dargestellt. Als Feldmaterial definiere ich Songtexte, Manifesttexte, Zine-Artikel und Interviews mit Frauen* über ihre Szeneaktivitäten.

Zur Ermittlung stehen folgende Fragen im Raum. Ist die Punk-Hardcore-Szene so stark männlich dominiert wie es auf den ersten Blick erscheint? Werden innerhalb dieser Subkultur Frauen* ebenso unsichtbar gemacht wie es so häufig in verschiedenen soziokulturellen Sphären passiert? Welche Formen feministischer Veranstaltungskultur treten in der Post-Riot-Grrrl-Ära auf?[6] Im Mittelpunkt stehen die Justierung von Geschlechterverhältnissen und -zuschreibungen innerhalb musikalischer Subkulturen der

---

[5] Ich gehe nicht von einer in sich geschlossenen Frau aus, sondern es werden alle als Frauen gelesene oder sich identifizierende Personen inkludiert, egal welches Geschlecht ihnen bei der Geburt zugeordnet wurde. Wo ohne „*“ gearbeitet wird, ist die wirkmächtige gesellschaftliche Norm (cis-gender. Heterosexuell) gemeint.

[6] Die an späterer Stelle beschrieben wird.

Punk/Hardcore-Bewegung. Bevor ich szeneimmanente Sachverhalte diskutiere, zeige ich die Entwicklung vom DIY-Prinzip und dessen Bubble-Up zum Mainstream-Phänomen auf.

Längst hat das do-it-yourself-Prinzip die Grenzen der Sub- bzw. Gegenkultur überschritten und dient nicht mehr nur als deren gesellschaftliches Distinktions- bzw. Identifikationsinstrumentarium. DIY wird schon lange nicht mehr nur mit Punks oder dem Typus autonomer Hausbesetzer_innen assoziiert. Im 21. Jahrhundert findet eine regelrechte „Mitmach-Revolution“ statt (Hornung/Nowak/Kuni 2011). Die katalysiert durch Web-2.0-Anwendungen und ein breitgefächertes Angebot an Selbstbedienungsapplikationen, die Einzug im virtuellen wie im realen Raum halten. Diese manifestieren sich ökonomisch beispielsweise durch Customizing-Strategien multinationaler Konzerne oder Selbstscankassen (Müller 2012). DIY und Selbstgemachtes gewinnen in einer global vernetzten Welt, in der man für Geld alles kaufen kann, einen neuen Stellenwert und erfahren dadurch eine neue Bedeutung. Strategien des Selbermachens in vom westlichen Industriekapitalismus geprägten Gesellschaftsordnungen können nicht als per se kritisch wahrgenommen werden (Mason 2008; Heath/Potter 2004). Subversive Taktiken bieten zwar Möglichkeiten traditionelle Mechanismen zu umgehen, erfordern aber gleichzeitig Mittel und Fähigkeiten, um Konsumgüter selbst zu produzieren. Somit sind nicht nur Privilegien, wie das Verfügen über kulturelles und finanzielles Kapital, sondern auch die nötige Zeit zur Partizipation erforderlich. „DIY-Aktivismus kann als Oppositionsgemeinschaft zu herrschenden, patriarchal und hegemonial geprägten, globalen kapitalistischen Wirtschaftssystemen allein nicht dienen“ (Held 2015: 329). Die Entwicklung der DIY-Kultur wird in weiteren Beiträgen dieses Sammelbandes elaboriert.

Historische Kontextualisierung

Hardcore entwickelte sich als subkultureller Musikstil in den 1980er Jahren, in den von der Reagan-Politik geprägten USA. Ian MacKaye (Minor Threat, Fugazi, Labelgründer von Dischord Records in Washington, DC) beschreibt diese Phase als Zeit des Umbruchs.

> We wanted to create our own culture because we didn't feel connected to anything. Here was the perfect opportunity for that. You were instantly devoted to others around you. This was the first time Rock Music was being written by, performed by, shows were being put on by, fanzines being put out, networks were being created – all by kids, completely outside of the mainstream music business, for reasons that had very little or nothing to do with economic business; as you know, music has always been a really insidious marriage of art and incentive. It was a really important time in music history because music actually rose above business. (MacKaye zit. nach Brockheimer 2009: 10)

Bei dem aufgezeigten Umbruch und der Musikrevolution, die Punk- und Hardcore als Jugendbewegung verursachten, wurden häufig die tradierten Geschlechterverhältnisse, die auch im Mainstream-Musikgeschäft herrsch(t)en, weitergeführt. Als Einstieg zur Dekonstruktion von Geschlechterbildern analysiere ich den Song „Not Just Boys Fun“ der amerikanischen Hardcoreband 7Seconds (Album: s) aus dem Jahr 1984.

> Man you've gotta problem, who made you fuckin' king
> A macho pig with nothing in your head.
> No girls around you, their place is not at gigs,
> Don't want 'em on the dance floor 'cos they're weak.
> A woman's place, the kitchen, on her back,
> It's time to change that attitude, and quick.
> (Chorus)
> Showing us your phobias, you're scared to see 'em think,
> You'd rather dress 'em up in pretty lace,
> All nice and colored pink.
> You feel so fucking threatened,
> When they stand out in front,
> A stupid, passive piece of meat is all you really want
> But it's:
> Not just boys' fun (x4)
> There's girls who put out fanzines, others put on shows,
> Yet they're not allowed to get out on the floor.
> Some make the music, well that you can accept.
> Hell, maybe live you'll get some tits and ass
> You fucking moron, your brains have run amuck,
> A girl's only lot in life is not to fuck!

Der Song ist titelgebend für diesen Artikel und weist Schnittmengen mit den Forderungen der Riot-Grrrl-Bewegung auf, die in den 1990er Jahren Hochkonjunktur hatte. Er zeigt, dass man sich innerhalb der DIY-Hardcore/Punk-Szene bereits in den frühen 1980ern partiell mit genderbedingten Inhalten beschäftigte. Hier soll nicht der Eindruck entstehen, es handele sich um ein homogenes Bestreben aller Akteur_innen nach emanzipatorischen Entwicklungen innerhalb der Musikkultur. Vielmehr wurde Hardcore häufig vorgeworfen, (klein)bürgerliche Attitüden zu reproduzieren anstatt sie zu dekonstruieren, denn auch eine subkulturelle Sozialisation und das Verlangen nach Andersartigkeit schließen den Traum vom Reihenhaus mit Wohnzimmerschrankwand nicht kategorisch aus (Büsser 2000).

7Seconds greifen in „Not Just Boys Fun“ einige Anklagen und somit auch Forderungen auf, die einige Jahre später von der Riot-Grrrl-Bewegung an die Punk/Hardcore-Szene im Besonderen und an die Musikszene im Allgemeinen gerichtet wurden auf: Machistisches Verhalten, Frauen auf die häusliche Sphäre zu limitieren und öffentliche Teilhabe, in diesem Falle das Besuchen von Konzerten, abzusprechen. Des Weiteren forderten sie einen Habituswandel in Bezug auf Geschlechterrollen und -erwartungen. Gleichzeitig thematisierten sie die Angst vor emanzipierten Frauen und, dass sich Männer eigentlich keine eigenständige Frauen mit eigenen Interessen und Szenepartizipation wünschten. Es werden diskursive Szeneklassiker, wie Frauen auf Konzerten als Kleiderständer zu reduzieren, inkludiert. Sowie auch Objektivierungstendenzen und Oberflächlichkeiten sind Gegenstand des Songtextes, genauso wie körperliche Insuffizienzen, die Frauen die exzessive Teilnahme am Mosh-Pit nicht zugestehen bzw. diese verhindern durch aggressive und testosterongeladene Bockwurstparaden, die den Zugang direkt vor der Bühne erschweren. Es wird sichtbar gemacht, dass Frauen ein Teil der Szene sind und auf verschiedene Arten partizipieren, vom Zine publizieren über Konzerte organisieren sowie auf Bühnen stehen und in Bands spielen.

Auch Martin Büsser beschreibt in seiner Publikation „If the Kids are united“, dass in dieser Phase „[i]nnerhalb der Hardcore-Szene [...] Feminismus häufig diskutiert [wurde], aber fast nie Inhalt der meist männlich vorgetragenen Texte [war]“ (2000: 35). Somit kann dem Song durchaus progressives Potential im Sinne einer emanzipatorischen Entwicklung innerhalb der Szene zugesprochen werden.

Was hat sich seit 1984 geändert? Sind diese Entlarvungen, Anklagen und Sichtbarmachungen noch zeitgemäß oder gar heute noch existent? Geschah etwas, um dem misogynen Habitus der frühen 1980er entgegenzuwirken? Das lässt sich, zumindest teilweise, positiv beantworten, denn es gab und gibt (queer-)feministische Interventionen innerhalb der thematisierten Musiksubkultur. Allerdings gilt es die Auswirkungen differenziert darzustellen und zu betrachten. Die Riot-Grrrl-Bewegung gilt als das bekannteste und besonders einflussreiche Phänomen (Baldauf 2013). Im Rahmen meines Beitrages wird diese Bewegung nur in ihren Grundzügen erklärt und zur Vertiefung auf einschlägige Literatur verwiesen, da zum Gegenstand bereits vielfältig publiziert wurde (Engelmann/Peglow 2013; Marcus 2010; Downes 2013; Engelmann/Herzing/Melián et. al 2013).

Die Bewegung war signifikanter Teil des Third-Wave-Feminism und verband auf unprätentiöse Art die Punk- und Hardcoresubkultur mit einem feministischen Habitus. So wurden feministische Theorien vom trockenen Hörsaalcharakter entstaubt, auf die Straße getragen und somit einem Personenkreis zugänglich gemacht, der sonst möglicherweise keine Berührungspunkte mit feministisch-theoretischen Inhalten gehabt hätte. (Held 2016: o.S.)

Sie hatte als feministische, musikzentrierte Bewegung ihre Epizentren in Olympia, Washington und Washington D.C, USA. Getreu dem Motto „Bildet (Frauen)Banden“ wurde unter dem Slogan „Revolution Girl Style Now“ nach dem gleichnamigen Album der Band Bikini Kill ab Anfang der 1990er Jahre die (Untergrund-)Musikszene in den USA regelrecht überrollt.

Die Riot-Grrrl-Bewegung nutzte DIY als kulturelle Selbstermächtigung. Es wurden Netzwerke gebildet, DIY-Strukturen und Mechanismen der DIY-Punk-Hardcore-Szene für die eigenen Motive genutzt und feministisch umgestaltet. Im Riot-Grrrl-Manifest wird explizit darauf hingewiesen:

> [W]eil wir wissen, daß [sic!] leben mehr sein kann, als bloß physisch zu existieren, und uns bewußt [sic!] ist, daß die idee des do-it-yourself im punkrock zentral für die kommende wütende grrrl-rock-revolution ist, die die psychischen und kulturellen welten von mädchen und frauen in ihren eigenen begriffen zu retten versucht.[7] (Baldauf 2013: 14)

Zur Vernetzung wurden wöchentlich erscheinende selbstgebastelte Zines zu einem Unkostenbeitrag publiziert und verschickt. Diese waren neben regem Briefverkehr zwischen den Akteur_innen einer der Hauptkommunikationskanäle. Es entstand eine fast unüberschaubare Anzahl an Printmedien, die anteilig als Riot Grrrl Collection in der Fales Library der New York University archiviert und als Bildband publiziert wurden (Darms 2014).

[7] Kleinschreibung im Original.

Abb. 1: Ausgestellte Riot Grrrl Zines im Rahmen der „Alien She“ Ausstellung Museum for Contemporary Craft, Portland, Oregon im September 2015. Fotocredit: Sarah Held.

Es wurden Bands gegründet wie beispielsweise Tribe 8 (die vorwiegend Dyke- und Queercore etablierten, aber immer wieder im Zuge von Riot Grrrl erwähnt wurden bzw. werden), Bikini Kill, Bratmobile (alle drei aus den USA) oder auch Huggy Bear (UK), um nur einige der prominentesten Beispiele zu nennen. Im deutschsprachigen Raum wurde Riot Grrrl während der Hochphase in den 1990er Jahren wenig populär verhandelt. Daher gab es auch dementsprechend wenig Riot Grrrl-Bands, beispielsweise Parole Trixie aus Hamburg (Peglow 2013).

Gemäß des aus dem Punk kommenden Spielethos war es zweitrangig, ob die Instrumente tight und perfekt gespielt wurden.

Getreu der Devise, ein Song braucht nur drei Akkorde, wurden die antisexistischen, queer-feministischen und selbstermächtigenden Inhalte von Bands im gewollten und (teilweise) genretypischen Dilettantismus produziert. Im Anschluss beschreibe ich zeitgenössische Entwicklungen und das Nachwirken der Bewegung.

Post-Riot-Grrrl-Ära

Auch wenn von der Riot-Grrrl-Bewegung oft im Präteritum gesprochen wird, ist diese nicht obsolet (True 2016). Sie wird nur wie die Punk- und Hardcore-Kultur ebenfalls musealisiert und akademisiert. Es finden Ausstellungen zu Punk (z.B. „No One Is Innocent“, Kunsthalle Wien, 2008), Riot Grrrl („Alien She!“ Wanderausstellung z.B. im Museum of Contemporary Craft, Portland, Oregon), diversen (auto)biografischen Werken bzw. Oral Histories („Please, Kill me!“ oder „Zum Glück gab es Punk“) inklusive einer fast unüberschaubaren Anzahl mehr oder weniger stark akademisch konnotierten Auseinandersetzungen mit der jeweiligen Subkultur statt. Aus musikalischer Perspektive sind Frauen, die sich mit dem Habitus von Riot Grrrl assoziieren, weiterhin aktiv. Maren Volkmann liefert in ihrem Artikel „Riot Grrrl is not dead“ einen Abriss verschiedener musikalischer Aktivitäten von Riot Grrrl Musikerinnen der ersten Stunde (Volkmann 2013). Aktuell gibt es Bands wie Lucky Malice (Norwegen), Petrol Girls (Österreich/UK), War on Women (USA) oder Kenny Kenny Oh Oh (Deutschland), die sich in den musikalischen und feministischen Diskurs um Riot Grrrl einschreiben. So wird deutlich, dass es sich nicht um ein ausgestorbenes Phänomen handelt. Es lässt viel mehr Rückschlüsse auf Medienberichterstattung und -interesse schließen. In der Mainstreamkultur wurde der feministische Untergrund-Spirit der Riot Grrrls in Form der niedlich-frechen Girlies vermarktet. Die bekannteste Variante ist die ent-radikalisierte Girl Power, wie sie von der Retortenband Spice Girls propagiert wurde. Das Phänomen Boy- bzw. Girl-Bands ebbte in den Nullerjahren ab; es entwickelte sich das Konzept der Castingshow-Band.

Aufgrund dieser Entwicklungen konvergierte auch das Interesse der Massenmedien an den Riot Grrrls gegen Null. Generell standen Riot Grrrl Bands, allen voran die britische Band Huggy Bear, Popjournalismus sehr kritisch gegenüber, da sie oft eindimensional und limitiert dargestellt wurden. Am Beispiel von Huggy Bear zeigt sich eine drastische Reaktion, die Band verweigerte ab einem bestimmten Zeitpunkt jegliche (Mainstream)Presseinterviews. Nicht nur in den großen Medien wurde Riot Grrrl undifferenziert verhandelt (Büsser 2000). Die Germanistin Katja Kauer bezieht sich in ihrem Band „Popfeminismus! Fragezeichen? Eine Einführung“ an verschiedenen Stellen auf die Riot Grrrl-Bewegung. Der Band weist für Szenekundige eine Vielzahl an Kontroversen und Ungereimtheiten an diversen Stellen auf. Besonders markant fällt hierbei neben gewagten Thesen und Interpretationen auch die konsequent fehlerhafte Schreibweise von Kathleen Hanna auf (Kauer 2009).

Martin Büsser konstatiert in „If the Kids are united“ Mitte der 1990er, dass es im frühen Punk, bis auf wenige Ausnahmen, „kaum nennenswerte von Frauen geleitete Bands“ gab (Büsser 2000: 32). Hier widerspreche ich, denn gerade im Punk der späten 1970er Jahre und im Proto-Punk partizipierte eine Vielzahl von

Frauen in der Szene. Beispielsweise in den Bands Hans-A-Plast oder Nina Hagen Band in Deutschland, The Plasmatics, The Go-Go's, X-Ray Spex, The Slits oder die frühen Jahre von Blondie, als angloamerikanische Beispiele. Die DIY-Punk-Hardcore-Szene lebt von aktiven Personen, die sich nicht nur auf der Bühne, sondern auch im zugehörigen Subkulturuniversum engagieren. Dazu gehört neben Konzertveranstaltungen auch das Betreiben von Zines, Labels oder Herstellen von Band- oder Szenemerchandise (Markey/Schwartz 2012). In all diesen verschiedenen Sphären agieren Frauen* seit dem Bestehen der Szene - auch ohne feministische Intention, wie in der Dokumentation „From the Back of the Room" anschaulich gezeigt wird (Oden 2011).

Das Lady*fest/LaDIYfest/Lady_fest-Konzept

Aus der Riot-Grrrl-Bewegung haben sich verschiedene interventionistische Konzepte entwickelt. Eines davon sind feministische Kunst- und Kulturveranstaltungen, die unter den variationsreichen Termini wie Ladyfest, LaDIYfest, Lady*fest oder Lady_fest verhandelt werden. Das erste Ladyfest [damalige Schreibweise] fand 2000 in Olympia statt. Es war eine Reaktion und Intervention auf sexuelle Übergriffe und Vergewaltigungen von Frauen auf einem Nachfolgefestival des berühmten Woodstock-Festivals (Mooshammer/Trimmel 2008). Bei dem thematisierten Phänomen handelt es sich um queer-feministische, nicht-kommerzielle Kulturveranstaltungen, die grundsätzlich nach einem offenen Mitmach-Prinzip organisiert werden. So finden dort Workshops und Vorträge aller Couleur von Stricken bis Thaiboxen oder Musik machen bis Sexspielzeug selbst basteln sowie Konzerte und Parties statt. In den letzten 20 Jahren fanden in westlichen Industriekulturen mehr als hundert Lady*feste mit einem breiten Themenspektrum statt. Diese Veranstaltungen sind Indikator dafür, dass es innerhalb der DIY-Punk/Hardcore-Kultur und auch in verwandten linken Kontexten eine starke Szene gibt, die einerseits bereit ist, sich für queer-feministische und genderorientierte Inhalte zu öffnen und andererseits auch aktiv zu praktizieren, indem ehrenamtlich Freizeit und Energie in eine feministische Interventionskultur investiert wird.

Diese feministischen Kulturevents nutzen die Strukturen der DIY-Punk/Hardcore-Subkultur. Daher finden sie sehr häufig in links-autonomen und selbstverwalteten Räumen statt, die sich durchaus als anti-rassistisch begreifen. Wichtig ist an dieser Stelle anzumerken, dass in der Entwicklung Riot Grrrl und dem damit verbundenen Lady*festen, ebenso wie in der feministischen Forschung, die Thematisierung von intersektionalen Perspektiven zugenommen hat.[8] Die Verschränkung von postkolonialer mit feministischer Theorie erweist sich in Bezug auf aktivistische Strukturen, zu denen das Lady*festkonzept gezählt werden kann, als notwendige Konsequenz, um intersektionale Exklusionen sichtbar zu machen und dagegen zu wirken.

[8] Beispielsweise auf dem Ladyfest in Kassel, 2015: http://ladyfestkassel.tumblr.com/programm [13.06.2016].

Vor diesem Hintergrund, der eine besondere Form von Exklusion offenbart, tragen postkolonial-feministische TheoretikerInnen weiterhin zu einer Weiterentwicklung des feministischen Aktivismus bei, in dem untersucht wird, wie Allianzenbildung über die Grenzen von Race, Klasse, Kaste, Geschlecht und Epistemologie hinweg möglich und machbar ist. (Fink/Leinius 2014: 121)

Als Beispiel zur Diversifizierung sei hier das Afropunk-Fest aus New York City zu nennen und anzumerken, dass auf Ladyfesten sehr häufig Critical-Whiteness-Workshops angeboten werden. Wichtig beim Critical Whiteness-Konzept ist, dass es nicht eins zu eins in den deutschsprachigen Raum implementiert werden kann, da die soziokulturelle Einbettung in den USA historisch anders verankert ist als dort. Zudem gilt es das Konzept der Identitätspolitik zu hinterfragen, denn

> [a]n die Stelle des Widerspruchs zwischen Individuum und Gesellschaft ist jedoch die Identitätspolitik getreten, die letztlich nur die Differenz und Konkurrenz verschiedener personaler Identitäten kennt. Die Identitätspolitik wurde in den siebziger Jahren populär, genau zu der Zeit, als mit dem Produktivkraftschub der Mikroelektronik der Kapitalismus in eine tiefgreifende Krise geriet und sich das akademische linke Denken von der Ausbeutung zur Ausgrenzung hin verschob und damit vor dem Entstehen der strukturellen Arbeitslosigkeit und den damit einhergehenden sozialen Veränderungen die Augen verschloss. Der Historiker Eric Hobsbawm interpretierte die aufkommende Identitätspolitik selbst als Krisenphänomen und neue Form der Konkurrenzkämpfe der Mittelklasse. (Hayner 2016)

Als zeitgenössisches Beispiel, das sich weniger mit Identitätspolitiken als mit Widerstand und Aktivismus gegen gesellschaftliche Normative richtet, sei das Lady*Fest in Innsbruck 2015 aufgeführt. Die Organisator_innen bespielten über mehrere Monate Innsbruck und Umgebung mit queer-feministischen Veranstaltungen und verfolgten einen aufklärerischen Ansatz. Es wurden von Frühjahr bis Herbst 2015 verschiedene ländliche Räume mit genderreflektierenden Veranstaltungen bespielt, feministische Inhalte thematisiert, queere Performances inszeniert und Konzerte veranstaltet. Man stelle sich einen Werkzeugkasten voller Theorie- und Performancetools vor, mit dem in verschiedene Gebiete Tirols gereist wurde.[9]

Es soll nun nicht der Eindruck entstehen, dass Menschen aus ruralen Gebieten emanzipatorisches Verständnis abgesprochen wird, doch handelt es sich bei den bereisten Kleinstädten nicht unbedingt um Hotspots für queer-feministische Themen. Denn genau darum ging es den Macher_innen. Sie verfolgten einen aufklärerischen Impetus und trugen feministische Theorien und Praxen an Orte, wo sie tendenziell weniger populär verhandelt werden. Um den Interessent_innenkreis zu erweitern und aus den gewohnten Strukturen auszubrechen, halte ich diese Taktik für äußerst sinnvoll. Nach dem Motto „Raus aus dem theoretischen Elfenbeinturm" werden Inhalte und Themen der Gender Studies im Realraum angewandt und popularisiert.

Mittels Lady*festen wird seit 20 Jahren feministisch innerhalb und außerhalb der DIY-Punk-/Hardcore-Subkultur interveniert. Es

---

[9] Programmbeschreibung des Innsbrucker Lady*fests (2015): http://ladyfest-innsbruck.jimdo.com/programm/ [13.06.2016].

wurden und werden internationale Netzwerke geschaffen, um sich gemeinsam zu unterstützen und zu Themen zu arbeiten, die in der Mehrheitskultur oft ausgelassen werden. Hierbei liegt der Fokus besonders auf Themen bezüglich Rassismen, sexuelle Orientierung und damit zusammenhängenden Gewaltverhältnissen, die gesellschaftlich und auch innerhalb subkultureller Räume produziert und reproduziert werden.

So sollen in der Raumproduktion am Lady*fest Sexismus, Homophobie oder Rassismus keinen Platz haben. Frauen, Lesben und Transgender sollen die Möglichkeit haben, ohne große Kraft- und Nervenanstrengung ihren Raumanspruch zu erforschen und umzusetzen. (Mooshammer/Trimmel 2008: 140)

Eva Trimmel und Bettina Mooshammer beschreiben in ihrem Aufsatz zum Lady*fest das oben genannte Lady*space-Konzept als feministische Raumproduktion, das „wenn [es] aufgeht, [...] ein Umdenkprozess und in weiterer Folge auch ein verändertes Verhalten im Umgang mit Raum stattfinden“ (ebd.). Begründet wird ihr Ansatz mit Bourdieus Konzept des sozialen Verhaltens im physischen Raum (Barlösius 2011)[10]: „Wir dürfen [...] annehmen, dass sich auf dem Wege ihrer Realisierungen in den Strukturen des angeeigneten physischen Raumes die unausgesprochenen Imperative der sozialen Ordnung und die verschiedenen Ordnungsrufe der objektiven Hierarchie in Präferenzsysteme und mentale Strukturen“ einteilen (Mooshammer/Trimmel 2008: 144). Innerhalb des

[10] Der soziale Raum wird nach Bourdieu durch verschiedene Faktoren, die auf das Individuum einwirken, wie Klasse, Ethnie, Bildung und das Verfügen über die damit verbunden Kapitalformen (kulturelles, symbolisches und finanzielles) bestimmt.

Lady*spaces, der immer wieder von neuem performativ hergestellt werden muss, gilt das Prinzip des Self-Empowerments. Es gilt vor allem, Raum für einen rücksichtsvollen Umgang miteinander zu schaffen.

Betrachtet man die (Weiter-)Entwicklung von Riot Grrrl und Lady*festen, so fällt auf, das der frühen Riot Grrrl–Bewegung immanente sexpositive und provozierende Habitus aus der DIY-Punk-Hardcore-Szene in den Hintergrund gerückt ist (Flannigan 2004; Busch/Ortmann 2001). Explizit wird hierbei auf das offensive und herausfordernde Verhalten von Bands wie Tribe 8, Bikini Kill oder auch noch frühen Punkbands wie The Slits angespielt. Die Akteur_innen dieser Bands traten provokativ nackt auf und fungierten dabei nicht als Projektionsfläche männlicher Lust. Der weibliche Körper wurde von androzentrischen Lesarten zurückerobert und in roher Natürlichkeit bis gar brutaler Darstellung inszeniert. Tribe 8 Sängerin Lynn Breedlove schlitzte sich auf der Bühne auf, zog sich einen Umschnall-Dildo an und konterkariert machistisches Verhalten und ist dabei ostentativ politisch inkorrekt. Wenn sich Kathleen Hanna in großen Lettern „SLUT“ auf den Bauch schreibt und ihre Kleidung ablegt, werden Aktionsräume geöffnet, in denen Frauen* neue und unerwartete Handlungsmöglichkeiten eröffnet werden (Threat 2015). Die Frau* auf der Bühne aufgrund ihrer Kleidung oder ihres (sexuellen) Habitus als Slut zu bezeichnen wird obsolet, da es bereits durch einen Reclaiming-Prozess vereinnahmt wurde und seine Diskriminierungsmacht verliert. Ebenfalls von interessanter Natur ist das programmatische Ausziehen bei Tribe 8. Die Praxis dieser Selbstermächtigung nutzt Ironie als Instrumentarium hypermännliches Verhalten auf humoristischer Ebene zu dekonstruieren, denn „humour is always the best defense and weapon" (Waters 2017: o.S.).

Im folgenden Teil wendet sich der vorliegende Artikel einem Interviewbeispiel aus einem deutschsprachigen Punk-Hardcore-Zine zu, um aufzuzeigen, dass auch innerhalb vermeintlich genderreflektierter Strukturen häufig herrschende Mechanismen aus der Mehrheitskultur reproduziert werden.

Interviewanalyse

Gegenstand des hier dargestellten Fallbeispiels ist ein Interview in einem deutschen Zine „Punkrock!"[11] mit der Sängerin Tijana der schwedischen Hardcore-Punk-Band Beyond Pink. Die Band wird innerhalb der DIY-Szene populär verhandelt. Dass die Band aus fünf Frauen besteht, wird in Interviews und Reviews oft thematisiert. Dabei gilt es noch einmal hervorzuheben, dass es sich bei der Riot Grrrl Bewegung um eine queer-feministisch motivierte Strömung innerhalb der Punk- und Hardcore-Kultur handelt, denn die Tatsache, dass Frauen Musik produzieren, evoziert keine Assoziation qua ihres Geschlechtes mit der oben thematisierten Bewegung.

Bereits im Einleitungstext des Interviews wird die eindimensionale Lesart von Frauen als aktiver Teil der Musiksubkultur deutlich sichtbar.

[11] Das Zine wurde 2015 eingestellt, nachdem es wegen geringer Verkaufszahlen im Huber Verlag gescheitert ist.

> Mit ihrer zweiten LP „The New Black“ wirbelt das schwedische All-Female-Quintett 2010 die Hardcorepunk-Szene auf. Die Folgen sind zig Touren und energetische Auftritte, woraufhin ihnen bald der Ruf ihrer mitreißenden Shows vorauseilt. Aber eben auch der, der fünf toughen Frauen, die auf der Bühne mehr aus sich rausholen als eigentlich möglich ist. So dauert es nicht lange, bis man sie in die Riot-Grrrl-Schublade stopft. Eine Tatsache, die ihnen bis heute zum Hals raushängt und worauf Sängerin Tijana im Interview äußerst dünnhäutig reagiert. Ein Gespräch über das vierte und neue Album „Against the Universe“ und das Leben im All. (Beyond Pink 2012: o.S.)

Was hier als Gespräch über das neue Album der Band angekündigt wird, endet in einer Aneinanderreihung von Plattitüden und geschlechterbedingten Vorurteilen. Denn über das neue Album bzw. die musikalischen Aspekte wird im Interview nicht respektive kaum gesprochen. Viel mehr kreist der Interviewer mit seinem Frageschema um die Tatsache, dass die Band aus Frauen besteht:

> Interviewer: Obwohl ich eigentlich darauf verzichten wollte, auf das Thema „Frauenband“ zu sprechen zu kommen, nun habe ich doch eine Frage in diese Richtung. Inwiefern wird von euch erwartet, dass dieser Punkt thematisiert wird?
>
> Beyond Pink: Die Band gibt es jetzt bald seit 15 Jahren und es ist immer wieder überraschend, wie besessen die Leute davon sind, dass wir eine „All-Girl-Band“ sind. Wir hoffen wirklich, dass man endlich aufhört unser Ge-

schlecht in den Fokus zu rücken und sich stattdessen unserer Musik widmet. Inklusive dir, wird man dauernd von allen drauf angesprochen Wir haben doch gerade ein neues Album aufgenommen, da könnte man doch meinen, man bekäme Fragen zu unserer Musik gestellt. Wäre doch viel interessanter. Für unser Gespräch und auch für die Leser.

Interviewer: Bekommen Riot-Grrrl Bands deiner Meinung nach zu viel Aufmerksamkeit?

Beyond Pink: Keine Ahnung, es ist eine Ewigkeit her, dass ich mich mit solchen Bands beschäftigt habe.

Beim Lesen des Interviews wird förmlich spürbar, wie angespannt und unangenehm die Interviewsituation ist, die der Interviewer mit seiner starren und vorurteilsbehafteten Frageweise erzeugt. Das stört den Lesefluss auf Seiten der Rezipierenden immens. Das hier gezeigte Beispiel ist deckungsgleich mit Mainstream-Popjournalismus. Als Belegbeispiel sei an dieser Stelle Linus Volkmanns Analyse im Artikel „Popjournalismus als Männersprache-Dieser Schnipo-Schranke-Text in der FAZ“ mit der Band Schnipo Schranke aufgeführt. Volkmann analysiert den Artikel „Ketchup im Feuchtgebiet Schnipo Schranke mit Chanson-Pop im Frankfurter Zoom“ aus der Frankfurter Allgemeinen Zeitung als eindimensional und anthrozentristisch. Kurz gesagt beschreibt er sexistischen Popjournalismus, der Frauen* als Teil der Musikwelt kategorisch ausschließt.[12]

[12] Wurde als plakatives und anschauliches Beispiel gewählt wie Frauen* häufig dargestellt werden und spiegelt nicht meinen Musikgeschmack wider.

> Dass über Musikerinnen anders berichtet wird als über Musiker, ist business as usual im Popbetrieb. Eine Band, die aus Frauen besteht, darf sich in jedem Fall auf signifikant mehr Bewertungen ihres Äußeren und ihrer grundsätzlichen Kompetenz an den Instrumenten freuen als eine voller Typen. Zudem wurde in einer Art zurückgebliebenem Gentlemans Agreement irgendwann wohl auch mal beschlossen, dass das Geschlecht einer weiblichen Band immer wieder Thema zu sein hat. Unablässig. So will es der (zumeist männliche) Gralshüter in der Popjournaille. (Volkmann 2016: o.S.)

Auch im behandelten Fallbeispiel von Beyond Pink aus dem Szenejournalismus greift die Aussage Volkmanns. Nachdem der Interviewer das Genderthema angesprochen hat und trotz mehrfachen Hinweisen durch die Sängerin auf das neue Album der Band und einer direkten Zurückweisung bzgl. der Riot Grrrl und Geschlechterthematik, bleibt er bei seinem starren Fragenkonzept. Zudem schreibt er sich mit seinem Interviewstil in den Diskurs um männlichen Popjournalismus ein, indem er über Kleidung und Äußerlichkeiten, getarnt als szene-investigativen Journalismus, sprechen möchte.

> Interviewer: Ihr seid in der linken, politischen Hardcorepunk-Szene verwurzelt und auf dem Cover des zweiten Albums „The New Black“ trägst du ein Shirt der Cro-Mags. Bist du je dafür kritisiert worden? Denn der Band, insbesondere Harley Flanigan, wird ja nachgesagt äußerst konservativ zu sein und dass das Cover ihres Kultalbums „The Age of Quarrel“ homophobe Szenen zeige.

Beyond Pink: Tatsächlich sind wir deshalb noch nie angesprochen worden. Kann es sein, dass du da etwas verwechselst? Meinst du vielleicht das zweite Album „Best Wishes", weil das Artwork von „The Age of Quarrel" zeigt eine Atombombenexplosion und ich wüsste nicht, wie ein Atompilz homophob sein könnte."
[...]

Interviewer: „Gut, dann lasse ich das mal so stehen. Stattdessen habt ihr einige Reaktionen auf eure Klamotten bekommen.

Beyond Pink: Zu unserem Plattencover gab es eine Menge Reaktionen, die sich auf unsere Kleidung bezogen. Beispielsweise interpretierte jemand in seiner Besprechung unserer Kleidung und unseren Look als ein Statement gegen die Modeindustrie, was keinesfalls unsere Absicht war. Wir haben bloß die Klamotten angehabt, von denen wir dachten, dass sie cool sind und gut passen. Aber noch mal, auch hier sind die meisten Leute zu sehr auf unser Äußeres fokussiert als auf das worum es eigentlich geht, nämlich die Musik.

Das erzeugt besonders interessante Korrelationen, denn im Song „Not A Statement" (Pride & Prejudice, 2012) thematisiert die Band die Fokussierung und Überinterpretation ihrer Kleidungsweise. Schließlich inszenieren sie sich, wie primär jede Band, auf dem Plattencover sowie auf der Bühne als „cool".[13] Im Booklet

[13] Dies beinhalten auch Praxen, die darauf abzielen, besonders *trashig* bzw. unästhetisch zu wirken, da das gerade auf ironischer Metaebene innerhalb verschiedener Szenekreise als „cool" gilt.

zur Platte kann man im Songtext nachlesen: „So yeah we care about our looks / We wear what we like, just like you / Neither a reaction against mainstream fashion / Nor a statement about punk clichés“. Im Refrain wird sogar das besagte T-Shirt der New York Hardcore-Band Cro-Mags erwähnt (Beyond Pink 2012: o.S.).

Auch dieses Exzerpt zeigt deutlich, wie wenig der Interviewer die Band musikalisch ernst nimmt. Trotz häufiger Hinweise auf die musikalische Zentrierung des Interviews bleibt er innerhalb seiner kulturellen Matrix, in der es Frauen anscheinend nicht möglich ist, über andere Themen als vestimentäre Praxen zu sprechen und sich mit ihrem Gender auseinander zu setzen.

Ein weiterer Beleg für diese These findet sich in dem Review eines anderen Zines (Trust). So gipfelt dieser Habitus, wenn der Dreiklang Beyond Pink, Riot Grrrl und Gender ein paar Seiten später erneut aufgegriffen wird und der Verfasser die Band bzw. Sängerin Tijana direkt diffamiert.

> [D]er zweite Artikel ist über eine aktuelle norwegische Riot Grrrl Band, die im Gegensatz zu Beyond Pink in dieser Ausgabe nicht gleich miese Laune bekommt, wenn man sie auf das Thema [Riot Grrrl, Anm. der Verf.] anspricht. Eher ganz im Gegenteil, denn der Großteil des Artikels handelt davon. (o.A. o.J.: o.S.)

Bei dieser Review expliziert der Verfasser, der auch Interviewer von Beyond Pink ist, einen Habitus, der im Mainstream fest verortet ist. Eigentlich erwartet er keine Antworten von seiner Gesprächspartnerin, sondern hat eine scheinbar zementierte Vorstellung bezüglich des Bildes von Musikerinnen*. Dass er immer noch der festen Überzeugung ist, dass Beyond Pink der Riot Grrrl-Bewegung angehört, erweist sich als borniert. Es wird sichtbar, dass es für den Interviewenden nur wenige Partizipationsmöglichkeiten für Frauen* innerhalb der Punk-/Hardcore-Szene zu geben scheint. Nämlich, wenn sie sich in die Riot Grrrl-Bewegung einschreiben. Nicht nur das Kategoriendenken des Interviewers sticht dabei heraus, sondern es zeugt auch von fehlender Versiertheit seinerseits. Denn hätte er sich musikalisch mit der Band auseinandergesetzt, käme diese Einschreibung überhaupt nicht in Frage, da die Band einen völlig anderen Stil spielt als er im Riot Grrrl-Genre üblich ist.

Abschließende Betrachtungen

Frauen, die musikalisch innerhalb der Szene partizipieren, werden häufig gegen deren musikalische Intention als Riot Grrrl kategorisiert. Dazu kommt, dass Termini wie „Female-Fronted" oder „All Girl Band", die Frauen* immer noch eine exponierte Sonderstellung zuweisen. Nach meiner Lesart erweisen sich diese Labelungen als problematisch, denn sie exotisieren Frauen* innerhalb der DIY-Hardcore-Punk-Szene sowie auch innerhalb anderer Musikstile. Dadurch werden musizierende Frauen* tendenziell davon entfernt, auf selbstverständliche Weise Teil der aktiven Szene zu sein. Genau diesen Habitus kritisieren Beyond Pink im Song „Thanx to all the boys" auf ironische Weise. Zur Absicherung, dass die Nachricht verstanden wird, fügen sie im Booklet eine präzise Erklärung hinzu. „Special thanx to Retaliate who at Law&Order fest 2010 made the audience give a bound of applause to all the girls who came to the show for their own sake. This really made us feel like such a natural part of the scene“ (Beyond Pink o.J.: o.S.).

Im Interview mit Tijana, der Sängerin von Beyond Pink, wird deutlich erkennbar, dass der Interviewende eine sehr präzise und starre Vorstellung davon hat, wie Musikerinnen innerhalb der Szene partizipieren. Und auch, welche Reaktionen er von seiner Gesprächspartnerin bzw. von einem Gespräch mit Frauen erwartet. Ob bei einem Gespräch mit einem männlichen Interviewpartner Stylingthemen Gegenstand der Unterhaltung gewesen wären, gilt es zu bezweifeln. Meine Vermutungen bestätigen sich, wenn man - wie bereits oben aufgezeigt - das Review aus dem Trust Zine aus derselben Ausgabe des Punkrock!-Zines betrachtet.

Wichtig ist es anzumerken, dass die Beispielbeiträge keinen homogenen Konsens in der Szene widerspiegeln. Diese Berichterstattung ist anschauliches Beispiel dafür, dass es trotz emanzipatorischer Bestrebungen innerhalb der DIY-Punk-HC-Kultur zu solch engen Sichtweisen bzw. massenmedienkonformen Darstellungen kommt.

Frauen* in Bands innerhalb des Diskurses bewusst oder unbewusst aufgrund ihres Geschlechts eine Sonderstellung zuzuschreiben, führt in meiner Lesart tendenziell eher zu einem Backlash als zu einer ausgewogenen Justierung der Geschlechterverhältnisse.

Gerade die Band Beyond Pink wehrt sich dagegen, in die sogenannte Frauenbandschublade gesteckt zu werden, legt Wert darauf über die produzierte Musik wahrgenommen zu werden und nimmt beispielsweise auch keine Konzertanfragen für Lady*feste an. Es gibt innerhalb der Szene viele Frauen, die ohne feministischen Ansatz partizipieren, was die bereits erwähnte amerikanische Dokumentation „From the back of the room“ von Amy Oden aus 2011 belegt.

Abschließend kann festgestellt werden, dass es teilweise ein asymmetrisches Verhältnis zwischen Männern und Frauen* in der Szene gibt, diese aber dennoch keine reine Herrenrunde ist. Es existiert eine Vielzahl von Frauen*, die mit oder ohne feministischem Ansatz einen wichtigen Bestandteil der DIY-Hardcore-Punk-Szene im deutschsprachigen Raum und international bilden und sich aktiv auf diverse Weise an der (Sub)Kulturproduktion beteiligen. Somit bilden sie einen essentiellen Bestandteil der selbstverwalteten und -organisierten DIY-Hardcore-Punk-Szene.

In diesem Sinne möchte ich mit einem völlig nicht-akademischem Schlusswort enden: Up the female-punx!

Literaturverzeichnis

Alien She. The Riot Grrrl Exzibit. Museum of Contemporary Craft, Portland, Oregon, 2015.

Baldauf, Anette (2013): Riot Grrrl ist... Das Riot-Grrrl-Manifest. In: Engelmann, Jonas/Peglow, Katja (Hrsg.): Riot Grrrl Revisited. Geschichte und Gegenwart einer feministischen Bewegung. Mainz, 13-14.

Barlösius, Eva (2011): PierreBourdieu. Frankfurt, New York.

Beyond Pink (2012): Not A Statement, Pride & Prejudice. Berlin.

Brockheimer, Siri C. (2009): „Not Just Boys‘ Fun?“ The Gendered Experience of American Hardcore. MA Thesis in American Studies. Department of Literatur, Area Studies and European Languages. ILOS. Universität Oslo.

Busch, Uta/Ortmann, Sandra (2001): Step up and be vocal – Interview zu Queer Punk und Feminismus. o.O.

Büsser, Martin (2000): If The Kids Are United. Von Punk zu Hardcore und zurück. Mainz.

Darms, Lisa (2014): The Riot Grrrl Collection. New York.

Downes, Julia (2013): DIY Queer Feminist (Sub)cultural Resistance in the UK. Dissertationschrift an der University of Leeds. [Link: http://etheses.whiterose.ac.uk/2383/; 07.08.2020].

Engelmann, Jonas/Herzing, Eva/Melián, Michaela/Plesch, Hans/Plesch, Tine (2013): Rebel Girl: Popkultur und Feminismus. Mainz.

Engelmann, Jonas/Peglow, Katja (2013): Riot Grrrl Revisited. Geschichte und Gegenwart einer feministischen Bewegung. Mainz.

Fink, Elisabeth/Leinius, Johanna (2014): Postkolonial-feministische Theorie. In: Franke, Yvonne/Mozygemba, Kati/Pöge, Kathleen/Ritter, Bettina/Venohr, Dagmar (Hrsg.): Feminismen Heute. Positionen in Theorie und Praxis. Bielefeld, 115-128.

Flannigan, Tracy (2004): Rise Above The Tribe 8 Documentary. o.O.

Hayner, Jakob (2016): Das große Reinemachen. [Link: https://jungle.world/artikel/2016/35/54757.html; 07.08.2020].

Heath, Joseph/Potter, Andrew (2004): Nation of Rebels – Why counterculture became consumer culture. New York.

Held, Sarah (2015): Critical Crafting und Craftivism – Handarbeit, Feminismus und Widerstand. In: Lehmann, Sonja/Müller-Wienbergen, Karina/Thiel, Julia-Elena (Hrsg.): Neue Muster, alte Maschen? Interdisziplinäre Perspektiven auf die Verschränkungen von Geschlecht und Raum. Bielefeld, 322-339.

Held, Sarah (2016): Girl Gangs Against Street Harassment. Feministische Street Art als künstlerisch-interventionistische Raumaneignungspraxis. Feministisches Institut der Technischen Universität Hamburg-Harburg. [Link: http://www.feministisches-institut.de/girl-gangs-against-street-harassment-feministische-street-art-als-kunstlerisch-interventionistische-raumaneignungspraxis/; 13.06.2016].

Hornung, Annabelle/Nowak, Tine/Kuni, Verena (2011): Do It Yourself: Die Mitmach-Revolution, Ausstellungskatalog. Mainz.

Kauer, Katja (2009): Popfeminismus! Fragezeichen?. Berlin.

Lady*fest. Innsbruck, 2015. [Link: http://ladyfest-innsbruck.jimdo.com/programm/; 13.06.2016].

Ladyfest. Kassel, 2015. [Link: http://ladyfestkassel.tumblr.com/programm; 13.06.2016].

Marcus, Sara (2010): Girls To The Front. The True Story Of The Riot Grrrl Revolution. New York.

Markey, David/Schwartz, Jordan (2012): We Got Power!: Hardcore Punk Scenes From 1980s Southern California. Los Angeles.

Mason, Matt (2008): The Pirate's Dilemma – How youth culture is reinventing capitalism. New York.

McCain, Gillian/McNeil, Legs (1997): Please, kill me! The Uncensored Oral History Of Punk. New York.

Mooshammer, Bettina/Trimmel, Eva (2008): LADY claim your SPACE. Das Ladyfest feministische Raumpraxis. In: Ernst, Waltraut/ Gerards, Marion/ Oster, Martina (Hrsg.): Performativität und Performance. Geschlecht in Musik, Theater und MedienKunst. Hamburg, 139-145.

Müller, Stephanie (2012): Exklusiv! Mode und Handarbeit zwischen Austausch und Ausgrenzung. In: Villa, Paula-Irene/Jäckel, Julia/ Pfeiffer, Zara S./Sanitter, Nadine/Steckert, Ralf (Hrsg.): Banale Kämpfe – Perspektiven auf Populärkultur und Geschlecht. Wiesbaden, 121-138.

Oden, Amy (2011): From the Back of the Room. Selbstdistribution. Washington, DC.

Peglow, Katja (2013): Quiet Riot. Oder: Warum Riot Grrrl in Deutschland still blieb. In: Engelmann, Jonas/Peglow, Katja (Hrsg.): Riot Grrrl Revisited. Geschichte und Gegenwart einer feministischen Bewegung. Mainz, 166-170.

Punk. No one is innocent. Kunst-Stil-Revolte-Kunsthalle Wien, 2008.

Spencer, Amy (2008): DIY The Rise of LO-FI Culture. London, New York.

Threat, Ana (2015): Tribe 8: Die Kupf – Kulturplattform OÖ. [Link: https://kupf.at/de/medien/zeitung/kabinett-threat-rockkolumne-1562015/tribe-8; 07.08.2020].

True, Everett (2009): The 10 myths of Riot Grrrl. [Link: https://www.theguardian.com/music/musicblog/2009/sep/14/myths-riot-grrrl-cribs-takeover; 13.06.2016].

Volkmann, Maren (2013): Riot Grrrl Is Not Dead. Eine Spurensuche in den Nullerjahren. In: Engelmann, Jonas/Peglow, Katja (Hrsg.): Riot Grrrl Revisited. Geschichte und Gegenwart einer feministischen Bewegung. Mainz,171-178.

Volkmann, Linus (2016): Popjournalismus als Männersprache – Dieser Schnipo-Schrank-Text in der FAZ. [Link: http://www.kaput-mag.com/kolumne_de/popjournalismus-als-maennersprache/; 13.06.2016].

Waters, John (2015): Go out in the world and fuck it up beautifully. John Waters' commencement speech at RISD [Rhode Island School of Design]. [Link: https://dangerousminds.net/comments/john_waters_2015_commencement; 07.08.2020].

Wieners, Ute (2014): Zum Glück gab es Punk: Autobiografische Erzählungen. Hannover.

Selbermachen als feministische Ermächtigung – eine Jungimkerin erzählt

von Christin Sirtl

In meiner Familie hat das Imkern seit fast einem Jahrhundert Tradition. Dabei hat es sich von einem überlebensnützlichen hin zu einem zeitvertreibenden und altersvorsorgenden Hobby entwickelt. Die Familienbeschäftigung hat im Laufe der Zeit einige politische Systeme überlebt: die Weimarer Republik, das Naziregime, den Sozialismus in der DDR und nun den Kapitalismus. Es bleibt dabei nicht aus, dass sich die Motive und Zwecke des Hobbies ändern. Als was ich es einmal bezeichnen werde ist mir noch nicht klar – aktuell nutze ich es als feministisches und emanzipatorisches Ausdrucksmittel, eingereiht in die zahlreichen Möglichkeiten der Selbermach-Kultur.

Ich möchte anhand meines Familienhobbies erklären, warum das Internet toll und das Imkern feministisch ist und für mich wenig mit ökologischen Idealen zu tun hat. Dabei stützen sich meine Thesen auf meine eigenen Erfahrungen und Rechercheergebnisse, die keinen fixen Analysekriterien unterliegen. Mein Text möchte mit Hilfe kleiner ironischer Feinheiten sowohl unterhalten als auch patriarchale Strukturen in der Hobbyimkerei aufdecken.

Der Alltag in der Familienimkerei

Ich bin Imkerin in der mittlerweile fünften Generation. Aktuell arbeiten in den Sommermonaten drei Generationen zusammen: Meine Großeltern, mein Vater und ich. Und seit einem Jahr auch meine Mutter.

Aus den 1970er Jahren hat sich bis heute die Kleiderordnung erhalten: ein blauer, baumwollener Arbeitskittel, der in allen möglichen Handwerksberufen zu finden ist: Gießereimitarbeiter, Schlosser, Klempner etc. Die Frauen der älteren Generationen, die meist an der Honigschleuder zu finden waren, bevorzugen immer noch die Kittelschürze aus Dederon[1]. Auch meine Karriere hat dort begonnen, ich habe mich aber für einen weißen Baumwollkittel entschieden.

Zu unserer Imkerei gehören zwei verschiedene Standorte sowie ein Schleuder-/Lager- und Abfüllhaus. Wir arbeiten vorrangig noch mit sogenannten Hinterbehandlungsbeuten, die arbeitsintensiver zu betreiben sind als moderne Magazinbeuten.[2]

Während der Arbeitsvorgänge an den Bienen wird zur Beruhigung der Tiere im sogenannten Smoker[3] Rainfarn verbrannt. Ich hege dabei den dringenden Verdacht, dass dieser Rauch nicht nur die Bienen, sondern auch die MitarbeiterInnen beruhigt. Anders

---

[1] Dederon ist der Markenname einer Faser, die zur Herstellung von Stoffen vor allem in der DDR verwendet wurde.

[2] Hinterbehandlungsbeuten sind Bienenbeuten, die von der Rückseite aus bearbeitet werden und daher einem kleinen Schrank ähneln. Im Gegensatz dazu sind die modernen Magazinbeuten von oben zugängig.

[3] Ein Smoker ist eine übergroße Pfeife, die nicht geraucht, sondern durch einen Blasebalg in Gang gehalten wird. Durch den Rauch bleiben die Bienen auf den Waben sitzen, was eine einfachere Bearbeitung für den/die ImkerIn möglich macht.

kann ich mir die friedliche Stimmung bei einem Arbeitstag zwischen drei Generationen nicht erklären.

Imkern heißt bei uns in den Sommermonaten, permanent die Völker zu beobachten und zu schauen, ob 'alles in Ordnung' ist: Drohnenbrut ausschneiden, Königinnenzellen ausbrechen, um Schwärmen zu verhindern, Bienen beobachten, ob und welche Farbe der Pollen hat, und darüber spekulieren, wie das Wetter wird.[4]

Die Imkerei besteht in der Regel aus vier bis fünf arbeitsintensiven Monaten von März bis August. Den eigentlichen Honig in Hobbocks – Abfüllbehälter aus lebensmittelgeeignetem PVC – abzufüllen, ist auf die Sommermonate bezogen der Arbeitsgang mit einem eher geringen Zeitfaktor. Dafür aber der befriedigendste. Nach einem erfolgreichen Tag zwischen Zigtausenden von Bienen, dem Geruch von verbrennendem Rainfarn im Smoker und dem Honig ist es ein gutes Gefühl zu wissen, dass die eigene Arbeitskraft diese Mengen Honig in die Eimer gebracht hat.

In den restlichen Monaten ist die ImkerIn damit beschäftigt, die neue Saison vorzubereiten, indem sie neue Mittelwände in Rähmchen setzt und Mutmaßungen darüber anstellt, ob es nun zu frühe, zu milde oder zu trockene Herbst-, Winter und Frühjahrsmonate geben wird.

---

[4] Diese Vorgänge gehören zu den alltäglichen Vorgängen bei der Imkerei. Da jedoch die Sinnhaftigkeit dieser Tätigkeiten auch zu Diskussionen führen kann, überlasse ich es der/dem LeserIn bei Interesse nachzuschlagen, was sich hinter diesen Dingen verbirgt.

Selbermachen überdauert geschichtliche Epochen – was treibt uns an?

Angefangen hat alles mit Wilhem Diestelmeier – meinem Urur-großvater. Die Ehrenurkunde des Imkervereins zum langjährigen Vereinsjubiläum, das auch die Übergabe der goldenen Ehrennadel beinhaltet, hängt noch immer in unserem Bienenhaus. Gleich daneben hängt eine Urkunde anlässlich der Diamantenen Hochzeit, ausgestellt durch die 'Zentrale Fachkommission Imker der Kreisverbände der Kleingärtner, Siedler und Kleintierzüchter', Sparte 'Bienen'. Hierin wird dem Ehrenmitglied und Träger der goldenen Ehrennadel ausdrücklich versichert, für ‚seine Treue, aufrichtigen Charakter desgleichen humorvollen Eigenschaften' durch den Verein zukünftig in Ehren gehalten zu werden.

Mein Ururgroßvater Wilhelm Distelmeier hat ca. 1925 mit der Imkerei begonnen. Was der Grund dafür war, konnte ich auf Nachfragen bei meinen Großeltern nicht erfahren. Honig war beliebt und teuer. Deshalb hat er vermutlich angefangen, ihn selber zu ernten. Die Anfänge waren dabei etwas chaotisch, da er nach dem Prinzip 'Trial & Error' gearbeitet hat. Besonders die Zuchterfolge waren in der Familie gefürchtet. So gab es durchaus ertragreiche Jahre, in denen es aber unmöglich war, durch den Garten zu flanieren ohne sich einen Bienenstich einzufangen. Das Zuchtziel Friedfertigkeit erschien ihm erst mit zunehmendem Alter als sinnvoll.

Mein Großvater hat in den 1950ern mit dem Einzug in das schwiegerelterliche Vierseitengehöft auch die Bienenhaltung übernommen. Zu DDR-Zeiten hat er immer ca. fünf bis sieben Völker gehabt. Der Honig wurde in blecherne Milchkannen gefüllt und an die örtliche LPG[5] geliefert. Dafür gab es nach seinen Aussagen „gutes Geld“. Sehr gutes Geld in Form von Bestäubungsprämien haben die Imker und Imkerinnen auch für das Wandern in die jeweilige Blüte (Klee, Sonnenblumen o.Ä.) erhalten. Dabei werden die Beuten auf einen Wagen geladen, an ein blühendes Feld gefahren und abgestellt. Die Bienen sammeln den Nektar und bestäuben dadurch die Blumen. Für diese Tätigkeit wurden sie von der LPG entlohnt. Das hat jedoch meine Familie nicht gemacht.

Das Imkern gehörte in der DDR in die Reihe der kleinen Nebenerwerbszweige, mit denen die BürgerInnen die Mangelwirtschaft ausgleichen wollten, ähnlich wie Hasen-, Tauben- und andere Kleintierzüchtungen. Warum mein Großvater das Hobby seines Schwiegergroßvaters übernommen hatte, weiß er selbst nicht mehr. „Irgendwas nebenher hat halt jeder gemacht“, war seine Antwort. Auf mein weiteres Nachfragen haben beide Großelternteile von einem sehr regen Vereinsleben erzählt. Neben den inhaltlichen, interessanten Vorträgen handelten die Geschichten vor allem von fantastischen Vereinsausflügen und -festen und einigen durchzechten Nächten.

Nach der Wende fiel die wirtschaftliche Komponente beim Imkern zunächst weg. Der Honig wurde den Imkern nicht mehr abgenommen und auf Eigenvertrieb waren sie nicht vorbereitet. Auch das Vereinsleben veränderte sich, da viele Leute nicht mehr zu den Veranstaltungen kamen oder keine Bienen mehr hatten. Mein Großvater hat dann auch die Lust verloren, die Produktion

---

[5] LPG – Landwirtschaftliche Produktionsgenossenschaft; Zusammenschluss von BäuerInnen und deren Produktionsmitteln zur gemeinschaftlichen agrarischen Produktion in der DDR.

auf einen kleinen Eigenbedarf reduziert und nur ein bis zwei Völker bewirtschaftet.

Ende der 1990er Jahre hat mein Vater begonnen, vornehmlich aus der Sorge um die Finanzierung im Alter auf Grund seiner Selbstständigkeit, und sich entschieden, ein zweites Standbein als Imker aufzubauen. Daraufhin wurde die Völkerzahl über mehrere Jahre von 5 auf 30 aufgestockt.

Die Zucht haben mein Vater und Großvater größtenteils selbst übernommen und so tauchten in diesen Jahren immer wieder interessante, teilweise selbstgebastelte Gegenstände in unseren Gärten auf, die so manche BesucherIn irritiert haben und die der Königinnenzucht dienten.

Die fünfte Generation – meine Motivation als Imkerin

Seit 2009 bin schließlich auch ich in das Familienhobby bzw. den Familienbetrieb eingestiegen. Mittlerweile sind mir alle Vorgänge bekannt und ich beginne mit der Betreuung modernerer Magazinbeuten. Meine Entscheidung hatte wenig mit wirtschaftlichen Interessen oder ideellen/ökologischen Motiven zu tun. Das Gefühl, die Tradition fortzuführen, körperliche Arbeit zu leisten und etwas zu tun, wovor Andere Respekt haben, waren meine Beweggründe. Wenn ich davon berichte, dass ich mit dem Smoker vor 60000 Bienen stehe, diese auf mir krabbeln und mich nicht nervös machen und ich – wenn mich eine sticht – nicht panisch davonrenne, ernte ich Respekt. In meinem Beruf als Bauingenieurin ist es ein angenehmes Gefühl, über etwas reden zu können, zu dem meine Kollegen – vorwiegend ältere Bauingenieur-Herren – ausnahmsweise nichts zu sagen haben und sich etwas von 'mir' erklären lassen müssen.

Ich bezeichne mich selbst als Traditionsimkerin, da ich zum einen Wissen traditionell erlernt habe und zum anderen in Strukturen wie einem Familienbetrieb und einem Imkerverein wirke.

SpiegelOnline fasst die Situation einer solchen Traditionsimkerei schön zusammen: „In Bienenvölkern dominieren die Weibchen, unter Imkern die Männer" (Demling 2014: o.S.).

Seit 2014 bin ich Mitglied im Imkerverein 1837 Weimar e.V. Bisher ist das eher eine träge Angelegenheit. In monatlichen oder zweimonatigen Sitzungen werden 'Imkerfreunde' zu Themen begrüßt wie Königinnenzucht, Berichte über die Imkervereinsausfahrt nach 'Hinterhermsdorf' verlesen oder um die Entlastung des Vorstandes für das vergangene Jahr gebeten usw.

Das Durchschnittsalter in den Vereinen, durch die meine Familie gegangen ist, ist zwischen 55 und 65 anzusiedeln. Im Imkerverein Weimar 1837 e.V. ist dies nicht unbedingt anders. Daher werden dort oft auch die 'guten alten' Zeiten besungen, in denen es noch Bestäubungsprämien gab oder man sich nicht um die Vermarktung von Zusatzprodukten wie Propolis-Salbe, Kerzen, Met oder anderen Kleinigkeiten kümmern musste, um für neue KundInnen attraktiv zu bleiben. Als Jungimkerin fühle ich mich da eher etwas belächelt und häufig geschulmeistert für meine Aussagen und Anregungen.

Dass Frauen in den Vereinen dabei sind und auch gefördert werden, ist für die Herren neu. Seit den 2000er Jahren setzt sich der Deutsche Imkerbund e.V. (D.I.B.) dafür ein, mehr junge und weibliche Mitglieder zu gewinnen, um die Überalterung und damit das Schwinden der Bienenvölker und Imkervereine aufzuhalten. 2008 wurde dazu im Deutschen Imkerbund das 'Jahr der Frau in der Imkerei' (Kehres 2008) ausgerufen. Die Statistiken zeigen, dass fast die Hälfte aller ImkerInnen, die neu beginnen, in den durchgeführten Schulungen Frauen sind. Im Vereinsleben dann aber nur ca. 7,5 Prozent als Mitgliederinnen vertreten sind. Der Jahresbericht des D.I.B. e.V. 2008 stellt zudem fest, dass vor allem [Frauen] in urbanen Gebieten als Neu-ImkerInnen zu verzeichnen sind: So gibt es 2014 in Berlin 290 Frauen in den Vereinen – ca. 30 Prozent - in ganz Thüringen hingegen nur 308 Vereinsfrauen – 13,31 Prozent (Kehres 2008).

Als Ergebnis der Kampagne hat sich in Thüringen der Frauenanteil innerhalb von 4 Jahren um 3 Prozent gesteigert (Deutscher Imkerbund e.V. 2015). Als einen wirklich sprunghaften Anstieg kann man das jedoch nicht bezeichnen. Im Ortsverein Ostwestfalen-Lippe gibt es 8 Frauen bei 41 Mitgliedern – immerhin fast 20 Prozent bei einem Durchschnittsalter von 60 Jahren (Landwirtschaftliches Wochenblatt o.J.). Bei meinem Lieblingsverein – zumindest vom Namen her – der „Goldenen Weisel Gera e.V.“ - sieht es ähnlich aus: 8 Frauen bei 50 Mitgliedern und einem Durchschnittsalter von 54 (Gebhardt 2020: o.S.). Mein Ortsverein in Weimar hat ein Durchschnittsalter von 51 und ist damit einer der jüngsten Vereine Thüringens.

Der Deutsche Imkerbund sieht als Gründe für das vermehrte Bestreben der Frauen in die Imkerei folgende Punkte:

> Gründe für das wachsende Interesse von Frauen, die mit der Imkerei beginnen wollen, sind u.a. eine besonders große Naturverbundenheit, das hohe Gesundheitsbewusstsein, der Wille nach Selbstverwirklichung und das Suchen einer sinnvollen und spannenden Freizeitbeschäftigung. (Deutscher Imkerbund e.V. o.J.: o.S.)

Ich bin geneigt, diesen Satz in der Broschüre als Ironie zu verstehen – es scheint jedoch nicht so, als ob die AutorInnenschaft das intendiert hat. Naturverbundenheit und Gesundheitsbewusstsein wird Frauen als genetisch bedingte Eigenschaft zugewiesen, vermutlich, weil es zur fürsorglichen Familienversorgung passt. Es ist erstaunlich, dass diese biologistischen Ideen immer noch fest verankert sind, Frauen daran glauben und Männer und Vereine es weiter vorantreiben.[6]

Auch wenn sich die oben aufgeführte Motivationsliste eher wie eine verwunderte Beschreibung von Männern (die z.B. auch darüber staunen, dass Frauen Auto fahren) liest, ist zu beobachten, dass Frauen vermehrt öffentlich am traditionell männerdominierten Imkern interessiert sind.

---

[6] Ich teile nicht die Definition, geschlechtsspezifische Rollenzuweisung (Frauen als die fürsorglichen Mütter und emotionalen Versorgerinnen der Familie, Männer als die wirtschaftlichen Versorger) sei biologisch/genetisch bedingt. Stattdessen sehe ich diese aus macht- und wirtschaftspolitischen Gründen erwirkt. Über diese Art der Geschlechtsdefinition ist u.a. nachzulesen bei Beauvoir (2018), Lorber (1999) und Butler (2018).

Damit stehen die überalterten Vereine vor der Wahl: Frauen reinlassen oder dem Vereins-Aus entgegenblicken. Warum sich dieses gesundheitsbewusste Lebewesen namens Frau nun aber nicht so einfach in die Vereine integrieren lassen will, ist den meisten Ortsvorständen ein Rätsel.

Zudem prophezeit mir eine – vermutlich männliche Stimme – auf der Website „Wieviel Gleichberechtigung verträgt das Land", dass das Streben von Frauen in die Imkerei wohl nur kurz andauern würde. Diese sei Knochenarbeit, woraus ich schließen muss, sie sei nur von Männern ausführbar:

> Klingt alles ganz wunderbar. Wird aber trotzdem nichts werden [Anmerkung: gemeint ist ein verstärkter Frauenanteil unter den Imkern], denn die Imkerei ist echte Knochenarbeit. (DschinDschin o.J.: o.S.)

Auf internationaler Ebene stelle ich fest, dass es Sprachen gibt, in denen es für Imkerinnen gar keinen Begriff gibt, da es scheinbar noch nie nötig war, eine weibliche Begrifflichkeit herzustellen: „In Russia, beekeeping used to be traditionally men´s specialty (wise old man). Sadly, we have no word (in Russian) for woman-beekeeper" (cerezha 2013: o.S.).

Selbermachen als Ermächtigung – Internetimkern

Wenn ich also zwischen den Vereinsmännern sitze, mich dafür loben lassen muss, dass durch meinen Eintritt der Verein ja nun 'attraktiver' wird und ich lese, dass ich für das Hobby nicht geeignet wäre, frage ich mich schon: Wozu das Interesse am Traditionsimkern? Warum mache ich das?

Und damit begebe ich mich auf die Suche nach neuen Kontakten. Wo sind denn eigentlich die (urbanen) Imkerinnen? Warum wollen diese nicht in Vereine eintreten? Ich begebe mich auf die Suche im Internet und entdecke das, was ich als Internetimkern[7] bezeichne.

Ich finde eine Fülle an Informationen, die über die Imkerei in verschiedenen Formaten (Tutorials auf YouTube, Bastelanleitungen auf Blogs, Erfahrungsberichte in Foren und auch Online-Artikel in Zeitschriften u.v.m. (Flottum 2015) zur Verfügung stehen. Ich entdecke neuen 'Vereinsformate': Neue Initiativen, die sich in den verschiedensten Städten bilden, um stadtimkern/urban beekeeping zu präsentieren. So gibt es seit den 2000er Jahren die New York Bee Association (New York City Beekeepers Association o.J.), die regelmäßig unterhaltsame Weiterbildungskurse anbietet, 'How-to-Do'-Videos erstellt, sehr unterhaltsame Selfies postet und dabei personell sehr divers aufgestellt ist. In einer meiner Recherchen lerne ich, dass New York fest angestellte ImkerInnen in ihrem Police Department hat, die vor allem mit Schwarmfang beschäftig sind (Velez 2015).

Ich entdecke die NGO The BeeGirl Organization – gegründet von Sarah Red-Laird mit der Idee: „[…] to inspire and empower communities to conserve bees and their habitat." (Bee Girl Organisation o.J.: o.S.). Dabei kombiniert die Organisation attraktive

---

[7] Diese Wortschöpfung bezieht sich auf die Möglichkeit, im Internet viel über die Imkerei und ImkerInnen zu erfahren – unabhängig einer Vereinszugehörigkeit.

Konsumprodukte (Base Caps, T-Shirts u.Ä.) mit traditionellen Imkereiprodukten wie Honig, Kerzen etc.

Ich stoße auf weitere tolle Seiten – von städtischen Imkerinitiativen wie Der Stadtimker (IGATE Community - Freier Imkerverband o.J.) bis hin zu HOT BEEKEEPERS: Pick the cutest beekeepers (Emami 2010).

Ich habe viel Spaß daran, auf den Websites zu stöbern und viele nützliche und unnütze Dinge zu lernen. Es motiviert mich unheimlich, von Menschen/Frauen zu lesen, die ungezwungen neue Dinge ausprobieren und offen für Neues, Anderes und Andere sind.

Bei weiterer Internetsuche stoße ich auf das Profil der Historical Honeybee Articles – Beekeeping History (Historical Honeybee Articles - Beekeeping History o.J.). Das ist eine Gruppe von Menschen, die diverse Artikel/Fotos und andere Dokumente von ImkerInnen aus der Vergangenheit zusammensucht und teilt. Dabei liegt der Fokus vermehrt auf Gruppen/Minoritäten, die – wie so oft in der Geschichtsschreibung – nicht als selbstverständlich eigenmächtig handelnd auftauchen. Da ist zum Beispiel das Foto einer Imkerin, die in den 1960er Jahren einen Schwarm von einer Stoßstange eines 1957 AMC Rambler einfängt und dafür einen handelsüblichen Eiskratzer benutzt – Post vom 6. Februar 2014 (ebd.). Oder ein Foto einer Girls Scout Group Anfang des 20. Jahrhunderts, die Mädchen das Imkern näherbringen will – Post vom 13. Februar 2014 (ebd.). Dabei kümmern sich die Mädchen um alles was während der Betreuung eines Bienenvolkes anfällt – was selbst mit Teenager-Mädchen-Knochen zu funktionieren scheint.

Nicht zuletzt tauchen immer wieder Imkerfrauen auf, die für die amerikanische/weltweite Bienenzucht Besonderes geleistet haben. Eine Kategorie, die ich im Deutschen Bienenjournal noch nicht gefunden habe.

Was machen diese Fundstücke mit mir und meiner Einstellung zur Bienenzucht? Ich erinnere mich an die Aufzählung der Motivation des Deutschen Imkerbundes, warum Frauen Bienen halten/züchten wollen und an meine Motivationsgründe. Ich sehe da einen Gegensatz. Es mangelt mir durchaus nicht an sinnvollen Beschäftigungen und für die Naturverbundenheit könnte ich auch im Wald spazieren gehen, um für mein mir als Frau zugewiesenes außerordentliches Gesundheitsbewusstsein Kräuter zu sammeln. Ich hingegen sehe die Gelegenheit, männlich dominierte Bereiche diverser zu gestalten – mich zu 'empowern' und brauche dafür nicht die gnädige Legitimation des Deutschen Imkerbundes e.V., dass Frauen jetzt auch bei der Bienenzucht mitmachen dürfen.

Ich denke, dass Internetimkern von Frauen auch gerade deshalb gern genutzt wird, da wir uns dort einen Ort herstellen können, in dem wir bestimmen können, wer was zu sagen hat und nicht abhängig sind von der Gnade des Vereinsvorsitzenden, ob wir mehr machen dürfen als Protokoll führen und für sämtliche 'flotte Bienenwitze' herzuhalten. Ich werde aber trotzdem weiterhin in den Vereinssitzungen sitzen und mir anhören, dass eine Steigerung des Frauenanteils in den Vereinen innerhalb von 5 Jahren auf 5 Prozent als großer Erfolg gefeiert wird und unter dem Punkt 'Amüsement' am Samstagnachmittag in meine Liste der sinnvollen Freizeitbeschäftigungen aufnehmen.

Vielleicht werde ich in unserer Imkerei zusätzlich ein deutliches optisches Zeichen des Feminismus setzen und Heldinnen vergangener und aktueller Zeit als Orientierungspunkt für die Bienen an den Beuten anbringen anstatt der üblichen Kreise und Linien auf weißem Hintergrund.

Abbildung 1: Der Traum einer jeden feministischen Imkerin – die Heldinnen als Orientierungshilfe für die Bienen (Foto: Christin Sirtl).

Literaturverzeichnis

Bee Girl Organization (2011-2019): Bee Girl. Love Your Bees. [Link: www.beegirl.org; 20.08.2020].

Butler, Judith (2018): Das Unbehagen der Geschlechter. Frankfurt am Main.

Cerezha (2013): Beekeeper demographics - Ratio of male to female keepers. [Link: https://www.beesource.com/forums/showthread.php?286974-Beekeeper-demographics-Ratio-of-male-to-female-keepers; 20.08.2020].

de Beauvoir, Simone (2018): Das andere Geschlecht. Sitte und Sexus der Frau. Reinbek bei Hamburg.

Demling, Alexander (2014): Die Königinnen von Oldenburg. [Link: http://www.spiegel.de/panorama/gesellschaft/hobby-imkerei-auch-frauen-wollen-bienen-zuechten-und-honig-machen-a-966018.html; 20.08.2020].

Deutscher Imkerbund e.V. Aus- und Fortbildung (o.J.): Frauen in der Imkerei [Link: http://www.deutscherimkerbund.de/176-DIB_Nachwuchsfoerderung_Frauen_in_der_Imkerei; 20.08.2020].

Deutscher Imkerbund e.V. (2015): Jahresbericht 2014/2015 des Deutschen Imkerbundes e.V. [Link: http://www.deutscherimkerbund.de/userfiles/DIB_Pressedienst/Jahresbericht_2014-2015.pdf; 20.08.2020].

DschinDschin (2008): Immer weniger Imker. [Link: http://wgvdl.com/forum2/index.php?id=38287; 20.08.2020].

Emami, Gazelle (2010): Hot Beekeepers: Pick the Cutest Beekeeper. [Link: http://www.huffingtonpost.com/2010/01/26/hot-beekeepers-pick-the-c_n_435782.html; 14.03.2017].

Flottum, Kim (2015): DIY Backyard Beekeeping. A Guide for Beginners. [Link: http://www.popularmechanics.com/home/lawn-garden/how-to/g56/diy-backyard-beekeeping-47031701/; 20.08.2020].

Gebhardt, Rolf-Dieter (o.J.): Geschichte unseres Vereins. [Link: http://www.goldene-weisel.de/gwgeschichte.html; 11.03.2017].

Historical Honeybee Articles (o.J.): Beekeeping History. [Link: https://www.facebook.com/Historical.Honeybee.Articles/?fref=ts; 20.08.2020].

IGATE Community (o.J.): Freier Imkerverband. [Link: http://stadtimker.de/; 14.03.2017].

Kehres, Marianne (2008): Frauen imkern. Ein Werbefaltblatt zum Jahr der Frau in der Imkerei. [Link: http://www.diebiene.de/alt/2008-06_Frauen_imkern.pdf; 18.11.2015].

Landwirtschaftliches Wochenblatt (o.J.): Aus Freude am Imkern. [Link: http://www.imkerverband-westfalen-lippe.de/media/Fachbereiche/Oeffentlichkeit/Bilder%20Honigtag/Interview%20Krumme.pdf; 14.03.2017].

Lorber, Judith (1999): Gender-Paradoxien. Wiesbaden.

New York City Beekeepers Association (o.J.): New York City Beekeepers Association. [Link: https://www.facebook.com/pg/NYCBeekeepers/about/?ref=page_internal; 20.08.2020].

Velez, Natasha (2015): Meet the NYPD´s new beekeepers. [Link: http://nypost.com/2015/07/27/meet-the-nypds-new-beekeepers/; 15.11.2015].

Wie man *Harvard* (s)ein Gesicht gibt. *Making up oneself* in Class Album und Scrapbook

von Christiane Lewe

Harvard ist eine der besonders prestigeträchtigen und altehrwürdigen Eliteuniversitäten in den USA. Strenge Auswahlkriterien lassen schon die Zulassung zum Harvard-College zur Auszeichnung werden.[1] Absolvent_innen ist eine glanzvolle Karriere beschieden und viele Wissenschaftler_innen träumen von einer wie auch immer gearteten Assoziierung. Inwieweit wissenschaftliche Güte und Innovationsfähigkeit in Forschung und Lehre, finanzielle Ressourcen oder wissenschaftspolitische Strategien Harvards Exzellenz begründen, soll hier nicht im Mittelpunkt stehen. Ich widme mich in diesem Artikel der Frage, wie Harvard-Studierende auf institutioneller und individueller Ebene zurechtgemacht werden. Wie kommt diese elitäre Menschenriege in die Welt? Was ist zuerst da? Das Elite-College, das dann elitäre Studierende hervorbringt? Oder erlesene Individuen, die erst die Noblesse der Institution begründen? Wird durch den Harvard-Status erst eine gewisse Existenzweise begründet? Oder beweisen die Harvard-Studierenden durch ihren Lebenswandel die Güte der Harvard-Auszeichnung?

[1] Die Zulassungsrate für die Klasse von 2004 beträgt 4,92 % (Fu/ Kim 2020).

Ich entlehne meine Fragerichtung dem bekannt gewordenen Artikel „Making up people“ (Hacking 1999: 165) des Wissenschaftstheoretikers Ian Hacking, der darin dem Realismus/Nominalismus-Problem nachgeht und die Frage verfolgt: Wie kommen „kinds of people“ in die Welt, verstanden als Kategorien und als reale Entitäten? Was ist zuerst da, ein Mensch, der in eine Kategorie passt oder die Kategorie, die den Menschen erst hervorbringt? Welchen Anteil haben die Labels, die Menschen aufgeprägt werden, und welchen Anteil haben die Gelabelten selbst durch ihr Verhalten innerhalb dieser Kategorie? Als Mittelweg schlägt Hacking einen dynamischen Nominalismus vor. Seine These lautet: "The category and the people in it emerged hand in hand" (ebd.: 165). Dabei lässt sich die je spezifische Weise, durch die diese oder jene Person oder Menschengruppe zurechtgemacht wird, durch ein Schema mit zwei Vektoren bestimmen: „One is the vector of labeling from above, from a community of experts who create a 'reality' that some people make their own. Different from this is the vector of the autonomous behavior of the person so labeled, which presses from below, creating a reality every expert must face“ (ebd.: 168). Die "kinds of people", anhand derer Hacking seinen dynamischen Nominalismus exemplarisch vorführt, umfassen solche Kategorien wie "homosexual", "multiple personality" und "garçon de café". Individuen in diesen Kategorien werden zurechtgemacht, haben aber auch selbst Anteil an ihrer Zurechtmachung. Es gibt also sowohl ein Zurechtgemacht-Werden als auch ein Sich-Selbst-Zurechtmachen. Je nach Kategorie und sozialem Setting hat mal der eine, mal der andere Vektor mehr Gewicht. Im historischern Wandel technisch-sozialer Bedingungen emergieren immer wieder neue Kategorien und damit auch "[...] new ways for people to be" (ebd.: 161).

Mir geht es um das mediale Setting dieses dynamischen Nominalismus. Was sind die diskursiv-materiellen Bedingungen? Mich interessieren die Praktiken, Medien und Formate, durch die Individuum und Institution die elitäre Harvard-Persona hervorbringen. Insbesondere nehme ich zwei für die bürgerliche Medienkultur Nordamerikas sehr wichtigen Albenformate in den Blick: das College Yearbook und das Scrapbook. Zwischen diesen beiden Formaten besteht das von Hacking benannte Spannungsverhältnis zweier Vektoren, einer offiziellen Selbstdarstellung der Institution (labeling from above) und der individuellen Selbstartikulation (pressing from below). In dem einen gibt sich die Institution ihr offizielles Gesicht. In dem anderen rahmen und konservieren einzelne Studierende ihre (mehr oder weniger) individuelle Harvard Experience. Es handelt sich jedoch nicht um eine einfache dualistische Gegenüberstellung von disziplinärer Festlegung und ihrer Subversion. Beide sind – wie ich zeigen werde – von vornherein wechselseitig beeinflusst und verschränkt. In der Untersuchung des Scrapbooks wird sich zeigen, dass das Selbermachen nicht notwendig subversiv und dissident, keineswegs endgültig befreiend ist. Vielmehr haben wir es mit variablen Kräfteverhältnissen zu tun, die in einem wechselseitigen Vorgang auf dynamisierende Prozesse wiederum Institutionalisierungen und neue Festlegungen folgen lassen. Anhand eines Beispiels einer Social-

Media-Kampagne von Schwarzen[2] Harvard-Studierenden und People of Color (PoC) aus dem Jahr 2014 zeige ich, wie sich diese reziproke Dynamik zwischen Institutionalisierung und Wiederaneignung aktuell fortsetzt.

Harvard Class Album: Making up Harvard students

Im 17. Jahrhundert von puritanischen Flüchtlingen aus England als Ausbildungsstätte für Geistliche gegründet, ist Harvard von Anfang an eine Institution zur Produktion einer distinguierten Führungselite. Die Absolventen sind (oder vielmehr: werden) prädestiniert für ein Leben in Amt und Würden. Gerade im 18. und 19. Jahrhundert ist Harvard nicht primär ein Ort der Wissenschaft, sondern eine Stätte der bürgerlichen Erziehung, die aus Boys einen exklusiven Kreis von Gentlemen macht und sie in die Kultur und Selbstkultivierung der *weißen* Upper Class einführt (Wright 2004). Bis weit ins 20. Jahrhundert hinein entwirft, produziert und verteidigt sich Harvard als völlig homosoziale, uniforme Gemeinschaft *weißer*, bürgerlicher Männer. Im Jahr 1870 graduiert Richard T. Greener als erster Schwarzer Harvard-Absolvent (Sollors/Titcomb/Underwood 1993: 37-58). Dennoch bleiben

---

[2] Ich halte mich an die Schreibregelung des einschlägigen Bandes zur Rassismus- und Kritischen Weißseinsforschung von Maureen M. Eggers, Grada Kilomba und Peggy Piesche: „Hinsichtlich von *weiß* entschieden wir uns statt der Großschreibung für eine Kursivsetzung, um den Konstruktcharakter markieren zu können und diese Kategorie ganz bewusst von der Bedeutungsebene des Schwarzen Widerstandspotenzials, das von Schwarzen und People of Color dieser Kategorie eingeschrieben worden ist, abzugrenzen“ (Eggers/Kilomba/Piesche 2006: 13).

Schwarze Studierende und Lehrende noch lange die Ausnahme. Spätestens seit dem 20. Jahrhundert formuliert Harvard immer wieder Diversifizierungsziele in der Aufnahmepolitik. In der Aufnahmepraxis werden aber weiterhin *weiße*, protestantische Männer aus der Middle oder Upper Class gegenüber Katholiken, Juden, Frauen oder ethnischen Minderheiten bevorzugt. Erst im Zuge der Bürgerrechtsbewegung ändert sich die Aufnahmepraxis langsam (Synnott 2004). Selbstverständlich haben auch die marginalisierten Personengruppen in der Geschichte Harvards stets eine wichtige Rolle gespielt. Professoren wie Studenten profitierten von der Arbeit Schwarzer Sklav_innen und Hausbediensteter. *Weiße* Frauen hatten als Ehefrauen der Harvard-Männer im Hintergrund ebenfalls eine wichtige, aber marginalisierte Position. Für die Studenten spielten die Upper Class Damsels vor allem als ‚standesgemäße Heiratsoption' eine entscheidende Rolle. Für ihr eigenes Recht auf Bildung mussten Frauen allerdings lange und hart kämpfen. Erst 1975 wurde die Zulassungsbeschränkung für Frauen in Harvard aufgehoben. Bis dahin mussten sich Frauen mit einem faulen Kompromiss abfinden: seit 1894 durften sie im eigenen Radcliffe Frauen-College studieren. Bildung sollte ihnen zwar zugutekommen, aber nicht der Harvard-Abschluss (Schwager 2004). Das außenwirksame Gesicht Harvards sollte offensichtlich weiterhin exklusiv *weiß* und männlich bleiben. Diese Segregation setzt sich bis heute in den Archiven fort. Aus der institutionellen Trennung von Harvard und Radcliffe folgt auch die Unterscheidung der Archive. Radcliffe-Archivalien und damit wesentliche Zeugnisse weiblicher Geschichte in Harvard lagern auch nach der Integration des Frauen-Colleges in das Harvard College fast ausschließlich in der Schlesinger Library, die sich der „History of

Women" widmet, außerhalb des Harvard Yards. Auch das Archiv behandelt Frauen in Harvard als Sonderfall, der nicht Teil der allgemeinen Harvard-Geschichte ist.

Die Harvard University Archives (HUA) verschreiben sich der Mission, Dokumente, Manuskripte, Publikationen und andere Zeugnisse der 380jährigen Geschichte Harvards umfassend zu sammeln, zu organisieren, zu erhalten und zugänglich zu machen. Besucher_innen werden jedoch mit einer bestimmten vorselektierten Geschichtsschreibung konfrontiert. Dies wird noch deutlicher, wenn man die Aufmerksamkeit darauf lenkt, wie das Archiv seinen Besucher_innen entgegentritt. In der Pusey Library auf dem Harvard Yard befindet sich der Reading Room der HUA als Schleuse zwischen unzugänglichem Depot und Öffentlichkeit. Registrierte Besucher_innen können sich auf gezielte Anfragen per Formular freigegebene Archivalien aus dem Depot holen lassen und im Reading Room in Augenschein nehmen. Im Reading Room selbst lagern aber ebenfalls Archivalien, die man ziellos durchstöbern kann, ohne selbst eine gezielte Suchanfrage stellen zu müssen. Wenn für jedes Archiv nicht nur entscheidend ist, was archiviert wird, sondern auch, was zugänglich gemacht wird, dann findet mit dem präsentierten Material im Reading Room eine Selbstartikulation des Archivs statt.[3] Es tritt ein kleines Stück heraus aus dem Dunkel des Depots in die Halböffentlichkeit des Reading Rooms den Besucher_innen entgegen. Das Archiv und damit die Institution, der es zugehört, gibt sich ein Gesicht – in diesem Fall nicht nur im metaphorischen, sondern im ganz buchstäblichen

---

[3] „Das Archiv entscheidet, in welcher Form Geschichte verfügbar ist und was unter Verschluss bleibt" (Ebeling/Günzel 2009: 13).

Sinne: ein signifikanter Anteil des hier präsentieren Materials sind die mitunter auch Facebooks genannten Jahrbücher der Abschlussjahrgänge des Harvard Colleges: Harvard Class Albums.

Abb. 1: Harvard Class Album, Class of 1906, HUD 306.04.5 B RR, Harvard University Archives. S. 135. Links unten: Porträt von Lawrence B. Webster.

Das Class Album ist an sämtlichen nordamerikanischen Bildungseinrichtungen institutionalisiert. Zum jährlichen Commencement Day, an dem die Abschlussjahrgänge ihre Graduierung feiern, erscheint das Class Album als umfangreiches fotografisches Inventar des Colleges: Kern der Alben sind die Porträtfotos der Absolvent_innen, doch auch sämtliche Gesichter vom Freshmen bis zum Senior über Personal, Fassadenporträts relevanter Gebäude, sämtliche Teams, Clubs und Verbindungen bis hin zu Abbildungen von Sport-Events und romantischen Campusansichten ergänzt um Zitate berühmter historischer Harvard-Leitfiguren finden Eingang in diese Kompendien und bündeln sich zu einem alljährlichen Porträt des Harvard Colleges. Jede_r Absolvent_in bekommt ein eigenes Exemplar. Im Lesesaal der Pusey Library kann man sich durch ein ganzes Jahrhundert von Harvard-Gesichtern blättern, die bis in die 1970er Jahre des 20. Jahrhunderts ausschließlich männlich sind. Erst mit dem Class Album der Klasse von 1972 werden die Harvard-Absolventen und Radcliffe-Absolventinnen in einem Album zusammengefügt.

Zur selben Zeit findet die Zusammenführung von Harvard und Radcliffe auch in einem anderen Format statt. Neben den Class Albums stehen im Reading Room auch die Class Reports oder sogenannten Red Books zum Durchstöbern bereit: Für jeden Jahrgang erscheint regelmäßig, anlässlich der Graduierungsjubiläen eine Anthologie von kurzen Biografien der Absolvent_innen. 1973 finden zum zehnjährigen Jubiläum der Abschlussklasse von 1963 schließlich auch die Lebensgeschichten der Radcliffe-Absolventinnen Eingang ins Red Book, die bis dahin eigene Jahrbücher geführt hatten. Auch in anderen Colleges gibt es ähnliche Jahrbücher, diese sind aber zumeist in Aufwand und Umfang sehr viel bescheidener, werden von Freiwilligen und ohne Finanzierung der Hochschule erstellt und nur im privaten Kreis der jeweiligen Klasse publiziert. Harvards Red Book ist dagegen ein aufwändiges, prestigeträchtiges und von der Hochschule finanziertes Programm mit einem ganzen Team vollzeitbeschäftigter Redakteur_innen. In Zusammenarbeit mit freiwilligen Vertreter_innen aus der jeweiligen Klasse fordern sie die Absolvent_innen auf, für den jeweiligen Class Report in Form einer kurzen Ich-Erzählung ihr Leben aufzuschreiben. Erzählt wird von Karrieren, Hochzeiten, Familienstrukturen, Umzügen, Schicksalsschlägen, Krankheiten und Todesfällen. Umfangreiche redaktionelle Arbeit bringt die sehr unterschiedlichen Einreichungen in eine publikationswürdige Form (Smullyan 2007). Die meisten Biografien erzählen Erfolgsgeschichten eines durch Harvard vorgezeichneten Lebens. Doch selbst tragische Geschichten oder Erzählungen vom Scheitern bekommen in der Form der redigierten Lebensgeschichte im Harvard Red Book einen erzählwürdigen und damit bedeutungsvollen Charakter. Das Harvard Red Book monumentalisiert jede einzelne Harvard-Biografie. Neben den Informationen zum Verbleib der Kommiliton_innen findet sich im 25-jährigen Class Report auch ein Porträtverzeichnis. Sofern Absolvent_innen der Aufforderung nachkommen, ein aktuelles Porträtfoto einzuschicken, wird dieses dem alten Porträt aus dem Class Album gegenübergestellt. Die Vorher/Nachher-Bilder zeigen altersgemäße Veränderungen im Erscheinungsbild, allein durch die Gleichförmigkeit der Schwarz-Weiß-Porträts[4] wird jedoch vor allem Kontinuität in der Zeit ins Bild gesetzt: Einmal Harvard, immer Harvard. Das Red Book artikuliert die lebenslange Beständigkeit der Elite. Jedes einzelne Leben an der Spitze der Gesellschaft steht bis zum Tod im Zeichen Harvards.

Eine Medienarchäologie[5] dieser beiden Formate führt in die Aufschreibe- und Diskursivierungswut der Disziplinargesellschaft des 18. und 19. Jahrhunderts, die einschlägig von Walter Seitter untersucht wurde (Seitter 1985). Der Aufbau des modernen Staa-

---

[4] Erst im Class Report zum 50jährigen Jubiläum, also im Rentenalter der Absolvent_innen, sind informelle Schnappschussfotos mit Ehepartner_innen, Familienangehörigen und Freund_innen erlaubt (Smullyan 2007).

[5] Medienarchäologie im Anschluss an Michel Foucault rekonstruiert Wissensformationen, Machtwirkungen und Subjektivierungsweisen anhand ihrer historischen Medien, Techniken, Apparate und Praktiken.

tes in christlich-abendländischen Gesellschaften nach der Reformation geht einher mit der Installierung einer polizeylichen[6] Ordnung und mit der Verallgemeinerung eines Schulwesens, das der Ausbildung guter Staatsbürger dient. „Das Wesen des Staates konzentriert sich in der Selbst-Rekrutierung des Staates, der sich zu diesem Behufe zur Menschen-Erziehungs-Anstalt ausbaut“ (ebd.: 70). Das Schulwesen installiert umfassende Praktiken der Erfassung, Typisierung und Überprüfung von Menschen. Die polizeyliche Ordnung realisiert sich durch statistische Erhebungen sowohl auf der Makroebene der Bevölkerung als auch auf der Mikroebene der Individuen und sorgt an den Schulen und Universitäten für ein ganz neues Bücherwesen: „Hier [..] geht es darum, so viele neue Bücher herzustellen, daß über jeden Schüler, jede Dekurie, jede Klasse, jeden Lehrer, jede Schule usw. Buch geführt werden kann“ (ebd.: 76). Heutige Besucherinnen der HUA können in einer unüberschaubaren Menge von Class Books, Student Records, Secretary's Reports, Freshmen Register etc. Aufzeichnungen aller Art finden. Harley P. Holden, ehemaliger Kurator der Harvard University Archives, bewirbt in einem Aufsatz (Holden 1976) die Fülle von jahrhundertelangen Aufzeichnungen über Studierende in den Harvard-Archiven für Forscher_innen mit unterschiedlichsten Erkenntnisinteressen. Seit Gründung der Universität im frühen

---

[6] Anders als die heutige „Polizei“ bezeichnet „Polizey“ oder „Gute Policey“ zu Beginn der Neuzeit einerseits allgemein die „gute Ordnung“ des Gemeinwesens. Zum anderen wird damit die Gesamtheit einer ganzen Fülle von Gesetzen, Normen, Verwaltungspraktiken und Regulierungsmechanismen benannt, die zur Herstellung und Sicherung dieser guten Ordnung dienen soll und dazu bis tief in die Einzelheiten des alltäglichen Zusammenlebens reicht (Iseli 2009).

17. Jahrhundert liegen zahlreiche Datensätze vor, die sich auf Einzelpersonen beziehen. In den 1720ern formiert sich in Harvard eine Kommission, die die Leistungen und Verfehlungen der Studenten individuell diskutiert und protokolliert. Im frühen 19. Jahrhundert werden die Informationen für jeden einzelnen Studenten noch zahlreicher und detaillierter: Aufzeichnungen über Abwesenheit von Vorlesungen, belegte Kurse, Disziplinarmaßnahmen, Prüfungen, Abwesenheit beim täglichen Gebet usw. In der ersten Hälfte des 20. Jahrhunderts erweitern sich die bereits für die Einschreibung ermittelten Datensätze stufenweise noch einmal deutlich, sie umfassen nun ein detailliertes Protokoll der gesamten Kindheit und Jugend jedes Studenten bis zum Alter von 20 Jahren.[7] Im Laufe ihrer Harvard-Jahre sammeln sich in ihren Akten alle erdenklichen Informationen an. Es sind ganze Biografien, die vollständig vor dem Hintergrund der Harvard-Zugehörigkeit entstehen: Harvard-Biografien. "On the first two decades of the subjects' lives, most of the detail in them is based on Harvard student records" (ebd.: 464). Die Datensätze in der individuellen Akte machen Harvard zum Schicksal des Individuums. Rückwirkend qualifiziert sich sein Wesen von Geburt an als Harvard-Mitglied. Die

---

[7] "The typical Harvard folder over this period [..] contains an application form with date and place of birth; citizenship; father's and mother's names, place of birth, nationality, education, an occupation; parent's marital status; school attended by applicant; extracurricular activities; list of offices held; honors received; teams played on; names of persons recommending applicant; essays on why applicant wants to go to College and why to Harvard; a photograph; and the applicant's autograph. [...] Also in the folder are generally found the applicant's secondary-school transcript, a report on health, College semester grade reports, applications for house assignment, administrative board reports on academic status, and details of various College encounters and experiences such as probation and leaves of absence" (Holden 1976: 462f).

Akte konstituiert den Studenten schon lange vor seinem freshmen year und entlässt ihn als elitären Absolventen mit vielversprechender Zukunft, die ebenfalls fortlaufend dokumentiert wird: ein ganzes Leben unter dem Zeichen Harvards. So stellt Holden auch immer wieder die Ergiebigkeit der Akten besonders nobler Harvardianer heraus, deren Biografien immer schon im Zeichen des Erfolgs und im Zeichen Harvards stehen: John Adams, John Hancock, Theodore Roosevelt, T. S. Eliot, John F. Kennedy, Henry Kissinger uvm. (ebd.: 463f).

Folglich ist „Making up Harvard Students" nicht zuletzt eine Praxis der Buchführung in einer Disziplinarinstitution. In einer „Einheit von Erfassung und Belehrung" (Seitter 1985: 80) werden elitäre Staatsbürger herangezogen und schriftlich auf ihre Identität festgelegt. Class Album und Red Book sind öffentlichkeitswirksame Kulminationen dieser Dokumentationswut studentischen Lebens und Monumentalisierungen der Harvard-Existenzen. In diesen Bänden findet sich die Essenz, die auch Holden von Historiker_innen aus seinem Archiv destilliert wissen will: im Red Book die glorreichen Biografien von zum Erfolg prädestinierten Harvard-Absolvent_innen, im Class Album ein Inventar nobler Physiognomien, denen man die Exzellenz im Gesicht ansehen soll.

Letzteres führt auf einer weiteren medienarchäologischen Spur in die bürgerliche Medienkultur, die mit dem Aufkommen der Fotografie Mitte des 19. Jahrhunderts ihre Vorliebe für reproduzierbare Porträtfotos für sich entdeckt. Insbesondere in den USA fällt die Verbreitung der Porträtfotografie mit einer großen Popularität von Physiognomik und Phrenologie zusammen. Nach Überzeugung des physiognomischen bzw. phrenologischen Paradigmas lässt sich das wahre Wesen von Einzelmenschen oder

Menschengruppen, ihre intellektuellen und moralischen Vermögen und Mängel an ihren Gesichtern (Physiognomik) bzw. an ihren Kopfformen (Phrenologie) ablesen. Die fotografische Technik, verstanden als Wahrheitswerkzeug, mittels dem sich die Natur selbst auf der Fotoplatte einschreibt, (Talbot 1844) alliert sich bestens mit dem physiognomischen Paradigma und wird zu einem wichtigen Medium in dem Verfahren, das Hacking „Making up people" nennt. Das Bildprivileg, das vormals nur wenigen, herausragenden Figuren ihr eigenes Bildnis zugestand, wird durch die reproduzierbare Porträtfotografie radikal demokratisiert. Jede_r hat von nun an ein Bild von sich. Mit der kostengünstigen Reproduzierbarkeit von Fotografien gewinnen die sogenannten cartes de visite an Popularität. Diese kleinformatigen, schlichten Porträtfotografien kommen zunächst in Europa, dann auch in den USA in Mode. In den 1870ern sind die cartes-de-visite-Alben bereits eine feste Institution unter amerikanischen Sammelleidenschaften (Decker 2010: 109ff). Zum einen verbreiten sie sich klassenübergreifend – ähnlich den heutigen Visitenkarten – als privates, individuelles Identitätspapier, das man mit anderen teilen kann. Dies spielt vor allem für die Artikulation von familiären, freund- oder kameradschaftlichen Beziehungen eine wichtige Rolle. Zum anderen haben die Bildchen von Prominenten und Würdenträgern als Sammlerstücke großen kommerziellen Erfolg (Siegel 2010). Hier zieht sich – wie Allan Sekula gezeigt hat – in die demokratisierte Bildpraxis eine neue Hierarchie ein, die die Menschen erneut in Über- und Unterlegene einteilt und ihnen ihren Status fotografisch ins Gesicht einschreibt. „Every portrait implicitly took its place within a social and moral hierarchy. The private moment of sentimental individuation, the look at the frozen gaze-of-the-loved-one, was shadowed by two other more public looks: a look up, at one's 'betters', and a look down, at one's 'inferiors'" (Sekula 1986: 10). Die Porträtfotografie funktioniert einerseits nobilitierend, z.B. in den Harvard Class Albums, die kultivierte, gelehrte Physiognomien der Harvard-Absolventen zeigen. Andererseits funktioniert sie repressiv wie in der Kriminologie oder Forensik, die die systematische Porträtfotografie zur Vermessung, Klassifikation, Identifizierung und buchstäblichen Fest-Stellung der „Abweichenden" nutzt. In diesem physiognomischen Raster hat jedes Facebook in den Harvard University Archives also ein Äquivalent in der Form eines Mugbook[8] im Polizeiarchiv: „[...] every proper portrait has its lurking, objectifying inverse in the files of the police" (ebd.: 7). Besonders in den USA hat sich die Bertillonage, die standardisierte, anthropometrische Porträtfotografie von Festgenommenen nach dem Verfahren des französischen Kriminalisten Alphonse Bertillon, flächendeckend durchgesetzt, sodass der Mugshot zu einer Ikone der visuellen Kultur Nordamerikas wurde.[9] Der fotografischen Erfassungswut der Polizei entspricht spiegelbildlich die fotografische Sammelwut von noblen Porträts in den Salons der Middle und Upper Class. Polizeiarchiv und bür-

---

[8] Das Wort mug umfasst im Englischen viele verschiedene Bedeutungen: Becher oder Krug, aber auch Fresse, Visage, Trottel, Schurke; als Verb: ausrauben, überfallen und auch fotografieren. Als Mugbook wird bis heute ein Album mit mugshots bezeichnet, das Augenzeugen zur Identifikation von Verdächtigen vorgelegt wird. Mugshots sind Porträtfotos von Festgenommenen, die von der Polizei systematisch angefertigt und archiviert werden (McAllister 2014).

[9] Einen besonderen Reiz entfalten Mugshots, wenn in ihnen die noblen und die infamen Physiognomien in eins fallen – wie bei Mugshots von Prominenten oder bei Straftätern, die berühmt werden (Pellicer 2009).

gerliche Fotoalben bilden ein doppeltes physiognomisches, hierarchisches Archiv: „The general, all-inclusive archive necessarily contains both the traces of the visible bodies of heroes, leaders, moral exemplars, celebrities, and those of the poor, the diseased, the insane, the criminal, the nonwhite, the female, and all other embodiments of the unworthy“ (ebd.: 10). Wie Elizabeth Siegel deutlich macht, nimmt die Album-Praxis in den USA noch mehr als in Europa eine wichtige Funktion gegen transformierende Kräfte und prekäre soziale Zustände ein. Eine noch junge Demokratie, eine von Migration geprägte Bevölkerung und die Unruhen durch den Civil War befeuern den Drang nach visuell-materieller Fixierung des Selbst und der Nächsten. Eine breite Mittelschicht, die sich zwischen Gefahr des Abstiegs und Chance des Aufstiegs in dauernder sozialer Mobilität befindet, vergewissert sich im Fotoalbum permanent des eigenen sozialen Status zwischen „one's 'betters'“ und „one's 'inferiors“ (ebd.: 10; Siegel 2010: 4). Das gilt nicht minder für die Upper Class Gentlemen, die sich durch ihren Platz in den Reihen der noblen Harvard-Porträts ihrer sozialen Position vergewissern.

Hier tangieren wir bereits den Bereich des album-keeping als Praktik des Sich-Selbst-Zurechtmachens. Tatsächlich haben sich die bürgerlichen Fotoalben und die institutionellen College Yearbooks aus einem sehr viel ungezähmteren, individuellen DIY-Format entwickelt: Ein Vorläufer und wichtiger Protagonist in der Genealogie des Class Albums ist das Einklebealbum oder Scrapbook und damit verbundene Praktiken des Selbst.

Scrapbook: Sich selbst zurechtmachen

Die Harvard University Archives halten weitere Alben bereit, die sich allerdings etwas zu chaotisch, etwas zu launisch geben und zu schwer zu fassen sind, um im Reading Room ausgestellt zu werden. Sie lagern daher im Depot und werden nur auf gezielte Anfrage hervorgeholt. Es sind Zeugnisse der Harvard-Studierenden, die der polierten Fassade Harvards noch einen anderen Anstrich geben.

Lawrence Burns Webster[10], Harvard-Student in der Abschlussklasse von 1906, hat wie viele seiner Kommilitonen und andere bürgerliche Amerikaner_innen seine Zeit im College mit einem persönlichen Scrapbook begleitet. Darin bewahrt er alle möglichen Schnipsel einer Massenprint-Kultur auf, die sich zwischen zwei Buchdeckeln unterbringen lassen. Sammelnd und kuratierend dokumentiert er seine Harvard Experience: von Zeitungsausschnitten, über Eintrittskarten, Notizen, Postkarten, Fotos bis hin zu nur schwer identifizierbaren Papierschnipseln findet sich alles Mögliche, was dem Autor irgendwann einmal bewahrenswert erschien. Auch dieses Album porträtiert ein Leben im Zeichen Harvards, auch dieses Album trägt in goldenen Lettern den Namen der Hochschule. Das Scrapbook hat aber eine andere, sehr viel chaotischere Ästhetik als das aufgeräumte Class Album. Es erzählt auch andere Geschichten.

[10] Siehe Abb. 1, sein Porträt und seine Vita sind unten links.

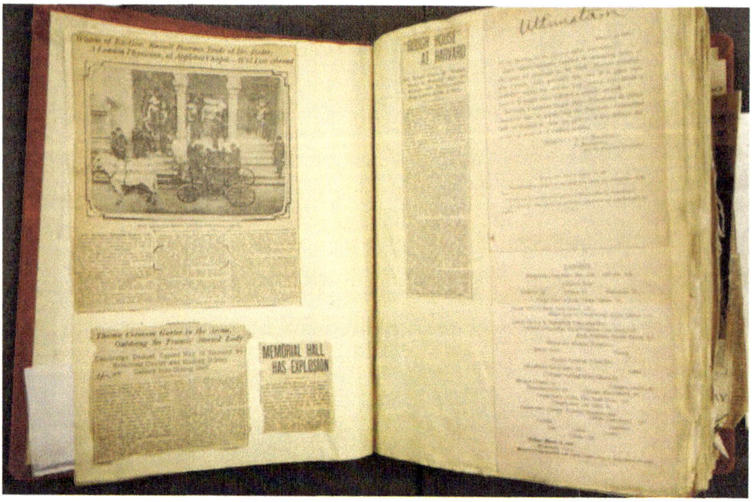

Abb. 2: Scrapbook of Lawrence Burns Webster, Class of 1906, HUD 902.93 Box 1, Harvard University Archives.

Auf einer Seite (Abb. 2) hat Webster z.B. ein paar interessante Zeitungsartikel eingeklebt, die ein anderes Bild der Upper Class Gentlemen zeichnen: In all diesen Artikeln ist von Streichen und Tumulten in der Memorial Hall die Rede, wo die Studenten ihr Abendessen einnehmen. In einem Artikel (handschriftlich datiert mit „April '04") wird von einem „hübschen Fräulein" berichtet, das einen Aufruhr in der Memorial Hall verursacht, weil sie ihr Strumpfband von der Galerie herunter in die Menge junger Studenten wirft, die da gerade zu Abend isst. Im Artikel heißt es: „[...] it looked for a while as though there was going to be a wrecked dining hall to tell from this visitation." Im Artikel daneben ist von einer Explosion in der Memorial Hall – ebenfalls zur Abendessenszeit – die Rede, verursacht durch einen Böller, der zwar keinen Schaden anrichtet, aber so viel Staub und Ruß aufwirbelt, dass das Essen ausgetauscht werden muss. Ein weiterer Artikel berichtet von einem Ereignis ein Jahr später: „Memorial Hall at Harvard last night saw its annual rough house. The occasion was the usual one – a balcony full of girls, with one a trifle more venturesome than the rest, a flower thrown from the balcony to the tables below, and then pandemonium.“ Es mündet in einer Essenschlacht. Der letzte Absatz wirft schließlich noch einmal ein anderes Bild auf den Tumult ein Jahr zuvor: „It was about a year ago that a freshman disguised as a girl, created a hubbub by taking of „her“ garter and throwing it from the balcony. The event this year was somewhat tamer.“ Und daneben schließlich eine Mitteilung des Executive Commitee, handschriftlich mit „Ultimatum“ überschrieben, in der die Schäden durch die Essenschlacht aufgeführt und die Schließung der Galerie für Besucher angedroht wird. Studierende werden auf ihre Pflicht hingewiesen, die Regeln in der Dining Hall einzuhalten, z.B. nicht mit Essen zu werfen.

Scrapbooks sind sehr heterogene Quellen (Helfand 2008). Das Sammeln und das Kuratieren stehen im Vordergrund, nicht das Erzählen oder eine narrative Kohärenz. Sie folgen einer nur schwer zu durchschauenden Ordnung, nicht selten sind es chaotische Konvolute unterschiedlichster Schnipsel: z. B. getrocknete Blumen, Fahrkarten, Kinotickets, Haarlocken, Briefe, Postkarten, Stofffetzen, Sammelbildchen, Geldscheine, Visitenkarten, Werbeanzeigen und allerlei unterschiedlichste Fund- und Erinnerungsstücke. Diese werden mal mehr, mal weniger kunstvoll arrangiert, manchmal schriftlich kommentiert oder durch Zeichnungen ergänzt. Ebenso heterogen wie die Materialien sind die Themen oder thematischen Rahmen dieser Sammlungen. Das sind z. B. bestimmte Sammelinteressen, erinnerungswürdige Ereignisse, Hobbys, Reisedokumentationen, Lebensabschnitte oder freundschaftliche Korrespondenzen, die im Scrapbook festgehalten werden. Nicht immer sind Autoren und Zeitspannen klar identifizierbar.[11] Deshalb sind die Kompendien für Archivar_innen und Historiker_innen manchmal schwer handhabbar. Ihre Inhalte sind chaotisch, diskontinuierlich und entziehen sich einfachen Deutungen. Wir wissen nicht, ob Lawrence B. Webster an all diesen Tumulten beteiligt war, ob er vielleicht sogar der Freshman in Drag war, der das Strumpfband warf. Wir wissen nicht, ob er vielleicht empört war über das ungehobelte Verhalten seiner Kommilitonen oder ob es ihn amüsierte und er an vorderster Front mitmischte. Sicher ist nur, dass er diese Artikel, die in einer Cambridger Zeitung erschienen, in seinem persönlichen Harvard-Scrapbook aufbewahrt hat. Sie sind in irgendeiner Weise Teil seiner Harvard Experience, setzen einen Kontrapunkt zur Ordnung, Etikette und Disziplin der Class Albums und überschreiten auch mal deren rigide Geschlechtersegregation.[12] Während die Harvard Class Albums die zukünftige Führungsriege ernsthaft und würdevoll ins Bild setzen, suggerieren manche Geschichten, die sich aus Scrapbooks destillieren lassen einen Blick hinter die wohlgeordneten Kulissen. Doch es wäre

[11] Typisch für solche College Scrapbooks sind die leeren Seiten am Ende. Das deutet darauf hin, dass das Album nicht erst nachträglich in Erinnerung an die Schulzeit und für die Augen anderer angelegt wurde. Vielmehr ist das Scrapbook eine Art Logbuch für Ereignisse, die sich als materielle Sammelstücke manifestieren und in Erinnerungsschichten sedimentieren. Unvermittelt hört das Sammeln dann irgendwann auf, wenn die Ereignisse der College-Jahre ein Ende finden.

[12] Für Harvard-Männer wie für Radcliffe-Frauen gelten lange Zeit rigide Kleidervorschriften. Auf beiden Seiten werden diese Vorschriften – vor allem in Theateraufführungen – immer wieder durch Cross-Dressing überschritten (McElheny 2004; Lepri 2004).

falsch, zu unterstellen, man fände in Scrapbooks wahrere Geschichten, die die polierte Oberfläche der Class Albums als bloß scheinhaft entlarven. Es gilt vielmehr zu beleuchten, wie sich in Scrapbooks und Class Albums die Harvard-Studenten auf unterschiedliche Weise entwerfen und zurechtmachen. Das eine ist nicht weniger wirklich als das andere.

Seit dem Ende des 18. Jahrhunderts ist das Scrapbook-Führen in den USA gängige und sehr verbreitete Praxis. Es geht einher mit der Entwicklung neuer Drucktechnologien (z.B. Chromolithografie) und der Verbreitung günstiger und massenhafter Farbdruckerzeugnisse, die – hatten sie ihren eigentlichen Zweck (Information, Werbung, Verpackung etc.) einmal erfüllt – entweder im Mülleimer oder im Scrapbook landen.[13] Für Schüler_innen und Studierende ist das Scrapbook ein nahezu obligatorischer Begleiter ihrer Zeit in Schule und Universität. Sie bilden ein informelles Pendant zu den autoritativen Aufzeichnungen über sie in den Verzeichnissen der Schuladministration. Als Gegenarchive erlauben sie den Individuen Anteil an der Erfindung ihres Selbst. Sie bilden eine Technik zur Konstituierung des Selbst[14] in deutlicher Abgrenzung

---

[13] Natürlich entsteht auch sofort ein Markt für die Scrapbook-Leidenschaft: "As caches for the booty of capitalism, scrapbooks fit seamlessly into the rituals of consumption [...]" (Ott/Tucker/Buckler 2006: 10).

[14] Im Sinne Foucaults lässt sich das Scrapbook als Technik des Selbst bezeichnen. In einem kleinen Text analysiert Foucault sogar antike Verwandte des Scrapbooks – die hypomnêmata: private Notizbücher, in denen Zitate und Textauszüge aus Büchern gesammelt, Erlebnisse verschriftlicht, Reflexionen und Gedanken festgehalten wurden. „Sie sind keine Selbstdarstellung. [...] Es geht nicht darum, dem Unsagbaren nachzugehen, Verborgenes zu enthüllen, das Ungesagte zu sagen, sondern darum, bereits Gesagtes festzuhalten, Gehörtes oder Gelesenes zu sammeln, und das zu einem Zweck, der nichts Geringeres ist als die Konstituierung des Selbst" (Foucault 2007: 141).

zu christlicher Bekenntnisliteratur und autobiografischen Subjektivierungsstechniken. Ein Scrapbook ist kein Tagebuch, das in kohärenter Narration die Innerlichkeiten der Seele aufdeckt. Es bildet nichts Verdecktes oder Vergangenes mittels vorhandenen visuellen Materials ab. Es repräsentiert nichts, was schon dagewesen wäre. Scrapbooks bedienen genau die entgegengesetzte Bewegung. In einem Strom massenhafter, ephemerer Druckerzeugnisse bilden sie materielle Gerinnungspunkte, durch die sich das Selbst manifestiert. Dieser Bastelprozess kommt zu keinem Ende, hält daher stets Möglichkeiten des Anderswerdens bereit. Die Arbeit am Scrapbook ist die unendliche Arbeit an sich selbst, ein stetes Sich-Selbst-Zurechtmachen. Und so folgt ein Scrapbook auf das andere, mit ihnen wandelt sich das Subjekt. Das Selbst besteht in diesem fragilen Gleichgewicht zwischen Dauer und Fluidität (Ott/Tucker/Buckler 2006: 25).

Auf Gegenerzählung folgt Re-Institutionalisierung

Scrapbooks haben die Potentialität eines Gegenarchivs. Deutlich existenziellere Beispiele als die Einklebealben ungezogener Studenten sind die alternativen Geschichtsschreibungen in den Scrapbooks von Afro-Amerikaner_innen, die Ellen Gruber Garvey untersucht hat (Garvey 2013). Als Korrektiv zur *weiß*gewaschenen Geschichtsschreibung sammeln Schwarze Amerikaner_innen Zeitungsartikel aus der *weißen* wie Schwarzen Presse, um 1.) die rassistische Unterdrückung und Misshandlungen sowie deren nicht minder rassistische Berichterstattung festzuhalten, 2.) die Rolle von Schwarzen als aktive Agenten in der Geschichte zu dokumentieren und auf diese Weise 3.) Schwarze Vorbilder und ein Schwarzes Selbstbewusstsein als soziale Gruppe zu generieren. *Weiße* Presse wurde so gegen den Strich gelesen und für eine eigene Schwarze Geschichtsschreibung instrumentalisiert. Scrapbooks ermöglichen entgegen der Hegemonie rassistischer Verzeichnung durch dominante *weiße* Diskurse eine eigene Schwarze Selbstkonstituierung jenseits diffamierender Stereotype.

Doch Scrapbooks sind nicht notwendig widerspenstig oder subversiv. Das legt der Vergleich der Black Scrapbooks mit den studentischen Harvard-Scrapbooks nahe: Die meisten, die man in den Harvard Archives findet, sind ausgesprochen gleichförmig und linientreu.[15] Strebsam und gewissenhaft in perfekter Verinnerlichung der Disziplin führen die Studenten darin Buch über ihre Leistungen, sammeln Examensergebnisse und Sporterfolge, entwerfen sich selbst als future leaders und noble gentlemen – so auch Lawrence Burns Webster. Seinem Scrapbook kann man nicht nur den Unfug in der Dining Hall entnehmen, sondern auch seine völlig kongruente Identifizierung mit Harvard, die sich z.B. in dem Sammeln von Zeitungsartikeln über Sporterfolge der Harvard-Teams äußert. Scrapbooks haben nicht nur ein widerspenstiges Potential, sondern auch ein erzieherisches. Im 19. Jahrhundert fand dieses Format auch stark Eingang in das Curriculum in Kindergärten und Schulen. Das Scrapbooking erwies sich als perfektes Instrument, Kindern das fokussierte Stillarbeiten beizubringen und sie dadurch zu ordentlichen Bürgern zu machen. Überdies ließen

---

[15] Hier greift natürlich auch wieder die Politik des Archivs, das entscheidet, was bewahrenswürdig ist und auch zugänglich gemacht wird.

sich über die Sammelinhalte bestimmte Werte vermitteln, Moralvorstellungen verinnerlichen und Geschlechterrollen einüben (Ott/Tucker/Buckler 2006: 9). Hier nutzt also wiederum ein staatliches Erziehungssystem eine ganz individuelle Selbsttechnik, um nützliche Staatsbürger_innen hervorzubringen.

Parallel zu seinem Scrapbook führt Webster auch ein kleines Fotoalbum, in dem er sorgsam beschriftete Schnappschüsse vom Campus, von seinem Wohnheimzimmer, von sich selbst beim gewissenhaften Studium, von Kommilitonen und Freunden, von seinen Clubs und von Sportereignissen bis hin zum Tag der Graduierung sammelt. Es ist zwar ein eher informelles Inventar für private Zwecke, doch dem Class Album sehr ähnlich: Es fixiert eine freundschaftliche Gemeinschaft gebildeter und kultivierter junger Männer, deren Verbundenheit von der Institution begründet und gerahmt wird. Und so trägt auch dieses Album die Aufschrift „Harvard Pictures".

Die Zugehörigkeit zur Kategorie Harvard-Student wird Webster also nicht nur disziplinär von oben aufgebürdet, sondern von ihm selbst mitgetragen: Class Book[16] und Scrapbook arbeiten Hand in Hand am Zurechtmachen der Harvard-Persona. Tatsächlich entsteht das erste Class Album – lange vor der ersten offiziellen Publikation durch das College selbst – gewissermaßen als DIY-Initiative der Klasse von 1852 an der Schnittstelle zwischen

16 Das Class Book ist ein vom Klassensekretär offiziell geführtes Register über jeden einzelnen Studenten und über Aktivitäten der Klasse auch nach der Graduierung.

Buchführung und Freundschaftsalbum.[17] Die jungen Männer wollen ihrer elitären, freundschaftlichen Gemeinschaft mit Hilfe der damals brandneuen fotografischen Technik eine materielle Form geben bevor sie das College verlassen und getrennte Wege gehen. Im Bostoner Studio des Fotografen John Adams Whipple werden Daguerreotypien angefertigt und im Salzdruckverfahren vervielfältigt. Sie lassen sich Alben mit allen Porträts anfertigen oder kleben die Aufnahmen in ihre persönlichen Freundschaftsalben, Notizhefte, Scrapbooks. Das Bewahren der elitären Gemeinschaft erfolgreicher Harvardianer nach der Graduierung gestalten die Studenten selbst. Doch die Schuladministration weiß die gut eingeübten Praktiken der Selbstdokumentation schnell aufzugreifen und für die Dokumentation ihrer Schützlinge zu nutzen. Die Salzdrucke der Klasse von 1852 finden sich schließlich auch in sämtlichen

---

[17] Scrapbook und Class Album haben einen signifikanten gemeinsamen Vorläufer im sogenannten Stammbuch oder Album Amicorum, das als Netzwerk- und Freundschaftsmedium seit dem 16. Jahrhundert in Europa vor allem in protestantischen und akademischen, aber auch aristokratischen Milieus zum Sammeln wichtiger sozialer Kontakte verbreitet ist. Albenbesitzer lassen sich von wichtigen Bekanntschaften, die sie an entfernten Orten treffen, etwas „ins Stammbuch schreiben“, darunter auch die Unterschrift mit Herkunft und sozialem Status des Schreibers. In der Struktur des protestantisch-akademischen Stammbuchs lassen sich Parallelen zum Class Album (und auch zum Class Report) klar erkennen: Für beide ist das Festhalten unter Bedingungen starker Mobilität wichtig. In beiden geht es um den Anschluss an einflussreiche Persönlichkeiten, die in den Alben in hierarchischer Reihenfolge angeordnet werden (so beginnt auch das Class Album oft mit einem Porträt des Gouverneurs, darauf folgt das akademische Personal, dann erst erscheinen die Porträts der Studierenden). Wie in den Class Reports werden in Stammbüchern oft kurze biografische Ergänzungen zum Schicksal und Verbleib der gesammelten Personen, vor allem engerer Freunde vorgenommen. Das Stammbuch darf auf jeden Fall als Social-Network-Medium gelten. Mit dem Scrapbook verbindet es das sammelnde Interesse und die gelegentliche Praxis, auch materielle Objekte (z.B. Haarlocken) als Zeichen der Verbundenheit darin zu bewahren (Schnabel 2013).

Formaten, die zum Verwaltungsarsenal der College-Administration gehören. Die Buchführung über jeden Studenten in den Class Books wird um das ID-Foto ergänzt. Das neue Medium der Fotografie, durch das sich die Studenten als freundschaftlich verbundene Elite entwerfen, eignet sich die Administration schnell an. Gegen Ende des Jahrhunderts macht sich die Harvard-Institution das Format des Class Albums völlig zu eigen und publiziert 1898 zum ersten Mal ein offizielles Class Album. So wird eine DIY-Initiative stückweise zu einer institutionalisierten Bildpolitik der Disziplinarinstitution.

Doch auch damit endet der reziproke Vorgang zwischen Dynamisierung und Institutionalisierung nicht. 2004 entwickelt Mark Zuckerberg zusammen mit ein paar Kommilitonen in einem Harvard-Studierendenwohnheim das Social Network Facebook (Kirkpatrick 2011: 20-44). Es steht zunächst nur Harvard-Studierenden offen und ist in seiner Funktionsweise einem College-Freundschaftsalbum nicht unähnlich. Für die Studierenden, die sich dort registrieren, hat die Möglichkeit, sich dort mit einem selbstgewählten Profilfoto online zu präsentieren etwas Emanzipatorisches. Sie erleben es als Befreiung, sich endlich selbst ein (semi-)öffentliches Bild zu geben, statt in den (mittlerweile auch online verfügbaren) Porträtverzeichnissen der Collegeadministration auf ein einziges ID-Bild festgelegt zu sein.[18] Doch auch aus

[18] "Clicking away late one night I couldn't help thinking how different these images were to those that would fill an official facebook, filled with Harvard ID photos resembling deer in headlights, stunned squirrels and other expressions of terrified confusion caught on film amidst the chaos of freshman week. Instead, the thefacebook.com scene includes reams of carefully coiffed, immaculately manicured, evening-garbed Harvard students grinning eagerly

Facebook, dem DIY-Online-Verzeichnis, das sich ein Stück weit der institutionellen Verzeichnung widersetzt, wird nach und nach eine Institution, die sich durch überaus angepasste Selbstpräsentationen auszeichnet. Durch eine auf Affirmation („Like“) setzende Struktur und eine an bedeutsamen „Lebensereignissen“ orientierte lineare Timeline setzt Facebook das Selbsterzählen von gelingenden Biografien und das Selbst-Zurechtmachen einer erfolgreichen Persona fort, das in College-Formaten wie dem Scrapbook, dem Class Album und dem Class Report bereits eingeübt wurde.[19]

I, too, am Harvard.

Das Wechselspiel von Institutionalisierung und Dynamisierung setzt sich also aktuell im Social Web fort. Im Frühjahr 2014 startete eine Gruppe Schwarzer Harvard-Studierender eine Social-Media-Kampagne, um auf den alltäglichen Rassismus an der Elite-Universität aufmerksam zu machen.[20] Unter dem Titel „I, too, am Harvard“ sammelten sie auf einem Tumblog Porträtfotos von Schwarzen Harvard-Studierenden. Sie halten alle eine Tafel in Händen, auf denen sie sich mit eigenen Statements zu Erfahrungen als Schwarze Harvard-Studierende äußern, auf rassistische Stereotype antworten oder diskriminierende Kommentare zitieren, mit

---

on page after page as we present our own ideal image of selfhood to fellow browsers" (Lester 2004).

[19] Mit einer medienarchäologischen Vorgeschichte von Social Network Media wie Facebook beschäftige ich mich in meiner Dissertation: „Subjects in facebooks. Eine Genealogie facialer Social-Network-Praktiken“.

[20] Die Kampagne wurde inspiriert durch ein gleichnamiges Theaterstück, das am 7. März 2014 auf dem Harvard-Campus uraufgeführt wurde.

denen sie konfrontiert wurden (Abb. 3). Die Kampagne war im Internet sehr erfolgreich und wurde auch von anderen Universitäten aufgegriffen (Horan 2014a).

Die Harvard-Administration bemüht sich seit Jahren durch verschiedene Programme um die Diversifizierung der Studierendenschaft. Mit fast 15% entspricht der Anteil Schwarzer Studierender in Harvard etwa dem Anteil von Afro-Amerikaner:innen an der US-amerikanischen Gesamtbevölkerung. Doch die Kampagne zeigt, dass die Erfahrung von Schwarzen Studierenden auf dem Campus weiterhin durch ausschließende Erlebnisse getrübt ist. "I go to Harvard, but I don't really feel *of* Harvard" (Bean 2014), so äußert sich eine Studentin in einem kurzen Video zur Kampagne. Eine ganze Reihe von den auf den Tafeln festgehalten Äußerungen zeigt, dass immer wieder eine Unvereinbarkeit von Harvard-Zugehörigkeit und Schwarzsein unterstellt und erfahren wird.[21] In solchen Äußerungen setzt sich Harvards jahrhundertelange Geschichte des rassistischen Ausschlusses von Nicht-*Weißen* fort.

I, too, am Harvard nutzt die fotografische Praktik des „Sign Holding", die als Form des Internet-Aktivismus seit etwa 2011 üblich geworden ist. Dabei teilen User_innen Porträts von sich, in denen sie eine Tafel mit einem Statement halten. Geteilt wird das Bild auf verschiedenen Social-Network-Plattformen unter einem designierten Hashtag.

---

[21] Einige Botschaften auf den abgebildeten Tafeln: "You're basically white"; "You don't sound black, you sound smart"; "You're really articulate for a black girl"; "You're the whitest black person I know"; "I don't even think of you as black" (I, Too Am Harvard 2014).

Abb. 3: I, too, am Harvard, tumblr 2014.

Diese Form wurde bereits für viele verschiedene politische Kampagnen genutzt, darunter z.B. eine Feminismus-Kampagne („I need feminism because...“) oder eine Kampagne gegen stereotype Kostümierung als bestimmte „Ethnie“ oder „Kultur“ („We are a Culture, not a Costume“), bei der Angehörige einer ethnischen Gruppe ein Bild eines entsprechenden stereotypen Kostüms in Händen halten (Horan 2014a). Die Bildkomposition reproduziert dabei das physiognomische Paradigma. In Korrespondenz mit den Informationen auf dem Schild, werden Betrachtende dazu angehalten, das Gesicht physiognomisch zu lesen: So sieht ein_e Feminist_in aus; so sieht eine Angehörige einer bestimmten ethnischen Gruppe aus; so sieht eine Schwarze Harvard-Studentin aus. Dies ist ein medialer Effekt des fotografischen Formats: Die Frontalporträts entsprechen der Bildkomposition von Mugshots (Abb. 4). In der ikonografischen Tradition von autoritativer Porträtfotografie zu Zwecken der polizeilichen Identifizierung und forensischen Typologisierung machen sich hier Individuen selbst zurecht als „kind of people“ – Feminist_innen, Afro-Amerikaner_innen, Schwarze Harvard-Studierende.

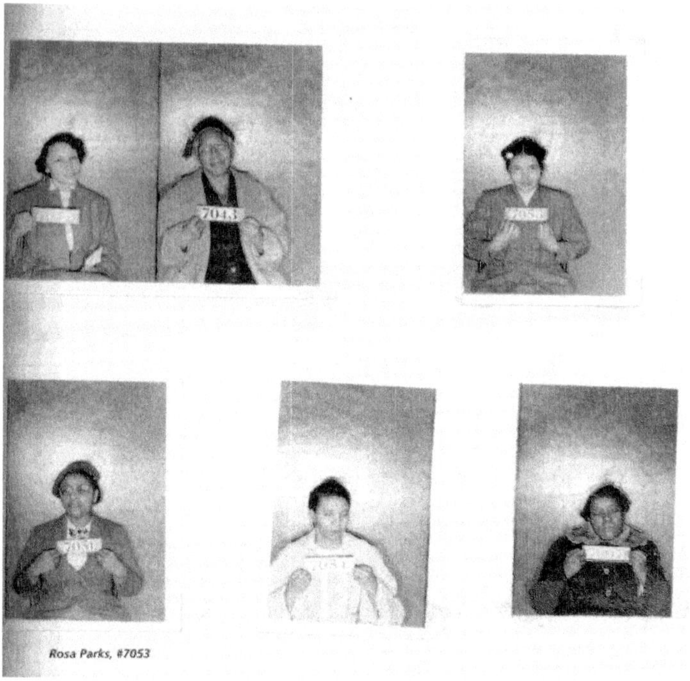

Abb. 4: Mugshots of Participants in the Civil Rights Movements, 23.02.1956, Montgomery County Archives (Ausschnitt) (Pellicer 2009: 215).

Die physiognomische Reproduktion von minorisierten Gruppen durch die Zitation polizeilicher Bildpolitiken erscheint problematisch. Um auf die Lage diskriminierter Gruppen aufmerksam zu machen, sind aktivistische Initiativen jedoch gezwungen durch Benennung (oder Verbildlichung) an ihrer sprachlichen/medialen/sozialen Konstruktion mitzuwirken. Indem ich etwa die Ungleichheiten in den Lebensrealitäten von Männern und Frauen benenne und gegenderte Sprache verwende, reproduziere ich Zweigeschlechtlichkeit. Im feministischen Diskurs ist dieses Dilemma als „Gender-Paradox" bekannt: „Das erste und oberste Paradox von gender ist, daß die Institution, ehe sie abgebaut werden kann, erst einmal ganz sichtbar gemacht werden muss, [...]" (Lorber 1999: 52). Das gleiche gilt auch für andere wirksame Kategorien wie z.B. race und class.

So geht es den Schwarzen Harvard-Studierenden unter dem Motto „I, too, am Harvard" nicht einfach nur um eine nahtlose Assimilation in die Gemeinschaft des Elite-Colleges, sondern darum, eine nach wie vor wirksame, institutionalisierte Differenz offenzulegen. In einem College, das Teil einer rassistisch strukturierten Gesellschaft ist, werden einerseits Schwarze Studierende als Schwarze Subjekte nicht gesehen („I don't even think of you as black.") (I, Too, Am Harvard 2014), nicht gehört und nicht repräsentiert, andererseits unterstehen sie als rassifizierte Objekte einer Hypervisibilität („The lack of diversity in the classroom does NOT make me the voice of all black people.") (I, Too, Am Harvard 2014). Die Fotokampagne reagiert auf beide Richtungen. Einerseits reihen sich die Gesichter der Studierenden formal ein in die repräsentativen Porträtverzeichnisse in den Harvard-Archiven. Über ihren minoritären Status in den offiziellen Verzeichnissen hinaus beanspruchen sie eine öffentliche Sichtbarkeit und politische Repräsentation als Schwarze Subjekte und Harvard-Angehörige mit eigener Stimme und eigener Botschaft. Andererseits zitiert die Fotokampagne die objektivierende Bildpolitik der Mugshots, die in der Hierarchie des umfassenden fotografischen Archivs im Sinne Sekulas Schwarze Gesichter stets den *weißen* unterordnete (Dyer 1997; Sekula 1986).[22] Sie besetzen die Schwelle

---

[22] Struktureller Rassismus u.a. im Strafsystem macht es für afro-amerikanische Männer im Vergleich zu *Weißen* bis heute wahrscheinlicher mit einem

zwischen dem nobilitierenden und dem repressiven Archiv und legen die Kontingenz des Diesseits und des Jenseits dieser Schwelle offen. Sie bringen die Bildpolitik, die Schwarze Gesichter tendenziell aus dem noblen Archiv ausschließt und auf eine diffamierte, kriminalisierte Physiognomie festlegt, wieder in Bewegung.[23]

DIY als agonales Kräfteverhältnis

Wie dieser Artikel in mehreren Schleifen gezeigt hat, sind Machtverhältnisse komplex, vielfach verschränkt und ständig im Wandel begriffen. Dichotomien von Repression und Subversion, von Institution und Subjekt, von Fremdbestimmung und Selbstbehauptung, von Zurechtgemacht-Werden und Sich-Selbst-Zurechtmachen haben höchstens einen analytischen Wert mit äußerst be-

---

eigenen Mugshot in einer Polizeiakte aufzutauchen als mit einem Porträtbild in einem College Album (Haney-López 2010).

[23] Die Kampagne unter dem Hashtag #iftheygunnedmedown operiert an genau der gleichen Schwelle zwischen nobilitierender und diffamierender Bildpolitik: In Reaktion auf die Berichterstattung über Schwarze, die von Polizist_innen erschossen wurden, stellen afro-amerikanische User_innen Bilder von sich gegenüber: eines in einem an bürgerliche Werte angepassten Kontext, z.B. in Robe und Doktorhut zur Graduierung; das andere in eher stereotyper Darstellung , z.B. mit Kapuzenpullover, mit Waffen oder Alkohol posierend oder im Hip-Hop-Style gekleidet. Die rhetorische Frage, die damit gestellt wird, lautet: Wenn ich erschossen worden wäre, welches Bild hätten die Medien dann verwendet? Die User_innen kritisieren damit die Praxis der Massenmedien, die durch die Auswahl ihrer Bilder, Schwarze als Kriminelle darstellen bzw. allgemein rassistische Stereotype perpetuieren. So werden von jungen *weißen* Kriminellen öfter die Porträts aus ihren College Yearbooks verwendet, Schwarze dagegen werden durch Mugshots abgebildet (Horan 2014c).

grenzter Gültigkeit. Selbermachen kann institutionalisierte Praktiken wieder dynamisieren und Veränderungen hervorbringen. Tendenzen der Stagnation und neuerliche Institutionalisierungen folgen auf dem Fuße. Selbermachen operiert nicht in einem Außen der Machtwirkungen, sondern ist selbst in diese Machtwirkungen verstrickt und von ihnen durchzogen. Michel Foucault hat immer wieder deutlich gemacht: Es gibt keine Freiheit außerhalb von Machtbeziehungen. Stattdessen sollten wir von einem dynamischen, produktiven und kämpferischen Verhältnis zwischen Machtwirkungen und Kräften des Widerstands ausgehen: „Machtbeziehung und Widerspenstigkeit der Freiheit lassen sich also nicht voneinander trennen. [...] Statt von einem wesenhaften 'Antagonismus' sollten wir hier besser von einem 'Agonismus' sprechen – einem Verhältnis, das durch gegenseitiges Antreiben und Kampf geprägt ist und weniger durch einen Gegensatz, in dem beide Seiten einander blockieren, als durch ein permanentes Provozieren“ (Foucault 2007b: 98). „Kinds of people“ emergieren im Spannungsfeld dieser reziprok aufeinander wirkenden Kräfte und verändern sich mit ihnen.

Literaturverzeichnis

Bean, Ahsante (2014): I, Too, Am Harvard (Preview). [Link: https://www.youtube.com/watch?v=uAMTSPGZRiI&feature=youtu.be; 20.08.2020].

Decker, Christof (2010): Visuelle Kulturen der USA. Zur Geschichte von Malerei, Fotografie, Film, Fernsehen und Neuen Medien in Amerika. Bielefeld.

Dyer, Richard (1997): White. London, New York.

Ebeling, Knut/Günzel, Stephan (2009): Einleitung. In: Ebeling, Knut/Günzel, Stephan (Hrsg.): Archivologie. Theorien des Archivs in Philosophie, Medien und Künsten. Berlin, 7-26.

Eggers, Maureen M./Kilomba, Grada/Piesche, Peggy (2006): Mythen, Masken und Subjekte: Kritische Weißseinsforschung in Deutschland. Münster.

Foucault, Michel (2007a): Über sich selbst schreiben. In: Foucault, Michel (Hrsg.): Ästhetik der Existenz. Schriften zur Lebenskunst. Frankfurt am Main, 137-154.

Foucault, Michel (2007b): Subjekt und Macht. In: Foucault, Michel (Hrsg.): Ästhetik der Existenz. Frankfurt am Main, 81-104.

Fu, Benjamin L./Kim, Dohyun (2020): Harvard College Admits 4.92 Percent of Applicants to Class of 2024. [Link: https://www.thecrimson.com/article/2020/3/27/harvard-admissions-2024/; 20.08.2020].

Garvey, Ellen Gruber (2013): Writing with Scissors. American Scrapbooks from the Civil War to the Harlem Renaissance. New York.

Greener, Richard T. (1993): The First Black Harvard College Graduate. For Good Government & Urban Politics. In: Sollors, Werner/Titcomb, Caldwell/Underwood, Thomas A. (Hrsg.): Blacks at Harvard. A Documentary History of African-American Experience at Harvard and Radcliffe. New York, London, 37-58.

Hacking, Ian (1999): Making Up People. In: Biagioli, Mario (Hrsg.): The Science Studies Reader. New York, London, 161-171.

Helfand, Jessica (2008): Scrapbooks: An American History. New Haven, London.

Holden, Harley P. (1976). "Student Records: The Harvard Experience", The American Archivist 39 (4): 461-467.

Horan, Molly (2014a): I, too, am Harvard. [Link: http://knowyourmeme.com/memes/i-too-am-harvard; 20.08.2020].

Horan, Molly (2014b): Sign Holding. [Link: http://knowyourmeme.com/memes/sign-holding; 20.08.2020].

Horan, Molly (2014c): If They Gunned Me Down [Link: http://knowyourmeme.com/memes/if-they-gunned-me-down; 20.08.2020].

Iseli, Andrea (2009): Gute Policey: öffentliche Ordnung in der Frühen Neuzeit. Stuttgart.

Kirkpatrick, David (2011): Der Facebook-Effekt. Hinter den Kulissen des Internet-Giganten. München.

Lepri, Karen (2004): 'Clothes Make the Man.' Cross-Dressing on the Radcliffe Stage. In: Ulrich, Laurel (Hrsg.): Yards and Gates: Gender in Harvard and Radcliffe History. New York, 227-240.

Lester, Amelia E. (2004): Show Your Best Face. Online social networks are a hop, click and jump from reality. [Link: http://www.thecrimson.com/article/2004/2/17/show-your-best-face-lets-talk; 20.08.2020].

Lorber, Judith (1999): Gender-Paradoxien, Wiesbaden.

McAllister, Hunter (2014): Mug Book: More Than Just Large Photospreads. In: Lindsay, Rod C.L. et al. (Hrsg.): Handbook for Eyewitness Psychology. New York, London, 25-58.

McElheny, Robin (2004): 'Feminine' Clothing at Harvard in the 1830s. In: Ulrich, Laurel (Hrsg.): Yards and Gates: Gender in Harvard and Radcliffe History. New York, 122-124.

Mühlberger, Knut (2013): Das Album Universitatis. Eine reiche Quelle mittelalterlicher und frühneuzeitlicher Universitätsgeschichte. In: Kramer, Anke/Pelz, Annegret (Hrsg.): Album. Organisationsform narrativer Kohärenz. Göttingen, 240-253.

o.A. (2014): I, too, am Harvard. [Link: http://itooamharvard.tumblr.com; 20.08.2020).

Ott, Katherine/Tucker, Susan/Buckler, Patricia P. (2006): An Introduction to the History of Scrapbooks. In: Ott, Katherine/Tucker, Susan/Buckler, Patricia P. (Hrsg.): The Scrapbook in American Life. Philadelphia, 1-25.

Pellicer, Raynal (2009): Mugshots. An Archive of the Famous, Infamous, and Most Wanted. New York.

Schnabel, Werner W. (2013): Das Album Amicorum. Ein gemischtmediales Sammelmedium und einige seiner Variationsformen. In: Kramer, Anke/Pelz, Annegret (Hrsg.): Album. Organisationsform narrativer Kohärenz. Göttingen, 213-239.

Schwager, Sally (2004): Taking up the Challenge: The Origins of Radcliffe. In: Ulrich, Laurel (Hrsg.): Yards and Gates: Gender in Harvard and Radcliffe History. New York, 134-181.

Seitter, Walter (1985): Menschenfassungen. Studien zur Erkenntnispolitikwissenschaft. München.

Sekula, Allan (1986). “The Body and the Archive”, October 39 (3): 3-64.

Siegel, Elizabeth (2010): Galleries of Friendship and Fame. A History of Nineteenth-Century American Photograph Albums. New Haven, London.

Smullyan, Deborah (2007): Red Books, Raw Gems. The College's Class Reports. [Link: http://harvardmagazine.com/2007/05/red-books-raw-gems.html; 20.08.2020].

Synnott, Marcia G. (2004): The Changing 'Harvard Student': Ethnicity, Race, and Gender. In: Ulrich, Laurel (Hrsg.): Yards and Gates: Gender in Harvard and Radcliffe History. New York, 291-320.

Talbot, William Henry Fox (1844): The Pencil of Nature (Der Zeichenstift der Natur). Budapest.

Wright, Conrad E. (2004): Creating a Fellowship of Educated Men. Forming Gentlemen at the Pre-Revolutionary Harvard. In: Ulrich, Laurel (Hrsg.): Yards and Gates: Gender in Harvard and Radcliffe History. New York, 21-50.

Archivalien

Harvard Class Album, Class of 1906, HUD 306.04.5 B RR, Harvard University Archives.

25th Anniverary Class Report, Class of 1906, HUD 306 25B RR, Harvard University Archives.

Scrapbook of Lawrence Burns Webster, Class of 1906, HUD 902.93 Box 1, Harvard University Archives.

Photograph Album of Lawrence Burns Webster, HUD 902.93 Box 2, Harvard University Archives.

Harvard Class Album, Class of 1852, (photo) UT.9 5.25 Pag.c. (1852) [Harvard College, Class of 1852] [graphic]. John Adams Whipple (photographer), Boston Athenæum.

Schreiben als Empowerment im Autor*innen-kollektiv

von Lena Eckert und Silke Martin

For most of history,
Anonymous was a woman
Virginia Woolf, 1928

Vorbemerkung

Was heißt es, als Wissenschaftler*in zu schreiben? Was heißt es, zu schreiben und sich in und mit dem, was man schreibt, zu positionieren? Sich innerhalb des Prozesses der Wissensgenerierung, innerhalb des Betriebes Akademia, aber auch in Hinblick auf sich selbst in diesem Gefüge schreibend zu behaupten und zu emanzipieren? Was heißt es, im Schreibprozess ein prekäres Selbst zu sein – insbesondere, wenn es ein weiblich* Positioniertes ist? Im folgenden Schreib_Gespräch unterhalten sich fünf Nachwuchswissenschaftler*innen darüber, was es heißt, zu schreiben. Sie reflektieren gemeinsam, was es heißt, sich als Frau* im Wissenschaftsbetrieb, der nach wie vor männlich dominiert ist, schreibend zu behaupten, die eigenen Texte ernst zu nehmen, das eigene Schreiben nicht zu bagatellisieren und zu marginalisieren. Sie sprechen schreibend darüber, was Selbstermächtigung sein kann, als Befreiung von Vorgaben und Erwartungen. Und sie schreiben über das, was in diesem Beitrag passiert, nämlich über die Praxis des Schreibens im Kollektiv, die es ermöglicht, sich gemeinsam zu ermächtigen, selbst und zusammen gegen etwas an_zu_schreiben.

Dieses Schreib_Gespräch zur Selbstermächtigung von Wissenschaftler*innen ist durch, mit und im Schreiben entstanden, im Autor*innenkollektiv nach gemeinsamer Lektüre von Virginia Woolfs *Ein Zimmer für sich allein* (1995). Die Schreibenden haben sich dazu für eineinhalb Stunden getroffen und jede* hat eine Frage formuliert, die durch die Lektüre inspiriert wurde. Anschließend wurde im Freewriting-Verfahren jede Frage von jeder Teilnehmenden beantwortet, rotierend, indem die Schreibenden nach jeweils fünf Minuten von Frage zu Frage bzw. von Laptop zu Laptop weiterrückten. Diejenige, die die Frage gestellt hat, kommt so nach 20 Minuten zu ihrem eigenen Platz zurück und beantwortet als letzte ihre eigene Frage. Die Methode des Freewriting bedeutet, ohne Zensur zu schreiben, ohne über Kommasetzung oder Grammatik nachzudenken, ohne über andere Hemmnisse nachzugrübeln, es geht darum, einfach zu schreiben, in einen Schreibfluss zu geraten und den Gedanken freien Lauf zu lassen, ohne die innere Kritiker*in die Oberhand gewinnen zu lassen. Die Hand bleibt immer in Bewegung, um so einen assoziativen Schreibfluss zu generieren, der auch Unerwartetes hervorbringen kann. Nach dem gemeinsamen Schreiben im Freewritingverfahren folgt eine kurze Überarbeitungsphase im Umlaufverfahren per Mail.[1]

---

[1] Eine Anleitung, wie diese Überarbeitung genau funktioniert sowie eine detaillierte Beschreibung der gesamten Methode finden sich in Eckert/Martin 2019.

Das Autor*innenkollektiv in verschiedenen Kontexten und Formaten

Das Autor*innenkollektiv trifft sich seit vielen Jahren zum Schreiben, in den unterschiedlichsten Kontexten, Formaten und mit leicht wechselnder personeller Zusammensetzung. Begonnen hat die Beschäftigung mit dem gemeinsamen Schreiben im Rahmen eines Peer-Tutorings an der Bauhaus-Universität Weimar, das von 2011 bis 2014 lief. Dort hat eine Gruppe von Wissenschaftler*innen mehrere Schreibworkshops bei der Schreibtrainerin Judith Wolfsberger besucht, die unter wechselnden Themen über mehrere Jahre stattgefunden haben. Zunächst ging es um die jeweiligen Qualifizierungsarbeiten (Doktorarbeiten und Postdoc-Projekte), schließlich um Überarbeitungsstrategien, dann um das Lehren von Schreiben und zuletzt um feministische und queere Aspekte des Schreibens. In Folge dieser Schreibworkshops entstanden verschiedene Formate des gemeinsamen Schreibens, wie regelmäßig stattfindende, thematisch ausgerichtete Schreibnächte, wöchentliche Schreibtreffs an verschiedenen Universitäten und Orten, um gemeinsam, aber jede* an ihrem* eigenen Text zu schreiben, sowie Workshops mit Tandem- und Gruppenschreibaufgaben, um Artikel und Gespräche gemeinsam schreibend zu produzieren, zum Beispiel zu hochschuldidaktischen Aspekten von Gender und Queer (Girgensohn/Jakob 2010; Eckert/Martin 2015). In diesem Zusammenhang ist ein weiteres Format entstanden, das sich mit queer-feministischen Themen auseinandersetzt: der monatliche Genderlektürezirkel. In diesem Lektürezirkel lesen wir zwar in erster Linie, doch geht jedem Schreiben immer auch Lesen voraus; somit ist Lesen als Voraussetzung des Schreibens zu verstehen, unabhängig davon, ob es sich um wissenschaftliches Schreiben handelt oder nicht (Woolf 2005). In Folge der oben genannten Veranstaltungsformate haben Lena Eckert und Silke Martin eine Ausbildung zur Schreibberatung und Schreibzentrumsarbeit an der TU Darmstadt absolviert und sind nun zertifizierte Schreibtrainerinnen.

Schreiben als Strategie des DIY

Schreiben ist ein Prozess, den man nicht nur selbst gestalten muss, sondern der auch aus dem Selbst kommt. Der Zusammenhang zum Do-it-yourself ist damit ein spezifischer: es geht um das eigene Selbst, das sich auf eine bestimmte Art und Weise sozio-kulturell, aber auch politisch verorten muss (oder will).

Virginia Woolf: *Ein Zimmer für sich allein* (1928)

Das Schreibgespräch, das im Anschluss der Tagung im Autor*innenkollektiv veranstaltet wurde, ist inspiriert von Virginia Woolfs *Ein Zimmer für sich allein.* Der Essay von 1928 wurde als Vortragsreihe an der Cambridge University von Woolf verfasst und 1929 publiziert. Gehalten am Girton College und dem Newnham College, die beide Ende des 19. Jahrhunderts für Frauen gegründet wurden, adressierten die Vorträge explizit die dort studierenden Frauen. In den Vorträgen beschreibt Woolf als eine der ersten die Situation schreibender Frauen in einer patriarchalen Gesellschaft. Ihre berühmte Forderung nach einem eigenen Zimmer und 500

Pfund im Jahr, um schreiben zu können, hat nicht nur in der Literaturwissenschaft, sondern auch im Feminismus Geschichte gemacht. Das eigene Zimmer steht ebenso wie die 500 Pfund für die materielle Unabhängigkeit, die Frauen damals verwehrt war, sowie für den eigenen Raum, in dem sie ungestört sein konnten. Schreiben ist, so die Ausgangsthese von Woolf, nicht möglich, wenn der Raum für Kontemplation und Muße nicht gegeben ist. Der eigene Raum steht aber auch metaphorisch für die Möglichkeiten der eigenen Erfahrungen, der eigenen Bildung und Arbeit sowie selbstgewählte menschliche Beziehungen, ohne ökonomische, politische, soziale und kulturelle Zensur und Beschränkungen. Der Zugang zum Literaturbetrieb und zur Wissenschaft ist hier selbstverständlich. Auch das Wissen über Literatur machte Woolf zum Thema sowie die Verortung der schreibenden Frau in einer weiblichen Tradition des Schreibens. Sie verlangt, dass wir „think back through our mothers if we are women“ (Woolf 2005: 75). Sie warnt jedoch auch davor, über das eigene Geschlecht während des Schreibens nachzudenken: „It is fatal for any one who writes to think of their sex... It is fatal... in any way to speak consciously as a woman" (ebd.: 102f.). Die Schriftstellerin Nathalie Sarraute formuliert dies 1984 wie folgt: „When I write, I am neither man nor woman, nor dog nor cat, I am not me, I am no longer anything" (Moi 2008: 261). Woolf geht es darum, dass eine Frau im Schreiben ihre eigene Stimme und ihre eigene Vision findet. Nicht spezifisch als Frau, sondern spezifisch als die Frau*, die sie ist. Das heißt, sie muss sich selbst schreiben.

Heute, fast 100 Jahre später, dürfen Frauen ihr eigenes Geld verdienen und besitzen. Sie sind materiell – zumindest in Deutschland und Großbritannien – zum großen Teil unabhängig von Männern. Der Zugang zu den Universitäten ist gegeben. Von den Studienabsolvierenden stellen Frauen im Jahr 2018 sogar über 48 Prozent, Professuren werden jedoch nur zu 24,7 Prozent von Frauen besetzt (gesis 2020). Die sogenannte *glass ceiling* ist dafür verantwortlich, dass sich Frauen, je höher sie im Wissenschaftsbetrieb hinauswollen, desto heftiger den Kopf stoßen (Williams 2005). Dieses Phänomen ist auch als Konsequenz der *leaky pipeline* bekannt: je renommierter und besser bezahlt die Position ist, desto weniger Frauen sind vorhanden, weil sie vorher aus dem System rausgedrängt werden. Schreiben ist zentral im akademischen Betrieb und damit ist die Rezeption der Texte von Frauen* im Gegensatz zu denen männlicher Autoren immer noch mit Vorurteilen belastet. Es gibt kein geschlechtsneutrales Rezipieren von Wissenschaft (Blackaby/Booth/Frank 2005). Damit ist Schreiben immer noch ein Thema, das nicht nur in der Wissenschaft, sondern auch in der Literatur unter Genderaspekten betrachtet werden muss. Das heißt auch, dass die schreibende Frau* nach wie vor mit anderen Anforderungen (auch denjenigen an sich selbst) zu kämpfen hat. So hat Virginia Woolfs Essay eine drängende Aktualität für die schreibende Frau* und andere durch Mehrfachdiskriminierung marginalisierte Personen in der Wissenschaft eingenommen. Der Kanon, auf den sich berufen werden muss, ist immer noch ein (wenn auch nicht mehr nur ausschließlich) männlich, dennoch aber ein patriarchal geprägter. Die Stimmen von weiblichen* Wissenschaffenden sind marginalisiert, weil die Wissenschaft dies durch Kanonbildung selbst verursacht. Zugrunde liegende Mechanismen sind vielfach beschrieben worden (Paul 2009). Sich als

Schreibende* dessen bewusst zu werden heißt, einen Bewusstwerdungsprozess im Schreiben zu durchlaufen, der dem eigenen Schreiben nicht gerade förderlich ist, sondern Mechanismen der Bewertung vor die Fertigstellung jedes Textes stellt. Traditionelle Anforderung an das wissenschaftliche Schreiben ist jedoch, dass sich Schreibende* auf andere Texte beziehen, um ein Argument in einem wissenschaftliche Kontext zu verorten, wenn die Schreibende* jedoch eine der ersten ist, einen bestimmten feministischen Aspekt zu beleuchten, sich also nicht Back-up durch bereits formulierte Forschung holen kann, wird das Geschriebene und damit auch die Schreibende* prekär und verletzlich. Das folgende Schreib_Gespräch ist in diesen Kontexten zu verorten.

Schreib_Gespräch[2]

Ch: *Ich möchte produktiv sein, viel schreiben, schnell schreiben und auch veröffentlichen (wo und wie auch immer). Wie schaffe ich es, ALLES was ich produziere auch ernst zu nehmen, zu würdigen als gute Resultate, selbst wenn es nicht perfekt ausgearbeitet ist, selbst wenn es kein lobendes Publikum gibt? Wie höre ich auf, meine eigenen Texte zu marginalisieren?*
Si: Das gelingt, indem ich immer wieder versuche, mich selbst anzuerkennen, das Hochstaplerinnen-Syndrom abzulegen. Was auf

[2] Wir benutzen hier den Unterstrich, um diesen besonderen Raum zwischen dem Schreiben und dem miteinander Sprechen deutlich zu machen, der hier entsteht.

jeden Fall immer hilft, ist sich ein lobendes Publikum zu besorgen, eine Gruppe zu finden, die versteht, was da geschrieben ist, die anderes Schreiben anerkennt, die aber auch kritisch ist. Beides ist total wichtig, Selbstanerkennung, aber auch verbunden sein, verbunden mit anderen im Schreiben – dann erscheinen die eigenen Texte plötzlich wertvoller, fühlen sich besser an, ihre Qualität ist besser zu erkennen.

J: Ich lausche den eigenen Stimmen im Kopf. Wo sind da eigentlich die Jubelierer? Die, die einem zurufen: Das hast du toll gemacht! Also erstmal kannst du dir ein Jubelkomitee im außen zulegen. Sehr empfehlenswert. Und dieses dann langsam nach innen verlagern. Dauert ein bissl, aber umgekehrt hat`s ja auch in jahrelanger mühsamer Internalisierungsarbeit geklappt. Und wie lese ich Texte eigentlich? Mit dem Ziel, jeden Satz gut zu finden oder eher in dem Bewusstsein, dass ich auf einer Insel herumwandere und vielleicht irgendwann überraschend einen schönen Schatz finde? Ein Gedanke, ein Satz, der mich durchfährt, den ich am liebsten polieren und mit nach Hause nehmen möchte, oder der sich nervend an mich kettet und mich nicht mehr loslässt. Ich weiß nicht, welcher Satz das sein wird, der an meinem Gegenüber hängenbleibt. Ich habe keine Kontrolle darüber. Nicht die geringste. Der Gedanke, den ich am schönsten finde, findet ein anderer banal und den, den ich zu platt finde, ist für jemanden eine Neuigkeit sondergleichen. Ich mache ein Geschenk. Ich weiß nur nicht welches.

C: Mein erster Gedanke - vielleicht naiv - würde sein: männliches Gedankengehabe antrainieren... Leider halte ich das aber für keine dauerhaft gesunde und zukunftsorientierte Variante. Warum wollten wir das Gehabe/Verhalten kopieren, das wir kritisieren?

Andererseits weiß ich, dass jede eine Stimme hat und diese ihre Daseinsberechtigung hat. Daher ist es auch legitim, daran zu glauben, was wir schreiben und denken. Das Wissen reicht allerdings noch nicht, um es auch umzusetzen. Wie also produzieren? Vielleicht mit dem Wissen, dass es irgendwo auf der Welt noch jemanden gibt, der deine Gedanken hat und unter dem Motto „Zwei Texte zu einem Thema sind ein Diskurs" an Veröffentlichungen herangehen. Wir wollen doch Diskurse!

S: Das ist eine sehr schwierige Frage, die mich auf jeden Fall auch selbst betrifft. Wenn ich an meine eigenen Texte denke, vor allem an die wissenschaftlichen, fällt mir aus dem Stand jeder negative und abwertende Kommentar ein, den irgendjemand irgendwann mal dazu gemacht hat. Jegliche positive Reaktion habe ich vergessen. Deshalb führe ich, so doof das klingt, eine Lobliste. Auf die kommt alles Positive, Bestärkende, was zu meinen Texten gesagt wurde und wird. Dieses bestärkende Feedback kann man auch einfordern, zum Beispiel von Freundinnen oder Kolleginnen, denen man vertraut. Das klingt vielleicht nach Selbsthilfegruppe und „die Mädchen haben das eben nötig" – aber es hilft. Denn natürlich haben Frauen* das nötig, denn ihnen wird die ganze Zeit abgesprochen, dass ihre Gedanken wert sind, geäußert zu werden, und das in einem Maße, dass sie selbst immer eher anderen glauben als sich selbst. Zusätzlich bin ich überzeugt, dass Schreibroutine hilft, also tägliches Schreiben, auch in anderen Formaten als wissenschaftlichen Papers und Büchern, also z.B. Freewritings, Kurzgeschichten, Schreibzirkel, Blogposts, Kommentare.

Ch: So ein Format hier hilft. In wenigen Minuten produzieren wir im Kollektiv einen publikationsfähigen Dialog. Das ist großartig! Aber auch sonst sollte ich vielleicht mit meinen Texten liebevoller umgehen. Auch mit meinen Gedanken. Ich sollte sie öfter zu Papier bringen und an einem würdigen Ort aufbewahren, auch, wenn sie zunächst niemand zu Gesicht bekommt. Juli Zeh sagt, ihre Romane entstehen immer aus Texten, die sie „Nur-so“ schreibt (2013). Die muss noch keiner lesen. Sie schreibt auch wahnsinnig schnell, sagt sie, und undiszipliniert. Nur, wenn sie gerade will. Daraus entstehen dann aber tatsächlich Romane. Sie ist eine Schriftstellerin, weil sie einfach schreibt. Welches Leben solche Texte danach noch führen, muss ich ja vorerst gar nicht entscheiden.

C: *Was mache ich mit meinem empowerten Text, nachdem ich ihn geschrieben habe? Wo ist der Raum dafür oder ist Empowerment nur individuell zu sehen?*

S: Auf keinen Fall sollte der Text im abgeschlossenen Kämmerlein bleiben! Raus damit! Ich mag ja diese Floskel nicht, aber: die neuen Medien! Also auf einen Blog, Facebook, als Leserinnenbrief an Zeitungen, Nachrichtenmagazine oder als Kommentare in sozialen Netzwerken. Dabei ist aber zu bedenken, dass das Internet kein diskriminierungsfreier Raum ist. Frauen und People of Color sind überdurchschnittlich oft Opfer von Hate Speech und das ist natürlich eine Strategie, ihnen den Raum zu nehmen, den sie sich mühsam erkämpft haben. Dennoch bin ich überzeugt, dass deine Gedanken auf jeden Fall raus in die Welt sollten. Deshalb: bildet Banden, sucht euch Verbündete, baut auf Sisterhood und bestärkt euch gegenseitig. Denn diese wichtige Aufgabe müssen wir nicht allein angehen. Und wenn dein Text da draußen ist, kann er als Vorbild arbeiten und das ist ebenso wichtig wie dass er dir zu deiner eigenen Stimme verholfen hat. Es gibt zu viele Mädchen und

Frauen, die ihrer eigenen Stimme nicht trauen, weil sie immer klein gehalten werden. Je mehr wir sind, desto besser.

Ch: Du meinst, welche größere, vielleicht strukturelle Wirkung die Texte haben, wenn man Frauen* dazu empowert, zu schreiben? Geht das über eine individuelle empfundene Stärkung und Bestätigung hinaus? Brauchen die Texte eine Öffentlichkeit, um wirksam und relevant zu sein? Vielleicht geht es dabei nicht um einzelne Text, sondern um das Schreiben selbst. Wenn Frauen* dazu gebracht werden, Schreibende zu werden, eröffnet sich ihnen ein Raum, der ihnen tendenziell verschlossen bleibt, oder zumindest schwerer zugänglich ist. Wenn sie aber schreibende Subjekte werden, erschließen sie sich diesen Raum und das kann dann auch zu einer Öffentlichkeit führen. Vielleicht erst zu einer kleinen Öffentlichkeit im Freundinnenkreis, und von da aus kann der Leser*innenkreis größer werden. Und damit verändert sich ganz viel. Dann wird Literatur viel weiblicher.

Si: Ja, das ist eine wirklich gute Frage: Ich kann so viel Empowerment machen wie ich will beim Schreiben, Texte erstellen, mich ermächtigen, aber wohin damit? Wozu? Welchen Zweck soll das Ganze verfolgen? Ist das nur für mich? Oder auch für andere? Dann aber muss es veröffentlicht werden, in der Gruppe rezipiert werden, darüber diskutiert werden, ein Raum geschaffen werden, um über das Geschriebene sprechen zu können. Empowerment braucht beides – die individuelle Handlung, das Schreiben, aber auch die Diskussion über das Schreiben, die Texte, es braucht eine Gruppe, eine Verbindung.

J: Weg vom entweder oder, hin zum sowohl als auch. Ich kann meinen Schatz für mich behalten, ihn im Kämmerchen bewahren und nur manchmal an besonders schönen oder traurigen Tagen herausholen, auf das er mich erquicken möge? Allerdings hat dann die Schwesternschaft nichts davon und der Text entfaltet eventuell auch nicht sein ganzes Potenzial und die Fülle seiner Lesarten, die andere Blicke aus ihm hervorlocken. („Wow, dieses Wort, wie treffend…“, „Hier hast du sicher auf xy angespielt?“ – „Äh nein, aber ab jetzt werde ich das behaupten.“) Ich stelle es mir auch als nettes Übungsfeld vor, im Internet erst einmal Dinge anonym rauszuhauen (ja, ein bisschen feige, aber scheiß drauf), um sich dann mit seinem Namen drunter mutig und stolz mit seinen Gedanken zu präsentieren.

C: An welche Personengruppe richten sich meine Texte frage ich mich. Welchem Genre gehören sie an? Mir fallen keine empowernden Texte in meinem Wissenschaftsbereich ein und ich weiß auch nicht wie das aussehen könnte. Mein Empowerment im Schreiben erscheint mir manchmal als ein Hobby neben meiner wissenschaftlichen Ingenieursdisziplin. Ich möchte das gerne zusammenführen. Ich möchte Empowerment nicht nur individuell verstehen – das wäre mir zu neoliberal: Dann sind wir wieder nur für uns selbst zuständig und müssen uns selbst optimieren bzw. in diesem Fall empowern. Ich finde die Stärke darin, dass andere Texte mich emanzipieren können und ich mich mitreißen lassen kann. Virginia Wolfs Gedanken, dass die Leserin mit dem Text machen könne was sie wolle, finde ich schön.

J: *An welche Texte erinnert ihr euch, die euch ermächtigt haben? Was daran war es?*

C: Die Texte, die mir Mut gegeben oder irgendwie motiviert haben, mich mit Feminismus und Ungerechtigkeiten zu beschäftigen, sind – glaube ich – alle von Frauen. Ich glaube, das ist ein Hauptgrund, warum sie mir etwas gesagt haben: Das (vielleicht

auch nicht immer zutreffende) Gefühl, dass ich mit der Autorin in Sisterhood verbunden bin. Die Texte, die das waren, sind ganz unterschiedlich. Ich glaube, ermächtigenden Texten, die ich vor zwei Jahren gelesen habe, stimme ich heute vielleicht nicht immer zu. Ermächtigungstexte – so beschreibe ich das heute vielleicht – sind Texte, die mir keine Wahrheit vorgeben. Sie fordern mich heraus, weil sie – vielleicht wie bei Virginia Wolf – es mir überlassen, was ich damit anstelle. Ich kann sie vergessen oder annehmen – die Verantwortung liegt bei mir. Das ist mir gerade in theologischen Texten meiner Jugend nicht begegnet. Da war es immer die Herausforderung, Auslegungen so anzunehmen, wie sie vorgegeben sind. Diese abzulehnen war/ist keine Option.
S: Für mich war das eindeutig die Entdeckung der feministischen Standpunkttheorie durch eine Freundin. Ich erzählte ihr von einer entmutigenden Konsultation mit einem Professor, der meine Recherche diskreditierte, indem er sagte: „Das ist ja alles ganz schön und gut, aber Sie müssen Ihre Beobachtungen mit denen anderer flankieren. Es reicht nicht, dass Sie allein das beobachten." In mir regte sich sofort Widerstand, denn wo ist denn der Gewinn der Arbeit, wenn nicht in meiner Sichtweise auf eine Frage? Die Freundin sagte: „Na klar, das heißt standpoint theory, ich schick dir mal ein paar Texte." Ich verschlang alle PDFs von Donna Haraway (1991), Nancy Hartsock (1983), Mona Singer (2008) u.a. noch am gleichen Nachmittag und hatte auf einmal einen Namen und einen ganzen theoretischen Kanon, auf den ich mich stützen kann: Meine Beobachtungen und meine Überlegungen reichen natürlich aus und müsse nicht allumfassend und repräsentativ sein, weil sie wie jede Wissensproduktion selektiv und situiert sind: Sie sind abhän-

gig von meiner sozialen, historischen, technischen, medialen Positionierung und wenn ich diese Positionierung sichtbar mache, trage ich zu einer besseren, da ehrlicheren und verantwortungsbewussteren Wissenschaft bei.

Ch: Meinst du Texte, die mich zum Schreiben ermächtigt haben oder generell ermächtigende Texte? Wenn ich jetzt anfange, Autorinnen aufzuzählen, wird die Liste entweder endlos oder ich vergesse letztlich doch die wichtigsten. Zum Schreiben ermächtigen mich Texte, die die Selbstverständlichkeit des Schreibens aufbrechen und die Mechanismen dabei offenlegen. Texte von Hélène Cixous (1977) zum Beispiel, um nur eine zu nennen. Damit werden meine eigenen Struggels plötzlich Teil eines strukturellen Problems und sind nicht mehr in meiner individuell empfundenen Unzulänglichkeit begründet. Und damit wird mein Schreiben auch politisch! Zuletzt habe ich die Poetikvorlesung von Juli Zeh „Treideln" (2013) gelesen. Sie schreibt sehr amüsant, sehr scharfsinnig über das Schreiben und de-mystifiziert es total. Man kann ein pragmatisches Verhältnis zum Schreiben haben und den Genie-Mythos endlich vergessen. Das finde ich ungemein entlastend.

Si: Ich weiß nicht, ob das immer nur Texte waren oder nicht vielleicht auch Gespräche und Workshops. Aber Virginia Woolfs *Ein Zimmer für sich allein* hat mich auf jeden Fall empowert. Vielleicht auch deshalb, weil sie über so viele Dinge schreibt, die für Frauen vor über 100 Jahren nicht üblich waren – und es leider bis heute nicht sind. Das zeigt mir, dass mein vages Gefühl stimmt, dass es viel Ungleichheit gab, aber nach wie vor gibt. Weiterhin fand ich einen Text von Susan Sontag (1972) sehr erhellend, über den Unterschied zwischen älteren Frauen und älteren Männern. Und auch Simone de Beauvoir (1977) hat mich sehr beeinflusst, ihre Schriften über das Alter gleichermaßen wie über das Geschlecht, und natürlich Judith Butler, Michel Foucault, Julia Kristeva.

J: Natürlich kann ich mich jetzt partout an keinen konkreten Text oder gar Autoren mehr erinnern. Also eher allgemein: Texte, die mir etwas erlauben, die mir nichts abschneiden…einen Gedanken, ein Gefühl, ein Bedürfnis. Die erst mal Ja sagen, die aber auch meine Normalität in Frage stellen und kräftig daran rütteln, so dass ich mich festhalten muss. Die mich mutiger machen. Ermächtigen…Macht, was ist das überhaupt? Ist ja extrem negativ besetzt und ruft gleich innere Bilder von Despoten und säbelrasselnden, großgrundbesitzenden Machthabern auf den Plan. Stattdessen Macht als Erweiterung und Nutzen meiner Handlungs- und Denkmöglichkeiten.

S: *Kann man wirklich sagen: Frauen schreiben anders als Männer? Ist das nicht irgendwie überkommener Differenzfeminismus? Inwiefern schreiben Frauen anders als Männer? Was hat Weiblichkeit mit Schreiben zu tun?*

Ch: Kann man wirklich sagen, es gibt Frauen und Männer? Auch wenn Weiblichkeit und Männlichkeit Konstruktionen sind, haben sie ja Wirklichkeitseffekte. Das ist beim Schreiben sicherlich nicht anders. Schreibende, die weiblich sozialisiert sind, schreiben anders als männlich Sozialisierte, oder haben mit anderen Schwierigkeiten zu tun, geben dem Schreiben eine andere Bedeutung. Geschlechterdifferenzen werden auch im Schreiben hergestellt. Sicherlich bestätigen Ausnahmen die Regel. Ich glaube, Hélène Cixous zählt auch einige Männer auf, die weiblich schreiben (1977). Sie hat ganze Bücher geschrieben, um diese Frage zu beantworten, und ist auch mit dem gleichen Essenzialismus-Vorwurf konfrontiert worden. Zu Unrecht. An einer wirksamen Differenz habe ich jedenfalls keine Zweifel, aber die ist natürlich nicht biologistisch begründet.

Si: Die Frage ist deshalb gut, weil sie ein Paradox beinhaltet, das vielen Genderfragen zugrunde liegt: wie über die Diskriminierung von Frauen sprechen, ohne sie nicht gleichzeitig zu thematisieren bzw. die Geschlechtertrennung neu zu produzieren? Ich glaube, dass Frauen anders schreiben, weil sie anders sozialisiert sind als Männer, auch und gerade im Schreiben. Wie ich über Körper und Film zu schreiben (z.B. Martin 2017) beispielsweise trauen sich bis heute überwiegend nur Frauen. Das ist einfach kein männliches Thema. Zudem ist das Ich und der persönliche Einstieg oder die persönliche Färbung von Texten nach wie vor eher bei Frauen zu finden. Zugleich ist es aber auch gerade das, was mich immer wieder daran erinnert, dass ich eine weibliche Autorin bin oder mich zumindest als eine solche zu erkennen gebe: das subjektive, persönliche Schreiben, das auch über den Körper nachdenkt, über Wahrnehmung, über Gefühle.

J: Die beliebte Frage nach dem Genderparadox. Gibt es dieses andere und wenn ja, wie sieht es aus, wie lässt es sich beschreiben? Weiblichkeit, Männlichkeit? Was verändert sich, wenn ich an den Anfang dieses Textes schreibe: Ich als Frau schreibe diese Zeilen nieder. Ich als Frau… Intuitiv würde ich sofort sagen: Klar, macht das einen Unterschied. Die Herausforderungen in meinem Leben sind andere. Ich werde als Frau gelesen, oft akzeptiere ich diese Lesart, auch wenn ich mit dem, wie es gefüllt wird, vielleicht nicht zufrieden bin. Ich positioniere mich in Bezug auf die Geschlechter um mich herum. Das wirkt sich auf mein Schreiben aus. Ich habe

Imaginationen im Kopf. Unsichtbare Zuhörer, denen ich etwas zurufe.

C: Ich schreibe anders als meine männlichen Kollegen. Diese ganze Meta-Ebene die mitschwingt ist anders, als bei männlichen Schreibenden. Auch wenn dieser Unterschied nicht biologisch begründet ist, halte ich ihn für körperlich manifestiert. Vielleicht liegt der Unterschied im Schreiben auch daran, dass Frauen in Räumen von Männern mit ihren Texten einfach nicht so gut ankommen – die Boys lassen sich ungern reinreden. Wenn also die Texte nicht ankommen und androzentrische Texte eh irgendwie nerven – warum dann nicht gleich anders schreiben? Also warum nicht neue Formate finden, in denen wir schreiben wollen: kurz, knackig, ausladend, bildhaft, mit Bildern oder Vielem anderen. Wie Frauen dann aber in den männlichen Universitäten mitspielen sollen, weiß ich allerdings auch nicht. Anders gefertigte Texte werden dann meist nicht so ganz ernst genommen in der patriarchischen Universitätsstruktur. Warum dann nicht gleich Revolution: Lasst uns neue Frauen-Universitäten gründen!? Vielleicht wie damals zu Virginia Wolfs Zeiten: ohne Schnick-Schnack. Es geht um die Steine, die das Haus bauen.

S: Weiblichkeit und Männlichkeit sind zunächst einmal nicht biologisch gemeint, sondern sozial: Wir werden zu Frauen und Männern erzogen. Diese Sozialisation hat Effekte auf alle Bereiche unseres Lebens, also auch auf unser Schreiben. Ein Effekt, den ich deutlich merke, ist, dass ich, anders als viele Männer in meinem wissenschaftlichen Umfeld, mein Schreiben viel mehr in Frage stelle, immer schon sämtliche mögliche Kritik vorwegdenke und deshalb oft gar nicht schreibe. Der innere Kritiker in den Schreibdidaktikbüchern wird nicht umsonst mit der männlichen

Form bezeichnet. Anders ist es bei Schreibarten, die eher weiblich konnotiert sind, also empfindsame, nach innen gerichtete Texte oder kreative Rumspinnereien. Die traue ich mir leichter zu, weil Frauen und Mädchen eher zu dieser emotionalen Arbeit erzogen werden als Jungs. Weibliches Schreiben, so könnte man vielleicht sagen, ist also fragiler und gefährlicher als männliches: fragil, weil es ständig und überall hinterfragt wird und gefährlich, weil Frauen öfter für ihre Stimme angegriffen und bedroht werden.

Si: *Wie kann heute Schreiben an der Universität empowernd sein für Frauen, wenn sie dauernd damit beschäftigt sind, bleiben zu können, eine Vertragsverlängerung zu bekommen, eine Perspektive zu finden?*

J: Freundinnen, Austausch, treffen und Gedanken teilen, auf andere werfen und schauen, was zurückkommt. Aber nicht auf diese fressenden Projektionsflächen. Nicht auf die, die es zerfleischen, zerhacken, sondern die, die es einem subtil verändert, verbessert, klüger zurückwerfen. Sich ermutigen lassen und dann aufschreiben. Den Mythos des einsamen Schreibenden zertreten. Gemeinsam wird ein Schuh draus. Oder draußen schreiben….nicht in diesem furnierten, buchenoptisch eingerichteten Unibüros seine Zeit absitzen, sondern einen Ort finden, in dem sich Gedanken ausbreiten können. Der Kampf und die Vertragsverlängerung immer im Hinterkopf. Ok, aber nicht ohne Verbündete. Offene und guerillamäßige Strategien entwickeln. Alles scheiße finden dürfen, zweifeln, hinterfragen, alles hinwerfen wollen, frustriert sein und dann wieder die Kurve kriegen. Aufgeben und dranbleiben, beides in Ordnung.

C: Diese Frage begegnet mir in meinem Hirn auch häufig: Ich drücke mich davor, Texte zu schreiben, da ich nicht weiß, ob sie gut werden – ob meine männlichen Vorgesetzten sie respektieren oder ob ich deren Respekt dadurch verliere. Ich beobachte, dass ich mit Textabgaben bis zur letzten Minute warte, nur um dann sagen zu können „Ach, na jetzt kann ich eh nix mehr daran ändern". Für mich ist jedoch der Gedanke, nicht dauerhaft an der Universität zu sein, aber auch hilfreich. Ich denke dann, dass es mir auch egal sein könnte, was die jetzt von meinem Text denken, da ich ja eh nicht ewig bleibe. Das hat allerdings zur Folge, dass ich gar nicht damit rechne, Karriere an der Universität zu machen. Diese ganze Meta-Ebene prägt den Arbeitsalltag enorm – ich habe auch keine Lösung für mich gefunden, wie ich mich motivieren kann, selbstbewusst Texte zu schreiben. Obwohl – ich kann mir vorstellen, dass es mit Austausch unter weiblichen Kolleginnen (Vorbildern) leichter fällt, meinen Gedanken zu vertrauen.

S: Mit den prekären Arbeitsbedingungen an deutschen Universitäten sind ja auch Männer konfrontiert, nur können sie im Gegensatz zu Frauen darauf vertrauen, dass sie in diese Räume gehören und ihnen zugehört wird. Diese Sicherheit haben Frauen nicht. „Denken Sie immer daran, wir gehören hier eigentlich nicht her" sagte eine Coach für Work-Life-Balance in einem Gleichstellungsprogramm und meinte mit „wir" „uns Frauen" und mit „hier" Universitäten. Wenn einer das sogar in Coachings gesagt wird, die eigentlich dazu gedacht sind, zu helfen – wie soll eine dann eine eigene Stimme entwickeln können und sich darüber ermächtigen? Denn die Macht, die ich im Ermächtigungsprozess übernehmen will, ist ja seit Jahrtausenden in der Hand der Männer. Und sie werden sie nicht von sich aus abgeben. Eine Strategie, mit dieser aussichtslosen Situation umzugehen, sehe ich aber doch: Wir müssen Netzwerke bilden und uns gegenseitig unterstützen.

Ch: Die Umstände prekärer Beschäftigung und andere Schwierigkeiten an der Universität erschweren das Schreiben massiv. Ist die Universität überhaupt noch ein Raum fürs Schreiben? Man sieht ja eigentlich fast überall, dass die eigentliche wissenschaftliche Schreibarbeit immer stärker ins Private und auch in die Freizeit verlegt wird, weil der Alltag in der Universität mit anderen Aufgaben überfrachtet ist. Wir müssen vielmehr gegen und trotz Universität schreiben und auch Gegenräume schaffen, um da zu schreiben. Das kann ja auch virtuell sein. Aber im Kopf muss das Schreiben auch eine Weigerung oder eine Kritik sein an allem, was uns innerhalb der Universität und der Wissenschaft feindlich gegenübertritt. Wenn das Schreiben rebellisch wird, kann es vielleicht auch in den Lücken stattfinden, die uns selbst eine prekäre Beschäftigung noch lässt. Keinesfalls sollten wir den etablierten Strukturen zu viel Glauben schenken und unser Schreiben daran anpassen. Die Antwort ist jetzt ganz schön abstrakt. Wir haben es hier ja mit sehr konkreten Schwierigkeiten zu tun.
Si: Schwierig, aber möglich: eine Gruppe, Verbündete finden, selbst Seilschaften bilden. Zugleich ist es auch immer wieder empowernd, wenn man eine weitere Stelle bekommen hat – ohne Beziehungen oder andere Unterstützung. Im Grunde genommen schreibt man immer in der Zeit und in dem Raum, die einer verbleiben: je nachdem, wie lange der Vertrag läuft, wieviel Arbeitslosengeld sich anschließt. Das reicht manchmal schon, um eine weitere Qualifizierungsarbeit fertigzustellen. Und auch das ist empowernd – wieder eine Hürde genommen zu haben. Und schließlich kann man auch aussteigen, was anderes arbeiten, und trotzdem weiterschreiben. Oder es einfach sein lassen, auch das ist eine Möglichkeit, die empowernd und erleichternd zugleich sein kann.

Im Grunde genommen sollte man loslassen, und schauen was kommt, was passiert.

Nachtrag

Empowerment – Ermächtigung – ist ein theoretisches Konzept und zugleich eine Praxis. Es geht um die Ermächtigung jener Personen, die marginalisiert sind und die in bestimmten Zusammenhängen keine Macht oder Handlungsfähigkeit besitzen. Die Kraft von Empowerment liegt im Wachstum von Selbstvertrauen und Selbstachtung, von Selbstbewusstsein und vom Verständnis der eigenen Handlungsmacht und -fähigkeit. Es geht auch darum, dem eigenem Selbst in einem größeren Zusammenhang ein Verständnis von *dignidad* (gleichzeitig Würde und Selbstachtung) bzw. das Gefühl des „being worthy of having a right to respect from others" zu geben (Rowlands 1997: 129f.). Es geht aber auch um das Bewusstsein des Respekts der anderen. Das heißt um die Bewusstwerdung dessen, dass man sich den Respekt der anderen nicht verdienen muss, sondern ihn bereits hat. Beim Schreiben werden Strategien benötigt, um weiterschreiben zu können, um nicht den Mut zu verlieren, um Kritik – auch positive – hören und mit ihr arbeiten zu können. Es geht beim Schreiben darum, den Strategien der Selbstverhinderung, wie z.B. den Text in letzter Minute abzugeben, um nichts mehr ändern zu können, die Stirn zu bieten und sich selbst zu überlisten, der Sprachlosigkeit keinen Nährboden zu geben, ihr entgegen zu wirken. Bewusstes Schreiben oder bewusstes Einsetzen von Schreiben kann ein sehr wirkungsvolles Instrument der Selbstwerdung/Selbstachtung sein.

Insbesondere in Kontexten, in denen Schreiben zur Definition und Ausformung des Kontextes gehört, wie in der Wissenschaft.

Frauen, die an Universitäten Studierende oder Wissenschaffende und somit auch privilegiert sind, fühlen sich dennoch oft sprachlos – denn im Wissenschaftsbetrieb sind Frauen immer noch marginalisiert. Die feministische Schriftstellerin Hélène Cixous hat sich mit dieser Sprachlosigkeit von Frauen auseinandergesetzt, die ihr zufolge eine „superverdrängende Wirkung" hat. Diese wird von der „Metasprache" verursacht, „d.h. vom Kommentar des Kommentars, von der Kodifizierung, so dass eine Frau, sobald sie den Mund aufmacht, gefragt wird – und zwar mehr als ein Mann – in wessen Namen sie spricht, von welcher Theorie sie ausgeht; wer ihr Meister ist und wo sie herkommt; kurz: sie hat zu deklinieren ... ihre Identität nachzuweisen" (Cixous 1977: 36). Frauen sind immer noch Rechenschaft schuldig, sie müssen sich rechtfertigen dafür, dass sie selbst denken und schreiben. Insofern müssen sie auch immer gegen das „Schreiben als Herrenrecht" anschreiben (ebd.: 53). Die US-amerikanische Schreibberaterin Joan Bolker bemerkt diesbezüglich: „Writing is dangerous for everyone" (Bolker 1997: 187). Schreiben ist gefährlich, weil man etwas von sich weggibt und damit rechnen muss, dass man es erstens nicht zurückbekommt und zweitens etwas damit gemacht wird, was man nicht beabsichtigt hat. Die Schreibende macht sich verletzlich, durchsichtig und benutzbar. Nicht nur deshalb scheint das Schreiben im Kollektiv vielversprechender: Empowerment durch Schreiben mit anderen Marginalisierten, die sich ebenso hergeben, macht Schreiben zum politischen Akt. Oder anders gesagt: Es macht das Schreiben zur Politik. Kollektives Empowerment ist machtvoller als individuelles, das kollaborative Tun gegen Strukturen, die unterdrücken und ausgrenzen wird im gemeinsamen Handeln so zur Ermächtigung und birgt auch gesellschaftliche Verantwortung in sich. Kathrin Girgensohn bezeichnet das Schreiben als grundsätzlich sozial: „Wir schreiben meistens für irgendwelche Leser und immer knüpfen Texte an andere Texte an, die schon vorher existierten. Schreibend treten wir also mit anderen Menschen und mit anderen Gedanken in Beziehung" (Girgensohn/Sennewald 2012: 113). Das heißt auch, dass der Mythos des einsam Schreibenden schon immer ein Mythos ist. Diese im Schreib_Gespräch explizit gemachte intrinsische Intertextualität ist auch ein Teil der Selbstermächtigung, ist ein Zerstören des Mythos, ist eine vielleicht „weiblich" zu nennende Schreibstrategie der Selbstermächtigung. Das Kollektiv explizit zu machen und zu leben – das ist schreibendes Empowerment!

Literaturverzeichnis

Blackaby, David/Booth, Alison L./Frank, Jeff (2005): „Outside Offers and the Gender Pay Gap: Empirical Evidence from the UK Academic Labour Market*", *The Economic Journal* 115 (501): 81-107.

Bolker, Joan (1997): The Writer's Home Companion: An Anthology of the World's Best Writing Advice. From Keats to Kunitz. New York.

Boros, Aniko (2016). Tagungsbericht: Do-it-Yourself! Subversive practices and informal knowledge, 18.11.2015-20.11.2015 Marburg. [Link: http://www.hsozkult.de/conferencereport/id/tagungsberichte-6381; 13.02.2017].

Cixous, Hélène (1977): Die unendliche Zirkulation des Begehrens. Weiblichkeit in der Schrift. Berlin.

de Beauvoir, Simone (1977): Einführung und Vorwort. In: de Beauvoir, Simone (Hrsg.): Das Alter. Reinbek bei Hamburg, 5-14.

Eckert, Lena/Martin, Silke (2015): Schöner Lehren. gegendert und gequeert. Marburg.

Eckert, Lena/Martin, Silke (2019): Schreib_Gespräch. In: Wymann, Christian (Hrsg.): Praxishandbuch Schreibdidaktik: Übungen zur Vermittlung wissenschaftlicher Schreibkompetenzen. Opladen, Toronto, 207-213.

Gesis. Leibniz Institut für Sozialwissenschaften, [Link: https://www.gesis.org/cews/unser-angebot/informationsangebote/statistiken/; 20.08.2020].

Girgensohn, Katrin/Jakob, Ramona (2010): 66 Schreibnächte. Anstiftung zur literarischen Geselligkeit. Ein Praxisbuch zum kreativen Schreiben. Baltmannsweiler.

Girgensohn, Katrin/Sennewald, Nadja (2012): Schreiben lehren, Schreiben lernen. Eine Einführung. Darmstadt.

Haraway, Donna (1991): Situated Knowledges: The Science Question in Feminism and the Privilege of Partial Perspective. In: Haraway, Donna (Hrsg.): Simians, Cyborgs, and Women: the Re-Invention of Nature. London, 183-201.

Hartsock, Nancy M. (1983): The Feminist Standpoint: Developing the Ground for a Specifically Feminist Historical Materialism. In: Harding, Sandra/Hintikka, Merrill B. (Hrsg.): Discovering Reality. Feminist Perspectives on Epistemology, Metaphysics, Methodology, and Philosophy of Science. Dordrecht, Boston, London, 283-310.

Klinkenhammer, Monika/Saul-Soprun, Gunta (2009): „Das „Hochstaplersyndrom“ in der Wissenschaft”, *Organisationsberatung, Supervision, Coaching* 16 (2): 165-182.

Kutzmutz, Olaf/Porombka, Stephan (2007): Erst lesen. Dann schreiben. 22 Autoren und ihre Lehrmeister. München.

Martin, Silke (2017): Berg und Film. Ästhetik und Kultur im deutschsprachigen Film der Gegenwart. Marburg.

Moi, Toril (2008): „`I am not a woman writer'. About women, literature and feminist theory today", *Feminist Theory* 3 (9): 259-271.

Paul, Barbara (2009): „Nach dem Kanon ist vor dem Kanon? Aktuelle queer-feministische Debatten in Kunst und Wissenschaft", *FKW//Zeitschrift für Geschlechterforschung und visuelle Kultur* 46: 48.

Rowlands, Jo (1997): Questioning Empowerment: Working with Women in Honduras. Oxford.

Singer, Mona (2008): Feministische Wissenschaftskritik und Epistemologie: Voraussetzungen, Positionen, Perspektiven. In: Becker, Ruth/Kortendiek, Beate (Hrsg.): Handbuch Frauen- und Geschlechterforschung. Theorie, Methode, Empirie. Wiesbaden: 285-294.

Sonntag, Susan (1972): „The Double Standard of Aging", *Saturday Review of the Society* 23: 29-39.

Todd, Zazie/Madill, Anna/Shaw, Nicky/Bown, Nicola (2008): „Faculty Members' Perceptions of How Academic Work is Evaluated: Similarities and Differences by Gender", *Sex Roles* 11 (59): 765.

Williams, Joan C. (2005): „The Glass Ceiling and the Maternal Wall in Academia", *New Directions for Higher Education* 130: 91-105.

Woolf, Virginia ([1928] 2005): A Room of One's Own. Harcourt.

Woolf, Virginia/Garland, P./Kersten, Karin (1995): Ein Zimmer Für Sich Allein. Frankfurt am Main.

Zeh, Juli (2018): Treideln. München.

Die Maker*innen Bewegung: Was die Mikroökonomie, die Feldtheorie und die Praxistheorie über sie zu sagen haben

von Lisa Conrad und Matthias Maier

1 Einleitung

In diesem Text geht es um verschiedene Weisen, die Maker*innen Bewegung ökonomisch und sozialwissenschaftlich zu beschreiben. Denn das Aufblühen der Maker*innen und DIY Bewegung seit etwa den 2010er Jahren wirft Fragen auf: Wie ist es dazu gekommen? Mit welchen umfassenderen Entwicklungen steht es in Verbindung? Ist das ein Hobby oder Arbeit? Was motiviert die Beteiligten? Warum entstehen so viele wichtige Innovationen in diesen Kontexten? Zur Bearbeitung dieser Fragen können verschiedene sozialtheoretische Rahmungen in Anschlag gebracht werden, die jeweils unterschiedliche Aspekte der Maker*innen Bewegung zum Vorschein bringen. Der vorliegende Text erprobt genau das. Er präsentiert drei verschiedene Rahmungen für das Phänomen der Maker*innen Bewegung – die erweiterte Mikroökonomie, die Bourdieu'sche Feldtheorie und die Praxistheorie – und skizziert ihre jeweiligen Einsichten.

Der Text ist in zwei Abschnitte geteilt. Der erste liefert eine (mögliche) Schilderung der Maker*innen Bewegung. Es geht um ihre Entstehung in der Überschneidung der Hacker*innenkultur mit der Arts-and-Crafts Bewegung, ebenso wie um die Räume, die

Ästhetik, die Praktiken und Narrative, die die Maker*innen Bewegung ausmachen. Anhand eines Beispiels, dem Projekt Plants & Machines, gehen wir näher ins Detail. Der zweite Textabschnitt präsentiert drei verschiedene wissenschaftliche Schablonen und was sie jeweils über die Maker*innen Bewegung auszusagen vermögen: 1) die auf Gary Becker zurückgehende Erweiterung der Mikroökonomie, 2) Pierre Bourdieus Feldtheorie und 3) die Praxistheorien. In ihrer Überlagerung liefern diese wissenschaftlichen Ansätze verschiedene Erklärungsmomente, Konzepte und Denkfiguren, um die Maker*innen Bewegung zu verstehen. Über diese Vorgehensweise wird auch deutlich, dass die Maker*innen Bewegung als empirisches Phänomen zu etwas anderem wird, je nachdem wie man sie konzeptionell bearbeitet (Mol 2003).

2 Entstehung und Merkmale der Maker*innen Bewegung

Über die Maker*innen Bewegung lässt sich sagen, was auch über viele andere Bewegungen zu sagen ist: Dass sich ihr Ursprung nur schwer festlegen lässt. Vielmehr emergiert die Maker*innen Bewegung im Zusammenfließen verschiedener Entwicklungen, von denen sich zwei prominent herausstellen lassen: Die Arts-and-Crafts Bewegung und die Hacker*innenkultur.

Die Arts-and-Crafts Bewegung entsteht im ausgehenden 19. Jahrhundert in Großbritannien. Sie dreht sich um die Wiederentdeckung des Handwerks im Angesicht seiner umfassenden und stetig weiter zunehmenden Überlagerung durch Maschinen. Die industrielle Produktionsweise führt aus Sicht der Arts-and-Crafts Bewegung dazu, dass viele der wertvollen und hart erarbeiteten

Handwerkskünste verloren gehen. Die Arts-and-Crafts Bewegung kritisiert auch, dass den Arbeiter*innen in den neuen maschinellen Konstellationen die Erfüllung und Befriedigung durch handwerkliche Arbeit abhandenkommt, ebenso wie ihre Selbstständigkeit als Mitglieder des freien Handwerks. Es geht also um den Verlust handwerklicher Fähigkeiten und der Qualität der so hergestellten Produkte, ebenso wie um das Problem der Entfremdung durch industrielle Arbeitsweisen und -verhältnisse. Die Arts-and-Crafts Bewegung vertritt dagegen eine Sensibilität für Materialien, Ornamente und die Nutzung von Werkzeugen, sowie die Frage nach guter Arbeit und einem gesunden Zusammenleben. Die Einheit von Entwurf und Produktion wird zu einem ihrer zentralen Merkmale, in dem diese Anliegen zusammenkommen: Designer*innen sollten die Materialien und die manuellen und maschinellen Verfahren beherrschen, die nötig sind, um einen Entwurf umzusetzen. Diese Haltung findet sich heute in den gängigen Ideen über die Kunst- und Design-Ausbildung wieder. Im 20. Jahrhundert lebt sie auch in der Do-it-Yourself-Bewegung weiter (Naylor 1980).

Die zweite Entwicklung, ohne die die Maker*innen Bewegung nicht denkbar wäre, ist die des Hackens. Sie bildet sich ab den 1960er Jahren im Kontext von Universitäten und Forschungseinrichtungen aus, wobei dem Massachusetts Institute of Technology (MIT) eine zentrale Rolle zukommt. Hacken bezeichnet eine Herangehensweise an Computertechnologien, die sich durch Neugier, Verspieltheit und die Ablehnung von Autorität auszeichnet, aber auch Rationalität und Transparenz hochhält. Außerdem geht es um eine Vision: Computertechnologien zur Steigerung der allgemeinen Lebensqualität zu nutzen und nicht lediglich, um bestehende Praktiken des Rechnens und Verwaltens zu beschleunigen

(Levey 1984). Die Hacker*innenkultur ist von Beginn an mit konkreten Orten verbunden, wie dem EAM-Raum am MIT für „Electronic Accounting Machinery". Im Jahr 1959 befand sich in diesem Raum einer der ersten Großrechner, ein IBM 704, an dem Studierende nachts heimlich herumbastelten (ebd.). Diese Szene wird zum Gründungsmythos der Hacker*innenbewegung: Computer auseinandernehmen, neu zusammenbauen und verändern – über diese *hands on* Praktiken eignen sich Hacker*innen die neue Technologie an. Heute sind Hackspaces die physischen Orte, an denen sich die Bewegung manifestiert und weiter entfaltet. Sie bieten Menschen die technische und räumliche Infrastruktur, um gemeinsam an Projekten zu arbeiten. Ab Mitte der 1990er Jahre breiten sie sich in europäischen und nordamerikanischen Großstädten aus. Erste und wegweisende Hackspaces sind die c-base in Berlin (1995), das Metalab in Wien (2006) und Noisebridge in San Francisco (2007).

Mehr oder weniger parallel zu den Hackspaces entstehen schließlich fabrication laboratories (FabLabs) als jene Orte, an denen sich die Hacker*innenkultur und die DIY Bewegung mischen und in denen sich auch die Maker*innen Bewegung kristallisiert.

Abb. 1: Hackerspace *Noisebridge*, San Francisco; Workshop „Arduino for Total Newbies" im Juli 2011; Foto von Mitch Altman (CC BY-SA 2.0) https://en.wikipedia.org/wiki/Noisebridge#/media/File:Noisebridge_Arduinos_For_Total_Newbies_workshop_July_2011.jpg

Das erste FabLab entsteht 2001 am MIT Center for Bits and Atoms. Es stellt eine Vielzahl von Werkzeugen zur Verfügung, die sonst für Privatpersonen kaum zugänglich wären: Laser-Cutter, CNC-Maschinen, 3D-Drucker, Press- und Fräswerkzeuge, industrielle Näh- und Strickmaschinen usw. Gründungsmitglied Neil

Gershenfeld nennt es die Grundausstattung „to make (almost) anything“. So lautet der Titel eines MIT-Kurses, den Gershenfeld seit 1998 anbietet und der ihm gezeigt habe, dass es bei den Nutzer*innen liegt herauszufinden, wie und wofür sich neue Technologien einsetzen lassen. Gegründet wurde das FabLab auch mit dem Ziel, die „Digital Divide“ zu überwinden:

> At the heart of this idea is the belief that the most sustainable way to bring the deepest results of the digital revolution to developing communities is to enable them to participate in creating their own technological tools for finding solutions to their own problems. (Mikhak 2002: 1)

Es geht also darum, Menschen Zugang zu neuen Technologien zu verschaffen und sie zu befähigen, eigene Werkzeuge zu entwickeln, um die eigenen, nicht von einer anderen Instanz definierten Probleme anzugehen. In Deutschland eröffnet das erste FabLab im Jahr 2009 an der RWTH Aachen, heute finden sich FabLabs in fast jeder größeren Stadt. Weltweit gibt es mehr als 400 FabLabs auf allen Kontinenten verteilt. Häufig ist auch synonym von Makerspaces die Rede.

FabLabs, aber auch die zahlreichen DIY-Blogs, Zeitschriften wie „Make“ oder die weltweit stattfindenden Messen, Maker Faires, sind seit einigen Jahren eine sichtbare Manifestation der Maker*innen Bewegung, doch sie lässt sich nicht darauf reduzieren. Die Maker*innen Bewegung ist eher als eine kulturelle Strömung zu begreifen, die Heimwerker*innen, Hobbyisten, DaWanda- und Etsy-Unternehmer*innen, Repair Cafés, Gemeinschaftsgärten,

Kreativmärkte usw. umfasst. Diese Gruppen und Institutionen teilen eine Haltung: Sie schätzen das Selbermachen, Ausprobieren, Lernen, Verstehen und Weiterentwickeln als eine Art von handwerklicher Auseinandersetzung mit Produkten und Technologien. Es geht auch darum, Wissen zu teilen, zu einer Gemeinschaft zu gehören und unabhängiger vom Markt bzw. als souveränere Konsument*innen auftreten zu können.

Anhand eines Beispiels lassen sich mehr Details darüber zutage fördern, was die Maker*innenpraxis ausmacht und umtreibt. Zumindest in unserem Beispiel scheint dazu vor allem das Verhältnis zu ihrer Umwelt zu gehören, zu den Institutionen, Praktiken und Annahmen der professionellen und marktorientierten Innovationsarbeit. Das Projekt Plants & Machines besteht aus einer Gruppe von (ehemaligen) Studierenden an der Bauhaus-Universität Weimar. Den Anfang nimmt Plants & Machines im studentischen Hackspace in Weimar, dem ‚Maschinenraum'[1]. Dort wird mehr oder weniger zweckfrei gebastelt, gehackt und Zeit verbracht. Ein kurzes Beispiel für die Basteleien, die im Maschinenraum stattfinden, ist der ‚twitterbot', der beim Problem des Zugangs zum Maschinenraum Abhilfe schaffen soll. Ein twitter-Account namens @mr_door_status sendet automatisch tweets darüber, ob die Tür zum Maschinenraum zu- oder aufgeschlossen ist.

[1] Begriffe in einfachen Anführungszeichen stammen von unserem Interviewpartner, einem Gründungsmitglied von Plants & Machines. Das Interview wurde von Lisa Conrad am 3.11.2015 im Arbeitsraum von Plants & Machines in Weimar geführt. Mehr und aktuelle Informationen über das Projekt finden sich hier https://plantsandmachines.github.io/.

Ein Sensor am Schloss registriert den Zustand der Tür und ein Aktor, eine Programmierung, sendet den tweet (Abb. 2).

Abb. 2: „Twitterbot“ des Maschinenraums. Account @mr_door_status

Die Idee zu Plants & Machines kommt einer Gruppe von Maschinenraum-Mitgliedern in einem ‚viel zu langen, deprimierenden Winter‘. Sie denken, dass es schön wäre, zuhause, in der eigenen Wohnung, einen grünen, blühenden Garten zu haben. Sie schreiten zur Tat und bauen einen ersten sogenannten ‚kubischen Garten‘ nach den Prinzipien der Aquaponik, die in der DIY Szene sehr beliebt ist. Der Garten besteht aus einer Reihe von transparenten Behältern, in denen jeweils Pflanzen oder Fische leben. Zusammen sollen sie einen in sich geschlossenen Wasser- und Nährstoffkreislauf bilden: Die Pflanzen werden in regelmäßigen Abständen mit dem nährstoffreichen Wasser aus dem Fischbehälter geflutet. Das Wasser wird dadurch gereinigt. Bakterien wandeln die Fischausscheidungen in Nitrat um, das einen Nährstoff für die Nutzpflanzen darstellt. Reguliert werden die einzelnen Behälter und die Verbindungen zwischen ihnen automatisch über Mikrocontroller und Computer. Ein Sensor registriert zum Beispiel, dass es nicht hell genug ist und löst daraufhin die programmierte Aktion aus, die Beleuchtung zu erhöhen.

Abb. 3: Darstellung eines aquaponischen Gartens, Graphik von *Plants & Machines* (CC BY-SA 4.0), online veröffentlicht unter https://plantsandmachines.github.io/

Den Prototypen baut die Gruppe zunächst ‚nur für [sich] selbst'. Doch die Idee, eine Firma zu gründen, ist ‚irgendwie immer präsent': Etwas machen und es dann auch verkaufen können, ‚da ist nichts falsch dran', sagt unser Interviewpartner. Heute sind Plants & Machines als Gesellschaft bürgerlichen Rechts (GbR) eingetragen. Sie finanzieren sich über verschiedene Förderprogramme: das EXIST-Gründer*innenstipendium des Bundesministeriums für Wirtschaft und Energie (ko-finanziert durch den Europäischen Sozialfonds) zum Beispiel. Die Gründungswerkstatt der Bauhaus-Universität, neudeli, stellt ihnen einen Arbeitsraum zur Verfügung. Außerdem erhalten sie Unterstützung durch die Accelerator-Programme der Städte Berlin und München.

Die Mitglieder von Plants & Machines sagen heute von sich: ‚Wir haben fast schon ein richtiges Produkt und sind fast schon keine Maker mehr.' Es ist dieses Aufeinandertreffen von Maker* und Unternehmer*innendasein, das bei Plants & Machines zentral verhandelt wird. Sie fragen sich, ob es gelingen kann, „eine neue Symbiose" herzustellen, das heißt, sich nicht für das Dasein als Maker*in *oder* als Unternehmer*in entscheiden zu müssen, sondern beides miteinander zu kombinieren. Sascha Lobos und Holm Friebes Buch *Wir nennen es Arbeit* stellt bei diesem Vorhaben eine explizite Referenz dar. Lobo und Friebe berichten von der neu entstehenden Gruppe der digitalen Bohème. Vertreter*innen dieser Gruppe gehe es in erster Linie darum, selbstbestimmt mit Freund*innen an eigenen Projekten zu arbeiten. Um dabei „nicht zu verhungern" (Lobo/Friebe 2006: 94) beschließen sie, „die Segnungen der Technologie herzlich zu umarmen und die neuesten Kommunikationstechnologien dazu zu nutzen, ihre Handlungsspielräume zu erweitern" (ebd.: 16). Die Formel lautet: „So arbeiten, wie man leben will, und trotzdem ausreichend Geld damit verdienen; das Ganze ermöglicht und befördert durch das Internet [...]." (ebd.: 15).

Das Element der Selbstbestimmung und der Zweckfreiheit zeigt sich bei Plants & Machines in der Motivation, im Fokus auf Gemeinschaft und Reputation und in ihren Visionen. Der Gruppe um Plants & Machines ist es zunächst wichtig, eine gute Zeit zu haben. Eine gute Zeit wiederum haben sie, wenn sie vor sich hin tüfteln, herumprobieren, experimentieren und dabei auch Risiken eingehen: ‚Wir sind alle Fatalisten', sagt unser Interviewpartner. Er zitiert das Motto: ‚Du weißt nicht, ob es fliegt, bis es fliegt.' Sie möchten Spaß an ihrer Arbeit haben und die Ungewissheit, ob etwas funktioniert oder nicht, gehört dazu. Freundschaften und Reputation aufzubauen ist ihnen ebenso wichtig und zwar nicht, um diese Freundschaften und Reputation in Gelegenheiten zum Geldverdienen umzuwandeln, sondern um ihrer selbst willen. Die Maker*innen-Gemeinschaft bietet eine Möglichkeit, um ‚Leute zu treffen und dadurch eine Stadt für einen selbst weniger anonym zu machen'. Reputation bedeutet, Erwähnung innerhalb der Maker*innen-Community zu finden über ‚coolen Code, coole Projekte, coole Beiträge'. Es geht um Anerkennung für die eigene Arbeit. Ein Ort, an dem sich Reputation entfaltet, ist zum Beispiel die Internetplattform hackaday.io. Dort haben sie ihr Projekt unter dem Titel ‚food replicator' vorgestellt und als Reaktion viele ‚likes' und ‚neue Follower' bekommen. Plants & Machines verfolgt die Vision der Open-Source-Gemeinschaft: Die Nutzer*innen sollen mit ihrer Entwicklung machen können, was sie wollen. Sie glauben an ‚Klauen und Zurückklauen' als Mechanismus, der schneller bessere Lösungen generiert als exklusive Nutzungsrechte, Patente und Lizenzen. Es bräuchte eine Art ‚Umerziehung', einen Wandel der Paradigmen: von der Konkurrenz zur Kooperation. Außerdem geht es ihnen um die Vision, Automation als eigentliche ‚high-end Technologie' simpel zu machen, sie auf ihre Grundelemente zu reduzieren und für Nicht-Expert*innen handhabbar zu machen. Roboter sehen sie als ‚sleeping giants', die in zahlreichen Kontexten Verwendung finden und Vorgänge wesentlich vereinfachen oder verbessern könnten. Das sei einfach ‚eine geile Vision', sagt unser Interviewpartner und ist sich seines überspitzten Technik- und Fortschrittsglaubens bewusst: ‚Etwas bauen und vielleicht die Welt retten.'

Das Element des Unternehmer*innentums übersetzt sich bei Plants & Machines in das Anliegen, ‚sich finanziell über Wasser zu halten', in ihre positive Einstellung zum Unternehmer*innentum, in ihr Sicherheitsbedürfnis und in ihren Glauben an Kooperation als ökonomisches Prinzip. Unternehmer*innentum ist für sie sinnvoll, solange es ihnen erlaubt, weiterhin mit Gleichgesinnten an Projekten arbeiten zu können, die ihnen wichtig sind. Es geht darum, eine Finanzierung für ihre Entwicklungsarbeit und das dafür benötigte Equipment sicherzustellen. Die Haltung von *Wir nennen es Arbeit* übersetzen sie in das Motto: ‚Mach' was du liebst und versuche dich finanziell über Wasser zu halten' – und wenn es mehr als nur das Nötigste zu verdienen gibt, umso besser. Unser Interviewpartner drückt seine insgesamt positive Einstellung zum Unternehmer*innentum aus. Den klassischen Vorwurf der ‚Profitgier' findet er ‚respektlos' gegenüber dem Einsatz, den das Unternehmer*innendasein verlangt, zumindest die anständige Variante davon. Es gebe gewiss zuhauf ‚verrohrte Unternehmenskulturen' und Skandale über die Umgehung staatlicher Regulierung. Er halte aber nichts von der ‚links-rechts-Rhetorik', die den jeweiligen Gegner dämonisiert. Eigentlich stellen beide Positionen verschiedene ‚*worst case* und *best case* Szenarien' zur Verfügung, mit denen sich arbeiten lässt. Doch wenn es um ihre eigenen Lebensentwürfe geht, schleichen sich immer wieder Fragen nach finanzieller Absicherung ein. Die Arbeit im Open-Source-Modus bedeutet, dass sie ihre gesamte Entwicklungsarbeit, jedes Bauteil, jede Zeile Code, dokumentieren und öffentlich machen. Dabei stellt sich gelegentlich das Gefühl ein, dass man diese Arbeit, statt sie ‚zu verschenken, auch in die Altersvorsorge hätte stecken können'. Trotz ihrer festen Überzeugung von der Richtigkeit und Überlegenheit des Open-Source-Ansatzes werden sie ‚ab und zu nervös' und fragen sich, ‚ob das gut geht'. Auf der anderen Seite sehen sie ‚closed innovation' und Patentierung nicht als Lösung an, denn das wäre ‚nicht rational'. Als kleine Firma scheint es ihnen vernünftiger, die Innovationsarbeit zu veröffentlichen und Kooperationspartner*innen zu finden. Im Open-Source-Modus zu arbeiten, ist auch rational, da es mehr Menschen involviert, die auf Fehler oder Probleme hinweisen können. In der Welt von Open Source nennt sich diese Annahme Linus's Law, benannt nach Linus Torvalds, einem der Hauptakteure der Bewegung: „Given enough eyeballs, all bugs are shallow" (Raymond 1999: 30).

Insgesamt legt sowohl die Makro- als auch die Mikro-Perspektive auf die Maker*innen Bewegung nahe, dass sie ein eigenwilliges Verhältnis zu ökonomischen Diskursen und Praktiken unterhält. Einerseits ist sie dominanten ökonomischen Annahmen (Professionalisierung, Konkurrenz, exklusive Nutzungsrechte usw.) gegenüber sehr kritisch eingestellt. Andererseits ist die Suche nach rationalen, effizienten und anwendungsorientierten Lösungen für Probleme ein fester Bestandteil der Bewegung. Die geschilderten Beobachtungen machen auch deutlich, dass es sich bei der Maker*innen Bewegung um eine Ansammlung von heterogenen Momenten handelt: Technologien und Maschinen; Personen und Gemeinschaften, die etwas basteln und produzieren; spezifische Orte kultureller und sozialer Praktiken; Organisationen, Institutionen, Regeln und Normen; Wissensformen und ein spezifisches Verständnis von Wissensvermittlung. All diese Momente treffen in der Maker*innen Bewegung zusammen und erlauben jeweils einen spezifischen Zugang zu diesem Phänomen. Daraus ergibt sich für uns die Frage: Wie begegnen Ökonomie, Soziologie, Organisationsforschung oder die Kulturwissenschaften jeweils dem Phänomen der Maker*innen Bewegung?

3 Ökonomische und soziologische Schablonen für die Maker*innen Bewegung

Im Folgenden werden wir die Beobachtungen über die Maker*innen Bewegung in verschiedene wissenschaftliche Rahmungen setzen und mit ihren jeweiligen Terminologien und Denkfiguren konfrontieren. Die Auswahl der Rahmungen ist dabei weder zufällig noch zwingend. Sie ist auf der einen Seite vom Gegenstandsbereich und andererseits von aktuellen Theoriediskussionen geprägt, hätte aber auch anders ausfallen können. Die drei verschiedenen Rahmungen sind

1) die erweiterte Mikroökonomik nach Gary Becker

2) Pierre Bourdieus Kapitaltheorie und seine Überlegungen zum literarischen Feld

3) die Gruppe der Praxistheorien wie Andreas Reckwitz sie skizziert hat.

Die Reihung dieser Theorieentwürfe sollte nicht zu voreiligen Schlüssen führen. Es handelt sich keinesfalls um eine aufsteigende Liste von Denkfiguren, von denen die erste weitgehend unbrauchbar ist und schrittweise eine Zunahme des Erklärungspotentials erfolgt. Vielmehr liefern die theoretischen Rahmungen jeweils unterschiedliche Elemente, um die Maker*innen Bewegung auszuleuchten. Es wird dabei die enge Beziehung deutlich, die zwischen empirischem Material und wissenschaftlichem Kontext (Disziplinen, Strömungen, Theorieschulen), in dem es behandelt wird, besteht. Empirisches Material ist nicht neutral, sondern als das Produkt jeweils spezifischer intellektueller Traditionen zu verstehen (Mol 2003: ix). In diesem Sinne präsentiert auch der erste Teil dieses Aufsatzes keine neutrale Beschreibung der Maker*innen Bewegung, sondern eine, die die konzeptuellen Rahmungen des zweiten Teils antizipiert.

3.1 Die mikroökonomische Perspektive

Gary Stanley Becker (1930–2014) war die meiste Zeit seiner wissenschaftlichen Karriere an der University of Chicago beschäftigt. In seiner Forschung befasste er sich mit vielfältigen Themen aus dem Schnittfeld von Ökonomie und Soziologie, wie zum Beispiel Kriminalität, Diskriminierung, die Organisation der Familie, Philanthropie oder Neid. Sein zentraler Referenzpunkt war dabei durchweg die Mikroökonomik. Im traditionellen mikroökonomischen Grundmodell gelten Unternehmen als produzierende, Haushalte dagegen als konsumierende Einheiten. Zwischen den Unternehmen und den Haushalten gibt es Märkte, die das Angebot der Unternehmen mit der Nachfrage der Haushalte verbinden. Daneben basiert das mikroökonomische Grundmodell auf der Annahme, dass Wirtschaftssubjekte vollständig informiert (es gibt keine Such- oder Vermittlungskosten) und vollkommen unabhängig voneinander sind (es gibt keine sozialen Wechselwirkungen zwischen ihnen).

Becker führt drei neue Elemente in die Mikroökonomie ein, indem er bestehende durch neue Annahmen ersetzt. Die Annahme, dass Wirtschaftssubjekte vollkommen unabhängig voneinander sind, ersetzt er durch die Annahme der sozialen Wechselwirkungen. Er entwickelt dazu das Konzept des sozialen Einkommens. Es umfasst die Summe aus dem Eigen-Einkommen einer Person (ihrem Verdienst etc.), und dem monetären Wert, den relevante Eigenschaften anderer Personen für sie haben. Es wird also angenommen, „daß eine Reihe von Charakteristika verschiedener Personen die Nutzenfunktion gewisser anderer Personen berühren" (Becker 1982: 285). Die „Wohlfahrt" einer einzelnen Person bestimmt sich nicht nur durch ihr eigenes Einkommen, sondern auch durch die soziale Umwelt, durch „die Einstellungen und das Verhalten anderer" (ebd.: 291).

Zweitens betrachtet Becker Haushalte nicht länger als passive Konsumenten, sondern als aktive Produzenten. Haushalte kombinieren demnach am Markt erworbene Güter mit eigenen Ressourcen, wie Zeit und bestimmten Fertigkeiten, um haushaltsspezifische Güter herzustellen, wie Erholung, Geborgenheit, Gesundheit und Unterhaltung.[2] Er verweist bei dieser Erweiterung des mikroökonomischen Grundmodells auf andere Forschungsarbeiten, die in gleicher Weise Haushalte als „kleine Fabriken“ verstehen, die Investitionsgüter, Rohstoffe, Energie und Zeit zusammenbringen (Cairncross 1958).

Drittens widmet sich Becker der Frage nach der Allokation von Zeit. Es geht ihm nicht nur um „die Frage der Aufteilung der Zeit zwischen Markt und Nicht-Marktbereichen“, sondern auch innerhalb des Nicht-Marktbereichs (Becker 1982: 97). Sein Ausgangspunkt ist die Beobachtung, dass „die Zeitspanne, die man der Arbeit widmete, nie ständig größer war als die Zeitspanne, die man anderen Aktivitäten widmete“ (ebd.). Das ist sogar der Fall, wenn eine Woche aus sechs Arbeitstagen zu je vierzehn Stunden besteht: Die Hälfte der Gesamtzeit steht immer noch zur eigenen Gestaltung zur Verfügung, so makaber das klingen mag. Becker konstatiert, dass sich die wöchentliche Lohnarbeitszeit beachtlich verringert hat und „die Arbeitswoche heute in den meisten Ländern unter 50 Stunden liegt, also bei weniger als einem Drittel der insgesamt verfügbaren Zeit“ (ebd.). Er leitet daraus ab, dass die Nutzung der Nicht-Arbeitszeit von großer Bedeutung ist und dass Ökonom*innen ihr mehr Aufmerksamkeit schenken sollten. Für die Ausgestaltung dieser Nicht-Arbeitszeit treffen Wirtschaftssubjekte zahlreiche „Verhaltensentscheidungen, bei denen es um eine Wahl unter konkurrierenden Zielen bei begrenzten Ressourcen geht – dies

[2] Z.B. Lebensmittel, Rezept, Zeit, Geschick = Mahlzeit; oder Abo bei einem Streaming-Dienst, Freund*innen bzw. Personen, die die eigene Nutzenfunktion erhöhen, Zeit = Unterhaltung.

entspricht ja einer gängigen Definition von Ökonomie“ (Becker 1982: 148).

Mit diesen Erweiterungen des mikroökonomischen Grundmodells handelte sich Becker eine Reihe von Vorwürfen ein, gleichzeitig erhielt er 1992 den Nobelpreis für Wirtschaftswissenschaften. Der zentrale Vorwurf lautete, dass er jeden Lebensbereich den Bedingungen der Ökonomie unterwerfe. Er erklärt alle Verhaltensweisen mit den Kalkülen des homo oeconomicus aus der Mikroökonomie: die „Entscheidung für eine Religion, für eine Ehefrau, für eine bestimmte Familiengröße, für eine Scheidung, für die Zugehörigkeit zu einer politischen Partei oder für einen ‚Lebensstil‘“ (ebd.: 148). Nichts entzieht sich der nutzenmaximierenden Rationalität. Doch gerade für diese radikale Ausdehnung des ökonomischen Ansatzes wird Becker auch gewürdigt, denn sie macht Konsumverhalten, Haushalte, Nicht-Arbeit und soziale Beziehungen für die ökonomische Analyse erst verfügbar. Becker selbst betont, dass er im ökonomischen nicht den einzigen und einzig richtigen Ansatz zur Erklärung menschlichen Verhaltens sieht. Er biete einen wertvollen, integrativen und „verführerischen“ Bezugsrahmen für ein breites Spektrum an sozialen Phänomenen, nichtsdestotrotz „stammen viele wichtige Begriffe und Methoden von anderen Disziplinen und werden auch weiterhin von diesen erbracht“ (ebd.: 13, 15). Laut Becker geht es darum, menschliches Verhalten nicht als „schizophren“ abzustempeln. Das ökonomische Modell betrachtet es stur so, „als habe man es mit Akteuren zu tun, die ihren Nutzen, bezogen auf ein stabiles Präferenzsystem, maximieren“ (ebd.: 15).

Es ist aufschlussreich, Beckers Forschung in ihrem historischen Kontext zu betrachten und mit langfristigen Entwicklungen zusammenzudenken. In der zweiten Hälfte des 20. Jahrhunderts, inmitten der industriellen Moderne, hat sich in den westlichen Gesellschaften eine stark ausdifferenzierte Form der Arbeitsteilung etabliert. Der Haushalt wird kaum noch als ein Ort begriffen, an dem gearbeitet und produziert wird. Im Gegenteil, er präsentiert sich als reiner Konsum-, Freizeit- und Beziehungsraum. Damit korrespondiert das bereits seit den 1930er Jahren bestehende Bemühen, den Haushalt zu rationalisieren und zu technisieren, sodass die Arbeit quasi daraus verschwindet (Haase 1992). In Anbetracht dieser Inszenierung des Haushalts wird seine Beschreibung als „kleine Fabrik" als Angriff auf diesen Gegenpol zur ökonomischen Logik verstanden. Ganz anders präsentiert sich die Situation, als Adam Smith 1776 die damals revolutionäre Idee der Arbeitsteilung und Spezialisierung in seinem Text zum Wohlstand der Nationen beschreibt (Smith 1776/1974). Zu dieser Zeit war der Haushalt noch eine Wirtschaftseinheit. Die Hausgemeinschaft erwirtschaftete alle Güter zum eigenen Bedarf und nur wenn sich dieser nicht vollständig decken ließ, bot sie diese auch zum Tausch an. Das Wort Ökonomik bezeichnet von der Antike bis ins 17. Jahrhundert die Lehre von der guten Bewirtschaftung des Hauses, des oikos, verstanden als die Lehre von der weitgehend autarken Bedarfsdeckung (Rabe 1974).

Beckers Intervention aus den 1960er Jahren stellt eine Verbindung zu diesem ökonomischen, vorindustriellen Haus her. Heute, also ein halbes Jahrhundert später, erscheint es weniger aufrührerisch, den Haushalt und die Nicht-Arbeitszeit als produktiv und durchdrungen von Nutzenmaximierungskalkülen aufzufassen. Vielmehr bietet es sich an, um die DIY-Bewegungen und ihr explizites Herausstellen der Produktivität jenseits der Lohnarbeit zu beschreiben. Mit Beckers Vokabeln ist das Tüfteln in der Nicht-Arbeitszeit ein Mittel zur Erzielung von zusätzlichem Einkommen. Verdienste nehmen die Form von Geldsubstituten an, wie Freude, Können, sozialen Beziehungen und Prestige, doch bisweilen entstehen auch Produkte, die den professionellen Produktionen Aufmerksamkeit und Geld streitig machen. Die Maker*innen Bewegung versteht sich auch als subversive Praxis: Sie feiert die Hobbybastler*innen, die sich während der regulären Arbeitszeit schonen und nach Feierabend verausgaben, wenn sie neue Objekte oder Medieninhalte kreieren. Die Produktivität jenseits der Lohnarbeit präsentiert sich hier als die Schaffung von Spielräumen, um im Hinblick auf die Austauschbeziehungen am Markt an Handlungsmacht und Souveränität zu gewinnen.

3.2 Die kapital- und feldtheoretische Perspektive

Ein zweiter Ansatz zum Verständnis der DIY und Maker*innen Bewegungen stellt die erweiterte Kapitaltheorie nach Pierre Bourdieu dar. Sie lässt sich unmittelbar an Gary Beckers Überlegungen anschließen. In den 1970er Jahren übernimmt Bourdieu Beckers Auffassung von einzelnen Akteuren als eigennützig und interessengeleitet und wendet sich damit von jenen soziologischen Theorien ab, bei denen Anpassung an soziale Normen im Zentrum steht (Convert 2003). Doch Bourdieu ist im Gegensatz zu Becker ein Klassentheoretiker. Er verfolgt die Frage, wie sich soziale Klassen konstituieren und reproduzieren. Er situiert das eigennützige und kapitalakkumulierende Handeln also im Kontext der Klassengesellschaft, womit er anerkennt, dass die einzelnen Akteure unterschiedliche Ausgangsbedingungen haben bzw. über in Quantität und Qualität verschiedenes Kapital verfügen. So sind beispielsweise die Chancen auf Profit durch schulische Bildung nicht für alle gleich, sondern variieren in Abhängigkeit von der „Verteilung des kulturellen Kapitals zwischen den Klassen" (Bourdieu 1983: 185). Neben dem ökonomischen Kapital sind für Bourdieu zwei weitere Kapitalformen von Bedeutung, um „die Reproduktion der gesellschaftlichen Struktur" zu verstehen: kulturelles Kapital und soziales Kapital (ebd.: 198).

Kulturelles Kapital steht für Bildung, Ausbildung und Habitus. Es liegt meist in inkorporierter Form vor: als Wissen, Fähigkeiten, Benehmen oder Sprechweisen. Kulturelles Kapital kann aber auch eine objektivierte und institutionalisierte Form annehmen: als Gegenstände (Bücher, Gemälde, Instrumente, Möbel) oder Bildungsabschlüsse (Titel, Auszeichnungen). Der zentrale und laut Bourdieu häufig übersehene Ort der Erlangung von kulturellem Kapital ist die Familie. Je nachdem, über wie viel Kulturkapital sie verfügt, ist „die gesamte Zeit der Sozialisation zugleich eine Zeit der Akkumulation" (Bourdieu 1983: 188). Unter dem Begriff des sozialen Kapitals fasst Bourdieu das Netz „von mehr oder weniger institutionalisierten *Beziehungen*" zusammen (ebd.: 190, Herv. im Orig.). Die Größe des Sozialkapitals bemisst sich aus der „Ausdehnung des Netzes" sowie aus der Kapitalträchtigkeit der Mitglieder (ebd.: 191). Sozialkapital verlangt nach permanenter Aufrechterhaltung: Es müssen regelmäßig Zeit, Geschenke oder Einladungen mit den betroffenen Personen ausgetauscht werden, um es zu erhalten und früher oder später Nutzen daraus ziehen zu können (ebd.).

Dieses erweiterte Kapitalverständnis wendet Bourdieu auch an, um den Bereich der kulturellen und künstlerischen Produktion zu untersuchen, einen Bereich, den er als „gesonderte Welt mit je eigenen Gesetzen“ versteht (Bourdieu 1999: 84). In seiner literatursoziologischen Arbeit *Die Regeln der Kunst* geht es darum, wie sich die „Ökonomie der Praxis“ (ebd.: 184) in diesem speziellen Feld ausspielt, das ein explizites Desinteresse an ökonomischem Kapital ausstellt. Dafür betrachtet Bourdieu das Paris des späten 19. Jahrhunderts, wo sich in Abgrenzung zur „Herrschaft des Geldes“ – zur Schicht der „Industriellen und Kaufleute mit riesigen Vermögen“ – eine neue soziale Gruppe herausbildet, die Bohème (ebd.: 84). Sie versucht, die sich immer weiter ausdehnenden Machtansprüche der Vermögenden einzuschränken. Dies gelingt ihr im Feld der künstlerischen und literarischen Produktion. Die Vertreter*innen der Avantgarde lösen sich von jeglicher Orientierung an der Nachfrage und stellen damit dar, dass sie „keinen anderen Herrn und Meister anerkennen wollen als ihre Kunst“ (ebd.: 134). Es ist eine Art Unabhängigkeitserklärung „gegenüber externen, politischen oder wirtschaftlichen Mächten” (ebd.: 104). Dieser Anspruch auf Autonomie und Legitimationsmacht im Feld der Kunst kommt im permanenten Bruch mit bestehenden Normen zum Ausdruck: in „Waghalsigkeiten und Überschreitungen“ und „nicht abbrechenden Provokationen“ (ebd.: 99, 110).

Bourdieu beschreibt den Avantgarde-Pol im Feld der Kunst als eine genuin anti-ökonomische Ökonomie. Doch es bleibt eine Ökonomie: Eine andere Kapitalform hat sich hier etabliert und wird mit Eifer akkumuliert und gehandelt. Er nennt es symbolisches Kapital. Dieses Kapital entsteht über Anerkennung innerhalb des Bereichs der reinen Kunst. Diese Anerkennung wiederum erhält man, indem man „absolute Unabhängigkeit vom Markt und seinen Ansprüchen“ unter Beweis stellt (Bourdieu 1999: 228). Es gilt die in gewisser Weise simple Maxime, dass ein Werk umso bedeutsamer ist, je weniger es sich an Wirtschaftlichkeit orientiert. Symbolisches Kapital kreiert sich also in dem Moment, wo auf ökonomische Verwertung verzichtet oder ökonomische Interessen *verleugnet* werden. Denn symbolisches Kapital – Prestige, Anerkennung, Ruhm – funktioniert wie ein Kredit (ebd.). In bestimmten Phasen kann es genutzt werden, um tatsächlich Geld zu verdienen oder anderweitig den Lebensunterhalt zu sichern. Anhand seines zentralen Falls, dem Autor Gustave Flaubert, zeigt Bourdieu allerdings auch, dass das Vorliegen ökonomischen Kapitals immer noch am besten „von den Zwängen und Dringlichkeiten der unmittelbaren Nachfrage" befreit (ebd.: 137). Flaubert, der Propagator des absoluten wirtschaftlichen Desinteresses, verfügte über eine umfangreiche Erbschaft.

Was bedeuten Bourdieus Konzepte für die DIY und Maker*innen Bewegung? Zunächst lenken sie die Aufmerksamkeit auf die Frage der Klassenzugehörigkeit. Woher kommen die Leute, die sich in Fablabs die Zeit vertreiben, die an Projekten arbeiten, weil es Spaß macht, weil sie innerhalb der community dafür Anerkennung und ‚likes' bekommen und mit denen sie vielleicht irgendwann in der Zukunft auch Geld verdienen können? Gerade das Vorliegen eines hohen Kulturkapitals könnte herangezogen werden, um die Maker*innen der 2010er Jahre von den Heimwerker*innen und Hauswirtschafter*innen der Nachkriegszeit zu unterscheiden. Es sind Personen, die nicht aus einem Mangel heraus handeln, sondern eine fehlende Effizienz und Zielgerichtetheit zur Schau stellen. Zweitens ist es eben die Verleugnung ökonomischer Interessen, die die Maker*innen mit Bourdieus Figur der Künstler*in teilen. Es geht in der Maker*innen Bewegung vielfach darum, innerhalb der community anerkannt zu werden, also innerhalb des recht autonom agierenden Feldes der Techies oder der digitalen Bohème. Diese Anerkennung gibt es für ,coolen Code, coole Projekte, coole Beiträge', wie unser Interview-Partner von Plants & Machines es beschreibt, und nicht für ökonomische Erfolge.

Dem Soziologen Andreas Reckwitz zufolge ist es ein zentrales Phänomen unserer Zeit, dass sich die Künstler*innen-Figur in Bereiche jenseits der Kunst ausdehnt. Die Forderung nach Kreativität gewinnt nicht nur in den neuen Berufsfeldern der sogenannten Kreativindustrie zunehmend an Bedeutung. Der ständige Ruf nach Innovation scheint auch mittlere und kleine Betriebe jeglicher Branchen erreicht zu haben. Laut Reckwitz hat dies mit der Entwicklung eines neuen hegemonialen Subjekts zu tun, die sich etwa seit den 1970er Jahren vollzieht. Er bezeichnet dieses Ideal-Ich als „konsumtorisches Kreativsubjekt" (Reckwitz 2006: 588ff.). Es vereint in gewisser Weise, was im Paris des 19. Jahrhunderts noch getrennt existierte: Die Figur des Bohemiens, die permanent mit Grenzen spielt und sie überschreitet, und die Figur vom erfolgreichen Kaufmann/Kauffrau, die ein Gespür für den Markt und die Dynamiken der Nachfrage hat. Die antagonistische Struktur, die Bourdieu zwischen dem kommerziellen und dem anti-ökonomischen Pol der kulturellen Produktion identifiziert, findet sich demnach in der Postmoderne wieder. Allerdings zieht sie sich durch das konsumatorische Kreativsubjekt hindurch: Es ist „Künstlersubjekt und Selbstunternehmer gleichermaßen" (ebd.: 591), eine „ästhetisch-ökonomische Doublette" (ebd.: 500). Dabei werden die Anforderungen nach „individueller Differenz" (ebd.: 603) auf der einen Seite und die Marktorientierung auf der anderen Seite „nicht als einander widersprechend" erlebt, „sondern als komplementär, einander ergänzend und sich gegenseitig verstärkend“ (ebd.: 599).

In Anbetracht dieser Analyse präsentieren sich die DIY und Maker*innen Bewegungen als Räume sozialerwünschter Ich-Gestaltung. Sie erlauben die Einübung des Spannungsverhältnisses zwischen ästhetisch-expressiver Selbstkreation und generalisierter Marktförmigkeit. Die Beherrschung dieser beiden Codes, des Künstlerischen und des Ökonomischen, strukturiert die heutige Subjektkultur.

3.3 Die praxistheoretische Perspektive

Eine dritte Rahmung, in die sich die Maker*innen Bewegung stellen lässt, ist die der Praxistheorien. Dieses „Bündel von Theorien mit ‚Familienähnlichkeit‘“ (Reckwitz 2003: 283) hat sich in verschiedenen Disziplinen und bei verschiedenen Autor*innen entwickelt. Häufig genannt werden Harold Garfinkel und die Ethnomethodologie; Anthony Giddens und die Strukturationstheorie; Michel Foucault, Gilles Deleuze und der Poststrukturalismus; Judith Butler und die Performanztheorie; oder Karin Knorr-Cetina, Bruno Latour und die Laborstudien. Auch die bereits hier verarbeiteten Autoren Pierre Bourdieu und Andreas Reckwitz gelten als Vertreter der Praxistheorien, wobei Letzterer insbesondere dazu beigetragen hat, den praxistheoretischen Ansatz theoretisch zu positionieren und zu explizieren (ebd.).

Innerhalb der Praxistheoriefamilie werden Praktiken als die kleinste Einheit des Sozialen gesehen und gleichermaßen als die zentrale Entität, in der sich Sozialität manifestiert. Demnach ist die Frage des Sozialen weder in individuellen Entscheidungsakten noch in gesellschaftsumspannenden Strukturen zu suchen, sondern in alltäglichen Praktiken des Lebensvollzugs. Diese Praktiken sind der Ort des Sozialen (Schatzki 2002). In ihnen wird soziale Ordnung produziert und aufrechterhalten, ebenso wie sie an neue Umstände angepasst und inkrementell modifiziert wird. Praktiken und soziale Ordnung sind damit aufs engste miteinander verschaltet. Praktiken sind Träger von sozialer Ordnung: Sie erzeugen die relative Gleichartigkeit und Vorhersehbarkeit von Handlungen „über zeitliche und räumliche Grenzen hinweg" (Reckwitz 2003: 292). Die eigentlich erstaunliche Geordnetheit der Sozialwelt ergibt sich aus Routinehandlungen, die sich wiederum aus dem impliziten Wissen über angemessenes Verhalten sowie angemessene Ziele und Wünsche und damit korrespondierende Lebensführungen nähren. Gleichzeitig sind es auch Praktiken, die die soziale Ordnung verändern. Sie sind nicht vollständig determiniert. Vielmehr finden sie immer in einem konkreten Kontext und einer konkreten Situation statt, die das Element der Unberechenbarkeit einbringen. Aus praxistheoretischer Sicht sind identische Wiederholungen von Praktiken nicht möglich, obwohl sie als solche wahrgenommen werden können. Vielmehr finden in Praktiken ständig Verschiebungen statt. Die soziale Ordnung ist auch deshalb in permanenter, wenn auch meist kaum wahrnehmbarer Bewegung, weil die Praktiken, aus denen sie besteht, nicht getrennt voneinander existieren. Ganz im Gegenteil, sie überlagern und kreuzen sich. Sowohl in bestimmten Situationen, an bestimmten Orten, als auch innerhalb einzelner Subjekte treffen verschiedene Praxiskomplexe aufeinander. Diese Überlagerungen können zu Spannungen und Konflikten führen, aber auch zu sozialen und kulturellen Innovationen.

Besonders im Hinblick auf Materialität und Verkörperung heben sich Praxistheorien von anderen Sozialtheorien ab. Oder anders gesagt: der starke Einbezug von Materialität und Verkörperung kann als zentrales Element gesehen werden, das Praxistheorien zu einer anderen Beschreibung der sozialen Welt führt. Theodore Schatzki beispielsweise beschreibt Praktiken als ein Amalgam von „doings and sayings“, das Artefakte wie Werkzeuge, Technologien oder Gegenstände umfasst, ebenso wie Räume und Körper (Schatzki 2002: 73). Sie sind elementare Bestandteile von Praktiken. Der Körper ist der Träger von Wissen, Fähigkeiten, Gefühlen und Gedanken. Im Zuge des Heranwachsens in einer historisch und kulturell spezifischen Konstellation wird er durch verschiedene Praktiken geformt und zu ihnen befähigt. Am Ende dieses Prozesses ist das Subjekt in der Lage, Praktiken ‚richtig‘ und intelligibel auszuführen, also auf eine Art und Weise, die von anderen wahrgenommen, verstanden und aufgegriffen werden kann. Dass eine Praktik nicht ‚gelingt‘, ist daran erkennbar, dass sie ignoriert oder sanktioniert wird. Die Praxistheorien betrachten auch den Geist – im Sinne von Wünschen, Zielen oder Glaubenssätzen – als Resultat und Teil historisch und kulturell spezifischer Praktiken. Statt von Intentionen, Interessen oder Vorlieben gehen sie von erlernten und Praktiken inhärenten „Motiv/Emotions-Komplexen“ aus (Reckwitz 2003: 293). Über Inkorporierung werden Subjekte letztendlich zu fähigen und zuverlässigen Trägern diverser von ihnen abverlangter (oder von ihnen angestrebter) Praktiken. Dabei muss die Ausführung nicht bewusst oder intentional ablaufen, sondern sie geht meistens routiniert oder automatisch vonstatten.

Materialität im Sinne von Artefakten und Umwelten ist für Praxistheorien zunächst insofern relevant, als das Subjekt den richtigen Gebrauch mit ihnen beherrschen muss. Über den gekonnten Umgang mit bestimmten Artefakten oder die Selbstverständlichkeit, mit der es sich in bestimmten Umgebungen bewegt und spricht, kann z.B. die Mitgliedschaft zu bestimmten Gruppen hergestellt werden. Daneben sind Objekte und konkrete Situationen aber auch stets eine Herausforderung und Provokation an gut eingeübte Handlungsmuster. Latour bringt den Aspekt mit diesem Fragenkatalog zum Ausdruck: Wenn wir handeln, wer handelt dann außerdem noch? Wie viele Handlungsträger sind außer uns noch präsent? Wie kommt es, dass wir nie tun, was wir wollen? (Latour 2007) Für die Praxistheorien emergiert Handeln im interdependenten Zusammenspiel von menschlicher und materieller Handlungsmacht. Gerade neue Technologien, wie beispielsweise der Fahrstuhl zu Beginn des 20. Jahrhunderts (Bernard 2006) oder das Smartphone an dessen Ende, stellen eine „kreativ zu beantwortende irritative Herausforderung“ dar (Reckwitz 2003: 285). Sie verlangen und ermöglichen neue Praktiken, indem sie Handlungsdruck ausüben.

Davide Nicolini, der die Praxistheorien für die Organisationsforschung aufarbeitet, schreibt: „Things seem to fall into place much better if we think of the fluid scene that unfolds in front of us in terms of multiple practices carried out at the same time.” (Nicolini 2012: 2) Wie fallen die Dinge also zusammen, betrachtet man die Maker*innen Bewegung im Hinblick auf verschiedene Praktiken, die gleichzeitig ausgeführt werden? Zunächst lassen sich die heterogenen Praxiskomplexe identifizieren, die sich in der

Maker Bewegung kreuzen und überlagern. Im Rückgriff auf den Fall von Plants & Machines sind das u.a. folgende:

- verstehen und gestalten im *hands on* Modus (Arts-and-Crafts Bewegung, Design, Kunst),
- experimentelles und zweckfreies Basteln mit Hightech (Hacker*innenkultur),
- Desinteresse an ökonomischer Verwertbarkeit (Bohème, Avantgarde, aber auch Wachstumskritik),
- Gleichgesinnte finden, sich vernetzen, Wissen teilen und tauschen (Open Source, Web 2.0),
- Start-up-Szene, unternehmerisches Denken und generalisierte Marktförmigkeit
- „Technological Solutionism" (Morozov 2013), apolitischer Fortschritts- und Technikglaube.

Es sind „doings and sayings" aus all diesen Bereichen, die die Maker*innen Bewegung aufruft. Sie ist aus ihrem Zusammentreffen entstanden und andersherum wirkt die Maker*innen Bewegung auf diese Praxiskomplexe zurück. Sie hat sich soweit konturiert und konkretisiert, dass Politik, Organisationsentwicklung oder Design sie in ihre eigenen Praktiken integrieren (z.B. EU-, nationale und kommunale Förderung; neue Bürolandschaften und Projektmanagementmodelle wie Scrum; Open-Source-Hardware und Open Design). Die verschiedenen Praktiken, die die Maker*innen Bewegung ausmachen, kreieren aber auch Spannungen. Zum Beispiel steht das zweckfreie Tüfteln im Widerspruch zu dem Wunsch, mithilfe von Technologie drängende gesellschaftliche Probleme anzugehen. Ebenso sind völlige Transparenz und das

Teilen des eigenen Wissens schwer vereinbar mit Marktbedingungen (Wettbewerb und Verknappung) und der Notwendigkeit, sich seinen Lebensunterhalt zu sichern.

Diese Gegensätze werden von den verschiedenen Beteiligten der Maker*innen Bewegung wahrgenommen und navigiert, doch die Art, wie dies geschieht und welche Verschiebungen sich ergeben, ist unterschiedlich. Denn die Personen handeln jeweils an konkreten Orten: in konkreten Hackspaces, Fablabs, Werkstätten, genauso wie sie konkrete Medieninhalte produzieren und rezipieren. Die „community of practice“ (Lave/Wengers 1991) der Maker*innen zerfällt bei näherer Betrachtung in verschiedene „communities of practice“, die sich jeweils anders entwickeln. Die eine sucht die Nähe zu Unternehmen und Investor*innen, die andere wendet sich Bildungs- und Forschungseinrichtungen zu, die nächste fokussiert politische oder ökologische Fragen. Praxistheoretisch tritt also auch die relative Instabilität – das Werden und Vergehen – der Maker*innen Bewegung zutage (Schäfer 2016). So erlaubt die Praxistheorie, die Maker*innen Bewegung als randständige, weitgehend gegenkulturelle Praxis zu betrachten, die aber durch die Überschneidungen ihrer Praktiken mit denen der reinen Ökonomie, der Forschung, der Bildung oder der Politik in der Lage ist, sowohl diese Kontexte, als auch ihre eigene Stellung zu verändern. Es bleibt damit zunächst offen, ob die Maker*innen Bewegung eine gesteigerte Ausprägung des kapitalistischen Geistes mit sich bringt oder ob sich durch sie solche Praktiken stärker ausformen und verbreiten, die der generalisierten Marktorientierung Konkurrenz machen (z.B. Bereitstellung und Nutzung von Gemeinschaftsgütern oder das Copyleft).

4 Zusammenfassung und Diskussion

Wir haben in diesem Text drei verschiedene „sozialtheoretische Optionen" (Reckwitz 2003: 284) vorgestellt und sie jeweils mit der Maker*innen Bewegung zusammengebracht.

Die Erweiterung der Mikroökonomie, wie Gary Becker sie vorgeschlagen hat, fasst die Maker*innen Bewegung als eine rationale, ökonomische Tätigkeit auf. Es geht um die Allokation von Zeit und Ressourcen zur Maximierung von Nutzen. Dieser Nutzen besteht demnach in der Ausbildung spezifischer Fähigkeiten oder im Konsum eines sozialen Kontexts. Die Nicht-Arbeitszeit wird genutzt, um andere Güter und Dienstleistungen herzustellen, wie Regeneration, Freundschaft und Reputation. Aus dieser Perspektive sind die Maker*innen eine Bewegung, die die Produktivität jenseits klassischer Marktbeziehungen fokussiert und ernst nimmt. Sie stellen die Produktivität der Nicht-Arbeitszeit explizit heraus, ebenso wie die Gewinne, die sie darüber erzielen.

Pierre Bourdieus Feldtheorie hilft, vermeintlich anti-ökonomische Verhaltensweisen im Maker*innen Kontext als Handlungen zu betrachten, die symbolisches Kapital generieren. Die verdrehte Ökonomie der künstlerischen und literarischen Produktion findet sich bei den Maker*innen wieder. Gerade das Desinteresse an einer Nachfrage machen ihre Produkte wertvoll und interessant. Aus eben dieser Verleugnung ökonomischer Interessen nährt sich laut Andreas Reckwitz auch das konsumtorische Kreativsubjekt, die aktuell hegemoniale Subjektformation. Das heißt, die Figur der Künstler*in, die Bourdieu als peripher beschrieben hat, wird heute immer zentraler. Das konsumtorische Kreativsubjekt der Postmoderne hat aber anders als die Künstler*innenfigur bei Bourdieu die

Aufgabe, die reine und die profane Kunst – desinteressiertes Experimentieren und aggressive Selbstvermarktung – gleichzeitig oder parallel zu vollziehen. Bei den Maker*innen wird das zum Beispiel in der Ablehnung des klassischen Unternehmer*innentums und der gleichzeitigen prinzipiellen Zuwendung zu Vermarktungsmöglichkeiten deutlich.

Die Praxistheorie erlaubt, die Maker*innen Bewegung als eine Praxis zu beschreiben, die aus einer spezifischen historischen und kulturellen Entwicklung emergiert. Sie wendet sich vom Textualismus und Mentalismus der Sozialwissenschaften ab und integriert den Anteil, den materielle Strukturen, Räume und Technologien an dieser Herausbildung haben. Sie inkludiert die Dinge, die herausfordern und Handlungsdruck erzeugen (z.B. Computer). Praxistheoretisch betrachtet sind es vor allem bestimmte Routinen, habitualisierte Umgangs- und Sprechweisen, die die Maker*innen Bewegung abgrenzen und in Existenz halten. Individuelle Rationalitäten oder gesellschaftliche Felder spielen weniger eine Rolle als vielmehr die ‚community of practice', die Gruppe, die sowohl virtuell und abstrakt existiert, als auch konkret und lokal. Es ist ein strikt relationaler Ansatz: soziale Ordnung formt Praktiken und Praktiken formen soziale Ordnung. An einem Ort wie einem Fablab treffen verschiedene Praktiken zusammen, die sich gegenseitig beeinflussen. Aus diesem Gemenge gehen neue Relationen, Entitäten und Praxiskomplexe hervor, wie beispielsweise die Start-up-Szene oder die Open Hardware Bewegung.

Die drei verschiedenen theoretischen Rahmungen weisen viele Überlappungen, gemeinsame Bezugspunkte und Komplementaritäten auf. In einer praxistheoretischen Sicht tauchen Kategorien und Elemente auf, die sowohl bei Becker als auch bei Bourdieu von Bedeutung sind, wie produktive Subjekte; soziale Wechselwirkungen; soziales, kulturelles und ökonomisches Kapital; Gewohnheiten und Habitualisierungen oder feldspezifische Normen und Wertigkeiten. Becker integriert soziale Wechselwirkungen in die ökonomische Analyse. Pierre Bourdieu integriert nichtmonetäre Kapitalsorten in die soziologische Analyse. Doch es gibt auch Inkompatibilitäten zwischen den drei vorgestellten Rahmungen: Die Praxistheorie widersetzt sich den mentalistischen und (hyper-)rationalistischen Vorstellungen, die bei Becker zentral sind. Zugleich widersetzt sie sich der Vorstellung von gesellschaftlichen Feldern, wie sie bei Bourdieu zu finden sind. Die Praxistheorie bewegt sich eher auf der Ebene des Mikrosozialen. Sie akzeptiert und fokussiert dabei auch die Beobachtung von Einzelfällen. Es ist damit weniger der Blick auf das ganze Feld der kulturellen Produktion wie bei Bourdieu, oder auf vermeintlich universelles, modelliertes menschliches Verhalten wie bei Becker, sondern eher der Blick auf eine konkrete „community of practice“, der für die Praxistheorie interessant und aufschlussreich ist.

Die drei Rahmungen stehen nicht in einem Verhältnis einer kumulativen Steigerung von Komplexität. Vielmehr weisen sie jeweils für sich ein komplexes wissenschaftliches Instrumentarium zur Betrachtung der Maker*innen Bewegung auf. Es ist wichtig, sie in ihren jeweiligen historischen und disziplinären Kontexten zu sehen. Welche Neuerungen bringen sie ein und wie verhalten sich diese Annahmen zu gesellschaftlichen Entwicklungen, in die sie eingebettet sind? Mit welchen aktuellen Entwicklungen kollidieren sie? Und welchen Status sollte man Theorieentwürfen wie denen von Becker und Bourdieu zuweisen – trotz der Kritik, die seither an ihnen geübt wurde? Wir halten es für sinnvoll und fruchtbar, ein konkretes und zeitgenössisches Phänomen wie die Maker*innen Bewegung mit verschiedenen theoretischen Entwürfen zu konfrontieren. Dieses Vorgehen dient einerseits dazu, das Phänomen intensiv und in verschiedenen Iterationsschritten zu bearbeiten und dabei jeweils andere Aspekte zu fokussieren. Andererseits bietet es die Möglichkeit, eine Sensibilität für das Verhältnis zwischen Theorie, historischem Kontext und empirischen Fällen zu entwickeln.

Literaturverzeichnis

Becker, Gary S. (1982): Der ökonomische Ansatz zur Erklärung menschlichen Verhaltens. Tübingen.

Bernard, Andreas (2006): Die Geschichte des Fahrstuhls. Über einen beweglichen Ort der Moderne. Frankfurt am Main.

Bourdieu, Pierre (1983). „Ökonomisches Kapital, kulturelles Kapital, soziales Kapital", *Soziale Welt*, Sonderband 2 „Soziale Ungleichheiten": 183-198.

Bourdieu, Pierre (1999): Die Regeln der Kunst. Genese und Struktur des literarischen Feldes. Frankfurt am Main.

Cairncross, A.K. (1958). "Economic Schizophrenia", *Scottish Journal of Political Economy* 5 (1): 15-21.

Convert, Bernard (2003). "Bourdieu: Gary Becker's Critic", *Economic Sociology* 4 (2): 6-9.

Haase, Ricarda (1992): ‚Das bißchen Haushalt...?' Zur Geschichte der Technisierung und Rationalisierung der Hausarbeit. Stuttgart.

Latour, Bruno (2007): Eine neue Soziologie für eine neue Gesellschaft. Frankfurt am Main.

Lave, Jean/Wenger, Etienne (1991): Situated Learning. Legitimate Peripheral Participation. Cambridge UK.

Levey, Steven (1984): Hackers. Heroes of the Computer Revolution. New York.

Lobo, Sascha/Friebe, Holm (2006): Wir nennen es Arbeit. Die digitale Boheme oder: Intelligentes Leben jenseits der Festanstellung. München.

Mikhak, Bakthiar/Lyon, Christopher/Gorton, Tim/Gershenfeld, Neil/McEnnis, Caroline/Taylor, Jason (2002): Fab Lab: An Alternate Model of ICT for Development. [Link: http://cba.mit.edu/events/03.05.fablab/fablab-dyd02.pdf; 11.8.2020].

Mol, Annemarie (2003): The Body Multiple. Ontology in Medical Practice, Durham & London.

Morozov, Evgeny (2013): To Save Everything, Click Here. The Folly of Technological Solutionism. New York.

Naylor, Gillian (1980): The Arts and Crafts Movement. A Study of Its Sources, Ideals and Influence on Design Theory. London.

Nicolini, Davide (2012): Practice Theory, Work, and Organization. An Introduction, Oxford, UK.

Rabe, Hannah (1974): Haus. In: Ritter, Joachim (Hrsg.): Historisches Wörterbuch der Philosophie. Basel, Stuttgart, 1007-1020.

Raymond, Eric S. (1999): The Cathedral and the Bazaar. Musings on Linux and Open Source by an Accidental Revolutionary. Sebastopol, CA.

Reckwitz, Andreas (2003). „Grundelemente einer Theorie sozialer Praktiken. Eine sozialtheoretische Perspektive“, *Zeitschrift für Soziologie* 32 (4): 282-301.

Schäfer, Hilmar (2013): Die Instabilität der Praxis. Reproduktion und Transformation des Sozialen in der Praxistheorie. Weilerswirst.

Schatzki, Theodore (2002): The Site of the Social. A Philosophical Account of the Constitution of Social Life and Change. University Park.

Smith, Adam (1776/1974): Der Wohlstand der Nationen. Eine Untersuchung seiner Natur und seiner Ursachen. München.

Kurzviten der Autor*innen

Lisa Conrad ist akademische Rätin am Institut für Soziologie und Kulturorganisation und assoziiertes Mitglied am Centre for Digital Cultures, Leuphana Universität Lüneburg. In ihrer Forschung und Lehre beschäftigt sie sich mit digitalen Technologien im Organisations- und Arbeitsalltag. Kürzlich erschienen sind der Aufsatz „Planning Table" im *Oxford Handbook of Media, Technology and Organization Studies* und das Buch *Organize* (zus. mit Timon Beyes und Reinhold Martin).

Sarah Czerney ist wissenschaftliche Mitarbeiterin im Gleichstellungsprojekt FEM Power am Leibniz-Institut für Neurobiologie in Magdeburg und Fellow der Frankfurt Memory Studies Platform an der Goethe-Universität Frankfurt/Main. Ihre neuesten Publikationen sind die Bücher *Zwischen Nation und Europa. Nationalmuseen als Europamedien* und *Mutterschaft und Wissenschaft. Die (Un-)Vereinbarkeit von Mutterbild und wissenschaftlicher Tätigkeit* (zusammen mit Lena Eckert und Silke Martin). Neben der praktischen Gleichstellungsarbeit umfassen ihre Forschungsinteressen feministische Theorie und Wissenschaftskritik, Medientheorie, Inszenierungen kollektiver Identitäten und European Studies. Darüber hinaus gibt sie Workshops zu kreativen Schreibmethoden in der Wissenschaft und zu kritischer Mutterschaft.

Lena Eckert ist promovierte Gender- und Literaturwissenschaftlerin und derzeit wissenschaftliche Mitarbeiterin im Projekt gender*bildet an der Martin-Luther-Universität Halle. Ihre Forschungsschwerpunkte liegen in den Gender und Queer Studies sowie der Bildungs- und Schreibforschung und der post-anarchistischen Theorie. Seit mehr als zehn Jahren ist sie zudem als Trainerin für Gender und Diversity in der Hochschuldidaktik und als Schreibcoach tätig. Sie ist Autorin und Herausgeberin gender-, bildungs- und medienwissenschaftlicher Publikationen, z.B. *Intersexualization. The Clinic and the Colony* (Routledge, 2016) oder *Schöner Lehren - gegendert und gequeert* (mit Silke Martin, Schüren 2016) und *Mutterschaft und Wissenschaft* (mit Sarah Czerney und Silke Martin, Springer 2020).

Ellen K. Foster ist promovierte Wissenschaftlerin der Science and Technology Studies am Rensselaer Polytechnic Institute. Derzeit ist sie Post-doc an der School for Engineering Education an der Purdue University und wohnt in Philadelphia wo sie mit dem Department of History der Drexel University affiliiert ist. Ihre Forschungs- und Theorieschwerpunkte liegen auf Maker und Hacker Kulturen, der feministischen Wissenschaftskritik von Science und Technology, der kritischen Pädagogik und kritischen Design Studies.

Sarah Held ist wissenschaftliche Mitarbeiterin an der Akademie der Bildenden Künste in Wien und Lektorin an verschiedenen österreichischen Universitäten zu den Themen Mode, Gender und queer-feministische Pornografie/PostPorn. Die Kunst- und Kulturwissenschaftlerin hat über affektive Interventionskunst als Handlungsmachtstrategie sowie zur Sichtbarmachung von sexualisierter Gewalt und Femicides promoviert.

Constance Krüger M.A. studierte Kunstgeschichte und Gender Studies an der Humboldt-Universität zu Berlin und der Jagiellonen Universität Krakau. Derzeit Dissertation zu polnischen Künstlerinnen der 1970er Jahre. 2018 bis 2020 wissenschaftliche Mitarbeiterin am Lehrstuhl für Kunstgeschichte Osteuropas am IKB der Humboldt-Universität zu Berlin in Vertretung. Seit 2019 Mitglied im Forschungsprojekt Gender Politics and the Art of European Socialist States. Forschungsschwerpunkt ist die Kunstgeschichte Ostmitteleuropas mit besonderem Augenmerk auf das 20. und 21. Jahrhundert.

Christiane Lewe ist Medienwissenschaftlerin und als wissenschaftliche Mitarbeiterin und Koordinatorin des DFG-Graduiertenkollegs Medienanthropologie an der Bauhaus-Universität Weimar tätig. In ihrer Forschung befasst sie sich schwerpunktmäßig mit dem Zusammenhang von Social Media/digitalen Kulturen, einer Medien- und Kulturgeschichte des Gesichts und der Geschichte nordamerikanischer College Yearbooks und Scrapbooks.

Silke Martin ist derzeit wissenschaftliche Mitarbeiterin an der Universität Erfurt, promovierte Film- und Medienwissenschaftlerin und seit vielen Jahren als Beraterin in der Hochschuldidaktik sowie akademischen Schreib- und Karriereplanung tätig. Ihre Forschungsschwerpunkte sind die Theorie, Ästhetik und Geschichte des Films, Gender/Ageing Studies sowie diversitätssensible Hochschulbildung und Schreibforschung. Sie ist Herausgeberin und Autorin verschiedener medienwissenschaftlicher und hochschuldidaktischer Publikationen, u.a. von *Berg und Film* (Monographie 2017), *Schöner Lehren – gegendert und gequeert!* (Sammelband

2016, mit Lena Eckert) und *FilmBildung* (Sammelband 2014, mit Lena Eckert).

Matthias Maier ist Professor für Medienmanagement an der Bauhaus-Universität Weimar. Seine Forschungsschwerpunkte liegen in den Bereichen der Neuen Institutionenökonomie, der Informations- und Netzökonomie sowie neuen Formen der Organisation.

Christin Sirtl hat Bauingenieurwesen studiert und arbeitet seit Anfang 2014 als wissenschaftliche Mitarbeiterin in Lehre und Forschung an der Bauhaus-Universität Weimar. Ihre Schwerpunkte liegen im Glas- und Stahlbau. In einem Fernstudienkurs hat sie sich zudem mit dem Thema „Theologie geschlechterbewusst – kontextuell neu denken" beschäftigt und sieht sich als feministische Bauingenieurin und Theologin. In die Imkerei ist sie ca. 2007 eingestiegen.

Register

Inter_Sections. mapping queer*feminist art practices

Tonia Andresen, Marlene Mannsfeld (Hg.)

Marta Press 2019, 120 Seiten, 20,00 € (D)
ISBN: 978-3-944442-81-5

Inter_Sections. mapping queer*feminist art practices

Inter_Sections nähert sich queer-feministischen Kunstpraktiken aus verschiedenen Perspektiven – von der Produktion künstlerischer Werke, die Themen wie Queerness und Geschlecht reflektieren, über kollektives Arbeiten und aktivistische Strategien. Die Beiträge untersuchen, wie Ungleichheiten und Hierarchisierungen zwischen sozialen Kategorisierungen – wie Geschlecht, sexuelle Orientierung, Klasse, (Dis-)Ability und vermeintliche ethnische Zugehörigkeit – zustande kommen und wie sie dekonstruiert und/oder produktiv genutzt werden können. Hierbei werden die Überschneidungen der oftmals als getrennt betrachteten Felder Kunst, Theorie und Aktivismus deutlich. Der Band vereint theoretische Aufsätze, ein Interview sowie experimentelle Essays und liefert vielfältige Anregungen von und für Forscher*innen, Künstler*innen und Aktivist*innen. Mit Beiträgen von Sophie Lembcke, Lorena Juan, Joke Janssen, Wiebke Schwarzhans, Eva Egermann und Lea Susemichel.